REINVENTING
THE FACTORY

REINVENTING THE FACTORY

■■■

Productivity Breakthroughs in Manufacturing Today

ROY L. HARMON
LEROY D. PETERSON

THE FREE PRESS
A Division of Macmillan, Inc.
NEW YORK

Collier Macmillan Publishers
LONDON

The Free Press
A Division of Macmillan, Inc.
866 Third Avenue, New York, N.Y. 10022

Collier Macmillan Canada, Inc.

Printed in the United States of America

printing number
1 2 3 4 5 6 7 8 9 10

Library of Congress Cataloging-in-Publication Data

Harmon, Roy L.
    Reinventing the factory : productivity breakthroughs in
manufacturing today / Roy L. Harmon, Leroy D. Peterson.
        p.   cm.
    Includes bibliographical references.
    ISBN 0-02-913861-2
    1. Industrial productivity. 2. Production planning.
I. Peterson, Leroy D.   II. Title.
HD56.H37 1989
658.5—dc20   89–16944
                                                CIP

Contents

Preface

EVERY MANUFACTURER NEEDS to heed the recent and continuing shifts in productivity leadership and the reasons behind the achievements of the emerging leaders, because powerful forces are reshaping and directing the flow of world trade, moving manufacturing away from the historic birthplaces of modern industry in Europe and North America. Increasingly, manufactured products are being produced and exported by developing countries. Their manufacturers capitalize on low labor costs and tightly control assets and overhead costs to finance the same type of equipment available to any manufacturer in the world.

Being a struggling company in a struggling country can be a blessing in disguise. The poor man has no money to waste; therefore, the poor man wastes no money. After working hard to accumulate money, the once-poor man usually continues his frugal habits. The emerging giants of manufacturing are typically like the once-poor man, carefully controlling even the smallest investments and expenses. For example, Mr. M. Takayanagi, President of the Nissei Electric Co., Ltd., facsimile factory in Japan, has devoted most of his efforts, recently, to developing foreign sources of components. His reason? Many Japanese component manufacturers are no longer cost-competitive vis-à-vis Singapore, the People's Republic of China, Taiwan, Hong Kong, Korea, and the Philippines.

Companies in developing nations have seen that success automatically leads to increased personnel costs. Employees should share in the benefits reaped, and in fact, personnel benefits among some of these new giants have risen to the point where total cost differences are no longer low enough to compensate for the transportation costs between their factories and their markets and raw material sources. To maintain worldwide supremacy, the giants have no alternative but to continuously improve personnel methods and factory automation, and to minimize required investments and expenses, or else find lower-cost sources of supply.

Factory automation is too often viewed as the area in which mature factories are deficient, and Western manufacturers have been chastised, and have chastised themselves, for a policy of short-term profitability at the expense of long-term investment. There is nothing wrong, however, with short-term profits! Too much attention has been paid to the panacea of spending on new plants and equipment to achieve productivity. Too little focus has been placed on low-cost opportunities to increase productivity. Simpler alternatives to high-cost automation may, in many companies, increase profitability, and provide funds for subsequent investment in the latest manufacturing technology. However, automation investments should be made only if they unquestionably contribute to increased profitability, both in the short and long term. Unfortunately, this is not always the case.

Some Western companies deserve chastisement, having unwisely milked their cash-cow factory, draining the proceeds of productive operations to distribute dividends or to finance new acquisitions or alternative investments. The majority of companies, however, have practiced sound fiscal responsibility, apportioning logical and limited percentages of earnings to capital investments. Moreover, while it has been popular to attribute the success of Oriental companies to their willingness to invest massively in automation and to accept short-term losses to ensure long-term growth, this myth is easily dispelled by examining their operating statements over a 10- or 20-year period. Most show few periods of low profitability or loss.

Manufacturing professionals who have worked in Japan, for example, see many old factories with equipment that is often older than that found in typical Western factories. They also note some very new factories that house the latest in manufacturing technology. However, the real reason for the remarkable growth of Pacific manufacturers has not necessarily been large investments in new plants and equipment. While Japanese, Korean, and other Pacific manufacturers have enjoyed explosive growth of both domestic and export demand, they have primarily increased demand through export sales. The newest plants and equipment were developed to meet that increase in demand, but only when the capacity limits of older plants were no longer adequate. In most cases, the output of both old and new plants is needed to meet total demand.

By contrast, most Western companies have had comparatively modest increases in real, noninflationary demand since they rely primarily on local markets for sales. Without major increases in either domestic or export markets, they suffer from the comparative maturity of their factories. The door is thus wide open for the new fast-growing companies with lower costs to take a large portion of their markets. In fact, the lack of Western competitiveness may not be due as much to failure to update existing factories, but rather to failure to aggressively increase either domestic market share or exports, thus generating a need for new plants and equipment.

One Japanese equipment purchase practice that could and should be emulated by companies everywhere involves the assumption that the company will win a dominant share of the worldwide market when planning plant and equipment investment for a new product or product line. Such plans appear risky since the company might not achieve the share and size of market anticipated. In most cases, however, aggressive plans turn into self-fulfilling prophecies. Further, to plan production facilities for the largest market share does not necessarily mean an immediate investment in plant and equipment required to meet the total volume. Increments of equipment designed as flexible modules should usually be added as actual sales are proven to equal or better the planned market share. Finally, new processes designed for the largest share of market will have the lowest cost per unit, and since higher unit volume supports the best in equipment and tooling, it should yield the highest possible quality.

Quality problems, incidentally, are still widely believed to be the fault of the worker. Worse, the solution is commonly thought to be the increased use of manual inspection, including statistical methods. In fact, virtually all quality problems can be eliminated by improving design specifications and by the use of equipment and tooling that are designed to either be incapable of defective production or, alternatively, designed to automatically reject any defective unit produced.[1]

While being the highest-volume producer is still important, the superior manufacturing techniques described in this book can help to reduce the volume necessary to be internationally competitive. For example, automobile assembly plants have historically had breakeven points of 250,000 units per year versus 40,000 for the best of today's factories. Ultimately, the automobile company that achieves the lowest

---

[1]Shigeo Shingo, *Zero Quality Control: Source Inspection and the Poka-Yoke System* (Stamford, CT: Productivity Press, 1986).

breakeven points in its plants will most likely be the world's superior manufacturer. General Motors, the world's largest automobile manufacturer, for example, is working zealously to adopt new superior techniques to reverse its loss of market share to smaller competitors.

To become or to remain the best manufacturer in the world is not the responsibility of manufacturing management alone. Every level in each branch of an organization must aggressively pursue the common goals of increasing personnel productivity and return on investment while reducing operating costs. The engineering organization is in a position of paramount importance because opportunities exist to maximize company productivity by designing products that have the highest practical value yet the lowest practical manufacturing and material cost. Outside suppliers should also play a major role in productivity improvement. More than 60 percent of most companies' product costs are for purchased materials and components. Further, many companies frequently reject some or all of each lot of material received. The opportunities to reduce product cost by simultaneously lowering supplied material and component value are epic in proportion.

While few aspects of the superior manufacturing techniques described in this book are entirely new, the combined results of adopting every idea have produced dramatic improvements and have been proven to be applicable in dozens of countries, in hundreds of companies, and for every conceivable type of manufactured product. There is only one vital prerequisite to the successful route out of the manufacturing past and into the factory of the future. The magic ingredient is a management team committed to achieving improvements of astounding new dimensions. The secret, simply stated, is something we have known all along— where there is the will, there is a way.

Nowhere is this made clearer than on a plaque widely distributed among the personnel of American Greeting Cards by Irving Stone, the company's chairman. It reads, "At every crossway in the road that leads to the future . . . each progressive spirit is opposed by 1,000 men appointed to guard the past." Overcoming resistance to change is one of industries' greatest challenges.

SIMPLIFICATION: KEY TO PRODUCTIVITY

Imagine the benefits that could result from a scenario where every manufacturing executive, manager, and employee would have SIMPLIFY tattooed in bold, bright red letters on the back of each hand! The single most important secret of leading-edge, productive manufacturing is simplification. The person who is constantly reminded to simplify, or to keep simple, has endless opportunities to:

1. *Reduce the number of components in the product.* With fewer components, the product is not only easier and less costly to produce; it will probably have better reliability and require less repair.

2. *Reduce the number of steps in the process flow,* with emphasis on elimination of steps that do not add to the value of the product. This applies to any process, whether factory operations or office procedures.

3. *Reduce the number of components in the fixtures and tooling used for machining.* The simplest fixtures and tools require the least time and cost to alter when a machine is changed from producing one item to producing another.

Many product and process designers have done a technologically superior job of designing complex solutions for basic problems. These designs have been developed because too many problems are accepted as inevitable components of the manufacturing process. For example, one die cast plant operated grinding operations for years to remove excess flash on every die cast part produced. By improving the quality of the dies used and by correcting the erroneous belief that die castings hidden within the structure of the final assembled product must have near-perfect surfaces, the company almost entirely eliminated grinding operations.

The beauty of this new simplification methodology is that the resulting designs have such elegant simplicity that the old concern for pioneering concepts that might not work disappears. There can be no doubt that the new, simple designs will work. The only applicable question is, "What fine-tuning might be necessary to make the new process work even better?"

With the reduction of both the number of operations and the number of employees, all aspects of manufacturing management become correspondingly simpler. For example, the size of the factory is reduced, and as a result of having a smaller area, fewer employees, and simpler operations, less supervision is required. Since there are fewer, simpler operations now performed in rapid succession, administrative costs of scheduling, tracking, and accounting are lower.

Simplification applies not only to the production process. It also entails the process of presenting the new methods to executive management for approval and the training needed by operating personnel to perform new and revised operations. Executives and operating personnel need simple, easy-to-understand presentations to efficiently approve new methods and get them into operation.

We might well ask why our executives and managers have permitted our products and processes to become overly complex. Perhaps one reason is that the nature of technical specifications makes it difficult or impossible to understand them, to say nothing of other alternative designs. Communication between our productivity improvement project teams and their executive and operating participants is never in the form of 10,000 elegant words or even 10,000 technical words. Rather, it takes the form of easy-to-understand sketches, photos, or key word visuals. Preparation of the usual technical specifications for simpler products and processes is still the responsibility of the project team. The secret of successful understanding and buy-in to the new, simpler designs is an understandable presentation of proposed methods. This is especially critical when dealing with top management who often have legal, financial, or marketing backgrounds, and thus a limited understanding of manufacturing operations. These individuals are constantly bombarded with lengthy written reports. Elegant and technical words complicate understanding and make effective communication difficult.

INVENTION: KEY TO MOVING BEYOND WORLD-CLASS MANUFACTURING

To stay or to become the world's best and biggest, every manufacturer working on the development of assembly and machining designs for new products or striving to upgrade or replace existing facilities must go beyond current world-class manufacturing performance. Since achievement of world-class status is not enough, the new hallmark of excellence must be continuous improvement to maintain a superior position! Very few factories have implemented every known superior manufacturing technique. In fact, not every manufacturing professional knows or even accepts all of the techniques that comprise the present body of knowledge. Even more important, there are an infinite number of new techniques still waiting to be invented.

In some factories around the world, the single most important question on the minds of executive management is: "Where are the factories that already have world-class techniques in operation?" If these executives ask to visit a factory where they can view what their factory should be doing, however, they are on the wrong track. Although company executives *should* have a professional interest in seeing similar operations, they should demand something even better or newer for their own company. The key to moving beyond the competition is not playing "follow the leader," but becoming the leader.

Some of the older and easier productivity improvement techniques that are presented here have been implemented in almost every Western factory improvement project. The newest and most difficult-to-accomplish techniques have been implemented in relatively few factories. In fact, some of the concepts are currently being developed for the first time in conjunction with new projects and/or as investments in research and development. Insistence on innovation is one of the keys to the success of the productivity projects described in the appendix.

HOW TO USE THE BOOK

The organization of this book parallels the structure we have found appropriate to best serve the purposes of various individuals in a manufacturing company, including those responsible for the strategic direction of the company and for productivity improvement projects. Topics of primary importance to executive management are in the first three chapters:

Chapter	*Title*
1.	Management Perspective: The Profit Motive
2.	Focused Factory Organization
3.	Future Vision: The Plantwide Plan

Individuals responsible for various departments in the organization should also review these initial chapters, but they may find it more satisfying to go directly to the material that directly relates to their responsibilities. For example, different individuals usually responsible for storage, assembly, machining, and changeover/setup may want to go directly to one of the following chapters:

Chapter	*Title*
4.	Assembly Process Design
5.	Machining Process Design
6.	Material/Product Storage
7.	One-Touch Changeover

Certain chapters affect several areas, however, and should be of secondary consideration to individuals with specialized interests. For example, some of the techniques and concepts of assembly and machining process design are applicable to both but are discussed mainly in one chapter or the other. Similarly, material storage should become the responsibility of the individuals responsible for assembly and machining in the factory of the future. Thus, it is important that they also review Chapter 6, "Material/Product Storage." Every area in the factory of the future needs drastically improved and simplified computer systems and manual procedures. Thus, not only systems personnel but all operating personnel, including executive management, should be interested in Chapter 8, "Productivity Systems: The Paperless Factory."

Executives and productivity improvement managers should be initially concerned with the secrets of successful projects. These are outlined in Chapter 9, "The Step-by-Step Approach." Most readers will recognize that numerous important techniques, problems, and issues of importance are not covered in this book. Such omissions were necessary to keep the book a practical size. The most obvious omissions are outlined in Chapter 10, "Other Productivity Issues." Finally, it seems important to many executives and managers to have proof that the techniques described in this and other books on the subject of productivity work in their parts of the world. The appendix, "The Achievers," identifies numerous companies, internationally, in which we have participated in projects to successfully design and implement improvements. Improvement achievement percentages are included in the appendix.

This book is not a book of slogans; nor does it advocate a single, simplistic gimmick for improving productivity and quality. Although people and motivation are vital ingredients for success, the book is not an inspirational work that depends on changing a company's culture to achieve success. Instead, it offers a nuts-and-bolts approach to myriad detailed improvements that, when taken together, make the difference between being one of the pack or being the superior manufacturer. Although the techniques that contribute most to success are clearly identified, most successful achievers will be those who pay attention to blockbuster improvements and to every other small but vital detail, such as container design, regardless of the size of the improvement gained. Any program of productivity improvement must be an eternal fight to lower costs and improve product quality and value. Therefore, it is no longer acceptable to manage a company without current improvement projects underway or to be satisfied with the project just completed. Ultimately, productivity improvement will have to be built into every employee's job description. Temporarily changing hardware used in the factory and simplifying procedures will greatly improve the productivity of most operations. Continuous improvement of company culture, however, will be a necessary aspect of becoming and remaining the world's superior manufacturer.

Roy L. Harmon
Leroy D. Peterson

1

□□□

Management Perspective:
The Profit Motive

PRODUCTIVITY AND INTERNATIONAL COMPETITION have become increasingly important issues for manufacturing firms here and abroad. With this in mind, the primary goal of this book is to demonstrate that any company, anyplace in the world, can achieve superior productivity technology. With even modest investment, the factory output of high-quality products per employee hour can be substantially increased. In fact, major advances can be achieved by the simple reorganization of people and equipment. For several years in the late 1970s, Andersen Consulting studied productivity problems when it served as a consultant to Yamaha Motor Co. in Iwata, Japan, and worked with Yamaha's customer, the Toyota Motor Co. One of the most important lessons Andersen learned from this relationship was how to set targets for improving productivity. Some of the more startling revelations of this endeavor were:

1. When management set unbelievably high targets, it expected improvements of 50 to 90 percent and more. Surprisingly, these high targets were almost always matched and surpassed.

2. Since management had no specific basis for establishing targets, entirely new manufacturing methods needed to be invented to achieve these objectives.

3. Little or no time was spent justifying the cost of the project. The

1

full-time project teams responsible for designing and implementing changes were charged with the responsibility of inventing low-cost solutions that were expected to generate savings in 6 to 12 months or less. Infrequent exceptions were handled through normal capital investment procedures.

In countries other than Japan, executives have recently started to adopt the same ambitious targets, and they have had the satisfaction of knowing firsthand that potential for productivity gains is not restricted to any single global area. Equally important, they have learned that these gains do not require a complete change in either national character or company culture. These executives also know that the most important secrets to success are setting high goals, discarding old ways of working, and inventing new, simpler, and lower-cost methods. The setting of seemingly impossible goals thus becomes self-fulfilling prophecy, but not by any magical formula, as radical goals demand radical departures from accepted ways of operating. When enlisting and insisting on the committed and enthusiastic participation of every manager, supervisor, and employee in the drive to achieve performance beyond the levels of competitors, executive management performs its most important role.

MANAGEMENT GOAL SETTING

Today, manufacturers in every country are comparing themselves to the most productive companies in the world, and most conclude that they may be second- or third-rate at best. Usually, however, the measure of productivity used to reach that conclusion has little to do with how successfully the company can compete in the international arena. Several indicators of productivity are measurable; others, such as degree of factory automation, are not. None of the conventional measures—(1) man-hours of direct labor per unit produced, (2) man-hours (or employees) on the entire payroll per unit produced, (3) product cost per unit produced, (4) degree of factory automation—are valid for meaningfully evaluating the competitiveness of a company vis-à-vis a company in another part of the world. For example, in some countries, employee compensation and benefits are only a small fraction of what they are in other areas. As a result, the productivity of the factory, office, and executive work force can be lower and yet still place the company in a competitive position internationally. Even when labor costs are comparable, material and component purchases usually make up 60 percent or more of product cost. Thus, purchase prices usually have a greater impact on competitiveness than do payroll costs. Since different manufacturers have different degrees of vertical integration, the one that merely assembles a product has considerably lower payroll costs than the vertically integrated manufacturer that manufactures components and, as well, assembles the finished product. Therefore, total product cost, although less than a perfect gauge, is a more meaningful measure of international productivity. The customer deciding between competing products of equal value should select the product with the lowest delivered price rather than be concerned with the manufacturer's cost. In the same vein, degree of automation is a subjective, and frequently erroneous, criterion for evaluating competitiveness. Glamorous, high-technology automation is often viewed as modern and productive—even if the automation should be eliminated, as in the case of material transportation and storage, or if the automation itself costs more than simpler, manual techniques, or low-technology alternatives.

As long as world trade remains unregulated and stiff international competition prevails, market price is the only practical measure of productivity for manufacturers of products with identical value. Even delivered price has only short-term transient value, since a price can increase or decrease as a result of changes in the value of currency. For example, rapid and sharp appreciation of the German mark and Japanese yen from 1985 to 1987 caused the prices of products produced in those nations to rise sharply in most other countries. In some parts of the world, and especially in the United States, it has been fashionable to chastise manufacturers for losing their competitive position or, in developing nations, for never having achieved one. It is time to realize that large numbers of companies, worldwide, are working diligently to surpass the world-class manufacturers of today, their goal being to become the superior manufacturers of tomorrow.

To get started in this race, some companies have viewed a competitive benchmark project as the first phase of a productivity improvement program. But while completing extensive and arduous competitive comparisons, they have delayed work on factory improvements. While it is important to understand as much as practical about the competition, it is a mistake to put off improvements, awaiting study results in order to set targets. For one reason, meaningful comparisons range from extremely difficult to impossible to make, and are based on factors such as the degree of vertical integration, degree of automation, and value of the local currency. And, above all, the main issue is not the competition's stance today or what it will be in the coming year, but how to determine how much a company can expect to improve.

As quickly as possible, executive management must set new style factory improvements in motion. It is management's responsibility to specify aggressive targets that will demand quantum leaps forward in the international race for manufacturing superiority. It is not difficult for management to determine what its goals should be, throughout the company, or in individual departments. Experienced managers can suggest improvement targets based on a fast factory tour, Japanese style, albeit with a more logical basis. However, it is less important *how* the goal is set, than how *high* it is set. To explain this concept further, the remainder of this chapter deals with achievements of Western companies that now stand as reasonable goals for most manufacturers.

CHANGEOVER AND SETUP REDUCTION

One example of a management target is the reduction of the cost of machine changeover from producing one part (or product) to producing another. Based on studies of thousands of different types of machines around the world, experience on changeover reduction shows that the average cost reduction should be expected to be somewhere between 75 to 80 percent. Interestingly enough, after the first project team has designed and installed changes to achieve the initial major reduction, a second team (on a second project) has been able to reduce the remaining cost in the very same range—75 to 80 percent. Bringing new objectivity to the problem, the second team can see ways to further improve the changeover—ways the first team failed to recognize in its close proximity to the process.

Reduction, and even elimination, of changeover costs is one of the most important techniques required to achieve superior productivity. Higher-than-necessary changeover costs have three serious drawbacks:

1. They demand long production runs, which make it impractical to respond rapidly to unexpected customer requirements. Thus, customers are forced to wait until the end of the long run, at a minimum, before their new demands can be satisfied.

2. Large production runs result in sizable amounts of inventory. Exhibit 1–1 illustrates the basic relationship between lot size and average inventory attributable to lot sizes. When a lot is completed, in-

LOT SIZE INVENTORY

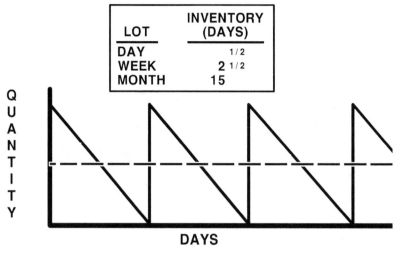

LOT	INVENTORY (DAYS)
DAY	1/2
WEEK	2 1/2
MONTH	15

QUANTITY

DAYS

EXHIBIT 1-1

ventory peaks. But over time, inventory decreases until the lot size is depleted. Then, a new lot is completed. The average inventory attributable to lot size is, therefore, half of the lot quantity. If every item is produced once a month, the minimum possible inventory is one-half the month's supply. If every item can be produced every day, the resulting minimum inventory could be one-half day's supply.

3. Large inventories require plant and stores/warehouse space, people and equipment to transport, stock, retrieve, and distribute.

SPACE UTILIZATION

Almost without exception every factory is twice as large as it needs to be to produce as much as double its current output. This being the case, the smallest factories should be the best factories, as suggested in Exhibit 1–2. Paradoxically, the physical size of a building hardly dictates the success of a company. A very large plant can be one of the best or one of the worst, depending on how its space is utilized. Experienced professionals can easily scan a factory, recognize opportunities for improvement, and establish targets for better use of space. Typical targets should be:

PLANT SIZE/COMPLEXITY

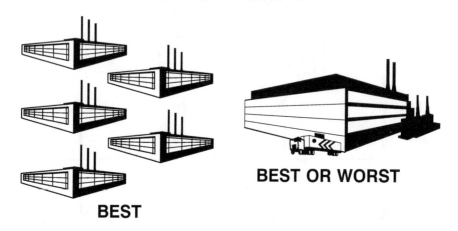

BEST OR WORST

BEST

EXHIBIT 1-2

Plantwide	50 percent
Machine process	50 percent
Assembly	80 percent
Stores/warehouse	50 percent

One important objective of improved space utilization is to reduce the required capital investment and depreciation expense for manufacturers that own their factories, or to reduce operating costs for those that rent space. Since lower-level management personnel are usually naive about the advantages of improved use of space, they often misconceive that improved space utilization means uncomfortable working areas for employees. But, in truth, working areas actually increase, as excessive inventory, conveyors or wide aisles, and wasted, unused space disappear. Also, these same managers often feel that if half the factory space is vacated, there are no savings since the space would just sit idle. Executive management, on the other hand, is often instantly able to envision dramatic savings associated with improved space utilization. For instance, it can see that:

1. Inventory, machines, etc., from other company plants and/or warehouses can be moved into the vacated space, and the other facilities can be sold or subleased.

2. New products or acquired product production can be moved into the vacated space.

3. With newly vacated space, existing plans for new factories and/or warehouses can be dropped.

4. Walls can be erected between the occupied and vacated space, and the vacant space can be sold or rented.

Vacated space can, by itself, be a source of major economic benefit. In most companies, however, improved utilization of space has many more important recurring productivity benefits. Processes designed to improve space utilization eliminate excess work-in-process inventory and the corresponding investment. Permanent reduction of inventory either reduces the carrying costs, or permits investment of the freed-up capital. In addition, smaller spaces minimize the unnecessary movement of staff—including both indirect personnel such as material handlers, supervisors, equipment repair employees; and direct workers who waste time moving about in areas that are larger than necessary to perform production operations. Improved space utilization also has some theoretical, intangible benefits that produce major economic results. For example, it improves communication among workers themselves, and between employees and supervisors. As well, the following unexpected changes typically occur: improvement of 90 percent in the number of defects, and a 75 percent improvement in equipment downtime. However, these performance improvements cannot be calculated based only on such concrete factors as time and motion, since they result largely from improved communications and team esprit de corps; nevertheless, management should establish targets for such improvements, remembering that setting the target high, and demanding its achievement, are two of the most important factors in success.

INVENTORY REDUCTION

For most manufacturing companies, reduction of inventory investment and of the associated costs of capital (or alternative investment return) is one of the most important internal sources of improved profitability. Although it is easier and faster to reduce work-in-process inventory, the largest amount of inventory (and, therefore, the area for greatest improvement) is in purchased materials and components and in finished goods. Permanent reduction of the latter inventory depends primarily on the implementation and operation of new manufacturing assembly and machining processes. For example, reducing changeover costs and the attendant ability to produce small production runs are paramount to finished goods reduction. However, achieving a permanent reduction of both finished goods and purchased inventories normally requires more time and effort than reducing work-in-process inventory. This involves implementation of new assembly and machining facilities since the physical layout and the process of the new facility control these inventory levels. When there is no space for work-in-process inventory, it cannot exist.

Sales and marketing staffs, as well as chief executive officers, should be skeptical of the premise that inventories of finished goods can be reduced while customer service is maintained or improved. Most manufacturers should plan to reduce these inventories only after demonstrating that reduced changeover costs have made it practical to respond rapidly to new and changed customer requirements, and that frequent, smaller run sizes improve customer service by increasing the frequency of receipts of finished stock. Significant, permanent reduction of purchased material and component inventory depends foremost on the implementation of a vendor program for most high-dollar-value suppliers. The reasons for large inventories, all of which can be changed, are:

1. Costs of vendor changeover cause production of large lot sizes.
2. Vendors frequently make late deliveries due to the unnecessary time required to process the latest schedule information into production schedules.
3. Even when the most recent schedules are available to vendors, deliveries are late because a long run already in progress needs to be completed. It is impractical to interrupt a long run because of the penalty of increased changeover costs.
4. Vendors frequently deliver defective materials and components that must either be reworked in house or returned to vendors for repair or replacement.

All the root causes of large material inventories can be addressed by a vendor program focusing on specific manufacturing process improvements. These include reduction of changeover costs, improvement of quality, and the provision of capacity flexibility to respond rapidly to new and changing customer requirements.

Factories that have designed and installed both productivity improvements and vendor programs for all major suppliers have found that typical targets for inventory reduction are:

Work-in-process	95 percent
Materials	75 percent
Finished goods	75 percent

But fearing disruptions in production, managers responsible for factory operations sometimes veto projects that could reduce work-in-process inventories immediately by as much as 95 percent. Accordingly, it is often wise to curtail such resistance by scheduling reductions over a lengthy period of time—two or three years. Yet, when the process is properly designed, a reduction of 95 percent or more occurs almost immediately, regardless of the target.

Clearly, inventory reduction and space requirements are interrelated. Although improved utilization of storeroom and warehouse areas might reduce required space by an average of 50 percent, the long-term target should include plans to decrease the amount of finished goods and material inventory by at least 75 percent. Thus, a combination of inventory reduction and better space utilization enables most factories to have 80 to 90 percent less storage space than historically needed.

SUPPLIER PROGRAM

In October 1980, Andersen Consulting organized one of the first of the "Japanese" productivity seminars, as reported by Robert Hall.[1] Six hundred executives met in the Ford Motor Company world headquarters auditorium and heard thousands of words describing key methods behind the success of the Japanese. Three words of these thousands were to catch the imagination of the Western world: "just in time." These words have come to mean, collectively, every technique of improvement in the reinvented factory.

Manufacturers and suppliers need to learn to work together as partners in profit. As suppliers provide defect-free materials and components at lower costs and just-in-time, they contribute to their customers' increased sales and accompaning success. Thus, both suppliers and manufacturers can share in the financial rewards. Successful supplier programs can also reduce the price of materials and components by 30 percent in two to four years, and by 5 to 10 percent each year thereafter. The reduction of suppliers' costs, coupled with maintenance or improvement of their profit margin, should be the basis for supplier price reductions. Since purchase prices represent 60 or 70 percent of the cost of most manufactured products, reduction of these prices will have a greater effect on profitability than will improvements in labor and overhead costs. These reductions should also reduce required inventory investment. For exam-

[1]Robert W. Hall, "Driving the Productivity Machine: Production Planning and Control in Japan," American Production and Inventory Control Society, 1981.

ple, a 30 percent decrease in the purchase price should, by itself, cause a 30 percent reduction in inventory investment. The benefits of supplier programs should not be limited to purchase and inventory investment reduction, but should include an 80 percent reduction in defective materials and components, and in packaging and container costs, as well as a 90 percent reduction in business communications costs.

In Japan, for instance, leading export-oriented manufacturers are supported by a network of supplying factories, including:

1. Factories owned and operated as integral units of the company
2. Fully owned subsidiaries, operated more or less as independent factories
3. Vendors who usually are as large as, or larger than, the customer or a subcontractor
4. Subcontractors whose inventories and schedules are usually controlled directly by the customer, and are often partially or wholly owned by the customer (subcontractors are almost always smaller than the customer)

These same types of suppliers are also found in the networks of many Western companies; thus, the Japanese philosophy of needing a supplier program, as opposed to a vendor program, may be applicable in the West.

LOW-COST AUTOMATION

Whenever machines and equipment can increase both short- and long-term profitability, they should be used to replace manual work. A manufacturing company that invests in state-of-the-art automation to stay abreast of new developments, but cannot justify the equipment on a normal basis, should acquire and operate it only as a research and development project. And, until such time that experimental use reveals how to operate the equipment within the target ranges of profitability, the company should not replace its workable manual systems. In recent years, numerous businesses have invested heavily, and with some blind faith, in factory automation. However much of this automation increased product costs and lowered profitability, with little or no prospects for future improvement.

In contrast, most Japanese improvement projects involve equipment upgrade, not equipment replacement. Worldwide experience has proven that making equipment improvements can usually produce the same target rates and quality of production as buying new equipment—and at a fraction of the cost. Even when new capacity is required, robots, machine centers, and flexible manufacturing systems are often not the best solutions. Rather, cells consisting of the latest conventional machine tools may not only cost less, but may also perform as productively as higher-cost alternatives. In 12 months of operation or less, productivity projects are expected to pay back their investment. A similarly short payback period of two to three years is reasonable for major equipment purchases.

Naturally, there is no single, magical solution for achieving superior manufacturing. Although changeover reduction and space utilization are notably key issues, there are hundreds of other factors that play minor roles. Yet, collectively, all these factors together produce astonishingly substantial gains in productivity and, thus, profitability. Although there are no simple individual keys to success, the executives of companies that achieve the best results establish goals for improvement that challenge the utmost capabilities of their employees. These goals, accompanied by active management support, then become self-fulfilling prophecies.

2

□□□

Focused Factory Organization

REKINDLING THE SPIRIT of entrepreneurial dynamism in manufacturing management is the fundamental goal of the focused factory organization. For superior results, the reorganization of existing plants into multiple, smaller "factories within a factory"[1] is the single most important feature of productivity improvement. In so doing, the entrepreneur must have the responsibility and authority to effect improvements unhampered by bureaucratic roadblocks and delays. Therefore, the new so-called focused subplant organization must include such functions as material management, engineering, and maintenance. In 1974 Wickham Skinner vividly described the problems of out-of-focus factories and offered the idea of establishing "plants within a plant" as a potential solution, already a long-established manufacturing practice in Japan. Later, in the 1980s, hundreds of international companies have shown dramatic improvements from creating focused "factories within a factory." Yet progress in focusing manufacturing operations has proceeded slowly except for outstanding companies dedicated to achieving superior manufacturing. Contributing to this lethargic tempo is resistance to reorganizing office staff and factory support functions in line with focused operations. Nevertheless, leading-edge companies have set some excellent examples of successful focus in the factory and factory-support functions.

Before proceeding further, it is necessary to describe both the focused

[1]Wickham Skinner, "The Focused Factory." *Harvard Business Review,* May–June 1974, pp. 113–121.

and out-of-focus organization. For plant modernization to be profitable, the organizational structure, or the company's employees, must keep pace. Therefore, as physical changes are made on the shop floor, personnel must be organized to fit new flows of production and new management techniques. Most senior manufacturing executives and managers have experienced working in, or observing, both focused and out-of-focus plants.

The focused factory can best be described as a small factory, with the following characteristics:

1. Communications are superb. Because the factory is small, people can talk to one another with ease. As a result, every employee, manager, and executive knows each important aspect of sales, production, product design, and process.

2. Manufacturing executives and managers control the factory on the factory floor, or nearby. When problems arise, executives and managers are on the scene, providing instantaneous decisions on how to proceed.

3. A lean administrative staff is located in the main plant rather than at a separate, remote headquarters that serves multiple plant locations. Thus, the staff is close to its employees, and also in close communication with the plant's vendors and customers.

4. Executives, managers, and supervisors wear many hats when a business is too small to warrant the hiring of specialists. For example, the shop foreman or supervisor often has responsibility for equipment maintenance until the business grows to the point of requiring a maintenance supervisor. Similarly, the owner/operator or the chief manufacturing executive, usually supervises product and process design.

5. Factory support services are often provided by machine operators and assemblers. Repairs, preventive maintenance, and housekeeping are part of their responsibilities.

6. Office staff is minimal and intimately familiar with factory operations, production, and inventory status. When questions arise, by exception, staff personnel can step into the factory to learn, realtime, the answer to current concerns.

7. Everyone in the organization feels directly involved in all aspects of procurement and production. For instance, a discussion between workers producing the part and assemblers using the component can quickly identify problems and produce solutions.

8. Limited funds and financing are available for a small factory. As a result, every responsible individual is aware of the need to economize. The results are minimal levels of inventory, and investments in assets that provide fast payback. New equipment is never purchased until existing equipment capacities are fully utilized. Often, bargain-priced used equipment is considered over new equipment.

As the factory grows, however, more and more products, processes, personnel, components, and materials are added. As a result:

1. Communications in the factory border on nonexistent. With so many employees, operators may never see or meet the assemblers who use their components. Office staff and factory workers rarely communicate.

2. Executives and managers direct the factory from offices far away from operations. Now there is a need for systems to collect and summarize the tens of thousands of transactions, and for memos to communicate between executives and the shop-floor workers. Problems are not anticipated, but are identified after the fact, when reported through formal systems. The lack of timely identification of problems finds expeditors, timekeepers, and inspectors substituting for any direct communication between managers and employees, and among employees themselves.

3. Specialized managerial jobs and supporting staff functions blossom. Procedures and systems that were unnecessary before now become vital to the expanded plant. Verbal communication gives way to company procedures requiring written documentation. Even worse, written communication requires multiple copies that are filed in numerous areas, as well as in the company's computer data base.

4. Factory support services are provided by higher-paid specialists. Since these support personnel are nonproductive, their number is kept at the bare minimum. Thus, critical services, such as equipment repair, are not given the necessary manpower to keep the plant at peak operation.

5. Office staff rarely visits the factory, but instead spends most of its time reviewing transactions. As a result, the staff issues reports on such matters as decisions regarding problems and operating rules, rather than communicating directly with employees.

6. Workers operate within the limited confines of their specific jobs, since others in remote factory areas or offices are responsible for key matters like material availability and quality assurance.

7. Employees who manage equipment investment are too far removed from the responsibility for earning profits. Because the company is sizable and has considerable assets, little effort is made to upgrade existing equipment to increase quality or output. The easy, expensive route of purchasing new equipment is usually the only alternative considered.

Recognizing the advantages of small versus large factories, knowledgeable executives and managers almost always decide to establish small plants within the existing plant. When they do, the major issues that arise are the nature of the subplant and how to reorganize existing operations within it.

THE FOCUSED SUBPLANT ORGANIZATION

To provide a foundation for discussing the focused organization, two relatively new terms—subplant and subplant cluster—require definition. Since the smallest manufacturing units are the most productive, one objective is to organize new factories of the smallest size practical within an existing factory. These compact entrepreneurial units are called *subplants*. A second objective is to organize manufacturing units along either product-family or component-family lines. The latter applies when the capacity of a machine or cell greatly exceeds that needed for any product family. A product-family facility usually consists of multiple subplants. These are called *subplant clusters*.

In terms of size and function, the precise definition of a focused subplant is difficult to articulate. In the 1970s when Andersen Consulting worked in Japan, this was not an issue since focused subplants already existed. Yamaha, Toyota, Hitachi, and other leading Japanese manufacturers generally accept 300 employees as the maximum number per subplant. Beyond that, the performance of the subplant starts to diminish. (The average number of employees per subplant is about 30.) To achieve maximum success in productivity improvement, people involvement is critical. The number of personnel in each organizational unit is almost always proportional to the resistance to change encountered when implementing improvements. Thus, the definition and implementation of a new focused organization are important steps toward achieving commitment and involvement. In addition, this broad range of employees per subplant—from 30 to 300—hints at the difficulty in defining the nature of the supervisory organizational structure. This contrasts sharply with the relative simplicity of defining the physical entities, such as cells and lines (which are similar to subplants) and subplants themselves. An assembly line, for instance, can become one or more subplants, just as existing machine lines or cells can become subplants. However, some small assembly lines or machine cells, with a few workers, might be too small to warrant assigning a supervisor or foreman to each. Conversely, a very large assembly line, with hundreds of employees, might be too large to be a subplant with a single supervisor or foreman. In the largest factories, such as those producing automobiles and major appliances, the line length and the area occupied are too great for supervision by any single individual. Thus, these types of factories are organized into two or more subplants—the most typical of which are prepaint operations, paint line, final assembly, and test.

Exhibit 2–1 illustrates the focused-product organization. In this example, subassembly facilities unique to the product are combined with the assembly facility. Likewise, machining operations that produce product components are physically organized in facilities adjacent to the product assembly. Both assembly and machining operations are the responsibility of a product manager. Not all businesses have sufficient volumes to justify machines, cells, and subassembly facilities dedicated to product lines. In these cases, the focused organizations of assembly and machining may be separated.

FOCUSED PRODUCT ORGANIZATION

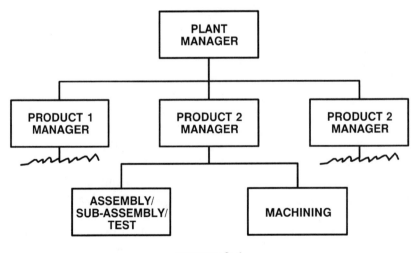

EXHIBIT 2–1

In productivity improvement projects, delegation of authority and responsibility to the subplant level, reduction of personnel, and simplification of the process are some of the factors that enable companies to reduce the total number of supervisory personnel and to increase the span of control. Western manufacturers suffer from too many levels of management. For instance, in the appliance factory, there is a danger that one manager will be placed over the three main assembly line subplants, another over machining, and yet one more over major subassemblies. These managers would report to the factory superintendent, creating three management levels; however, the new focused organization should have as its goal the elimination of middle-level management and the expansion of the factory superintendent's control to include direct management of subplants.

Equating the physical organization of a factory with the supervisory and management organization can be a major mistake, and commonly results in a wide disparity in the number of people reporting to different supervisors or managers. If one supervisor can supervise 30 workers, so can all others. If the smallest entity in the focused factory is a cell (synonymous with a subplant), three cell workers are too few to warrant assigning a full-time supervisor, or even a lead operator. Even a simple product subplant cluster could employ too few employees to warrant a full-time supervisor. Thus, a supervisor might manage two small subplant clusters, or one small cluster plus another large subplant.

PRODUCT VERSUS PROCESS FOCUS

In his pioneering work defining focus, Skinner suggested organization of subplants by product. Some of the most successful factories are focused this way, and in these, it is practical to have close relationships among the employees, the customers, and the vendors. Other profitable plants have broad product families and/or costly equipment that dictate focus by function. Perhaps most manufacturers need a mix of product and process orientations. Large businesses with broad product lines are most often organized as functional process factories. In this case, the functional factory is one type of vendor, whose customers are plants that use its products. If it is practical to reorganize the functional factory into customer-oriented focused subplants, moving the customer subplants into the customer factory would achieve the best results.

Where feasible, subplants organized by product are markedly superior to those organized by process. In a focused-product subplant, the manager can be given both the authority and the responsibility for monitoring all aspects of the business, including costs, schedules, and quality performance. Ideally, responsibility by product can also span every manufacturing process, including not only final assembly or finishing operations but also production of all manufactured components. Unfortunately, as most companies have grown, the primary trend has been towards process, rather than product, organization. However, there are several reasons for organizing component and subassembly production by process rather than by product. The most important is an imbalance in the speed and capacity of the final assembly/finishing operations and in subassembly and component production. Often, focus by *both* process and product is appropriate. The master plan for the Augusta, Georgia, plant of The Kendall Company (Exhibit 2–2) contains both product-oriented and process-oriented subplants. (Large, costly-to-move, existing processes such as sterilizers and bleaching are common to many products.) In this plant and another Kendall plant in Bethune, South Carolina, space savings of 50 percent made it practical for the master plan to include all health-care products in one factory. Incidentally, new docks in the areas of the wet dressing and paper package products were added to permit easier receipt and storage of necessary materials and components, thus reducing the amount of material handling required if this were done in the warehouse at the other end of the factory.

SUBPLANTS

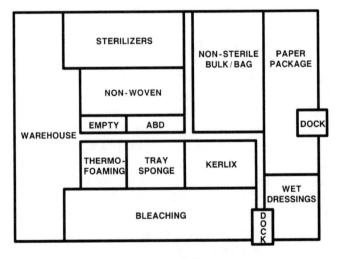

EXHIBIT 2–2

In many factories, final production facilities, especially assembly lines, have already grouped products by family. If there are three assembly lines, it is likely that three groups of products (or families of products) should be the basis of any new plant organization. For instance, Villares' Electric Motor Division in São Paulo, Brazil, assembled large electric motors in three factory areas. Subsequently, the project team found it appropriate to design three assembly lines, the rationale for which products to group into the three families being quite simple. In this factory, as in most, assembly facilities have evolved, naturally, according to logical criteria. For example, in the São Paulo plant:

1. The three types of motor families were small, medium, and large. The difference in size from smallest to largest was substantial.

2. The different sizes of motors on the assembly line dictated different transport methods. The smallest motors traveled on pallets on a waist-high conveyor line; medium-size motors traveled on cars on floor tracks; and the largest were moved by overhead crane.

3. The components for each family had some commonality within the group, but virtually no commonality with motors in other families. Thus, storage for each family consisted of a limited number of items unique to each. Each family's new storage area would thus be compact and manageable in contrast to the single, large, and complex storeroom previously used.

4. The tools and equipment required on each line were suitable for the size range of motors produced on that line.

5. The machines required to optimally produce components corresponded to engine sizes. For example, motor shafts for the smallest products were ideally machined on the smallest lathes, although theoretically they could have been produced on the largest. Shafts for the largest motors, however, must be machined on the largest lathes.

Exhibit 2–3 illustrates where product (vertical) focus or process (horizontal) focus applies for some of the major processes involved in manufacturing telecommunications switchgear. The factory produces six products that fall into two product families, A and B. Each family consists of three unique products. Family A consists of products A1, A2, and A3; family B consists of products B1, B2, and B3. In this factory, separate production lines and equipment were already used for test, assembly, and subassembly of the two families. Therefore, it was clear that it would continue to be feasible to organize one subplant, or a cluster of subplants, for product family A and another for product family B. In addition, most of

VERTICAL OR HORIZONTAL FOCUS?

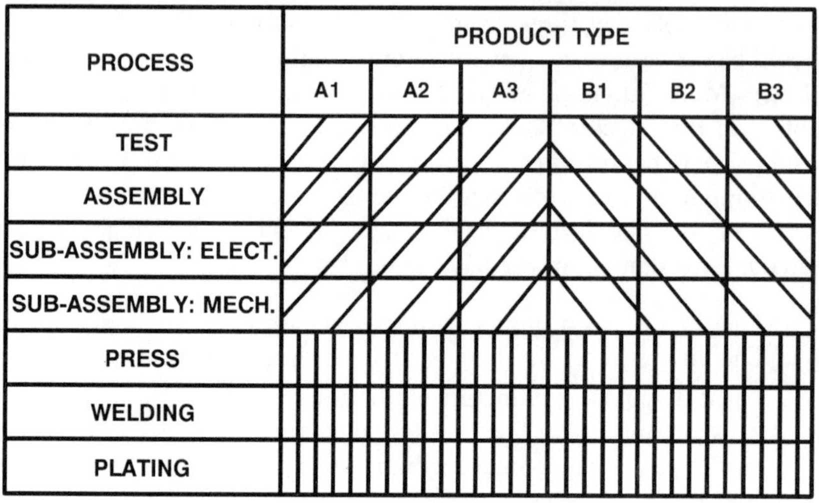

PROCESS	PRODUCT TYPE					
	A1	A2	A3	B1	B2	B3
TEST						
ASSEMBLY						
SUB-ASSEMBLY: ELECT.						
SUB-ASSEMBLY: MECH.						
PRESS						
WELDING						
PLATING						

EXHIBIT 2–3

the component manufacturing processes (press, welding, and plating) use one-of-a-kind machines or processes to supply components for both product families A and B. Consequently, process (horizontal) subplants, not product (vertical) subplants, were found applicable to component manufacturing. This illustration, however, raises several key questions. For one, what are the criteria for determining whether a specific process should be vertically integrated with other processes? And, for another, what are the criteria that determine whether different product types should be produced in the same or different subplants?

The critical factor for evaluating whether or not to integrate vertically one process with others that follow is the degree of balance between the capacities and speeds of the two processes. If they are well balanced, vertical integration as opposed to horizontal integration is most feasible. To illustrate this point, suppose there is a machine that has a capacity to manufacture components at the rate of 100 per minute. Since the assembly line that uses the components operates at the rate of two units per minute, it is probably not feasible to integrate machine and line vertically into one focused department. The machine speed is 50 times faster than the line speed, thus the machine would be utilized only 2 percent of the time if it were to be dedicated to the line. As a prerequisite to including the machine in the product subplant, balancing machine speed and line speed is important only if there are not enough machines for every product subplant. The requirement for 2 percent of the machines' capacity *could* be the *sole* requirement, in which case it *would* be practical to move the machine to the product subplant. In most factories, it is economically necessary to assign existing one-of-a-kind machine (or processes) to a subplant supplying several product subplants. When the one-of-a-kind machine, especially an expensive one, has more than enough capacity for all product families, it is difficult to imagine that the company would buy one or more additional machines and dedicate them to each product family. In the long term, since they complicate scheduling and synchronization of assembly and machining, one-of-a-kind machines should be avoided. Even worse, they have the potential to halt all production if they break down; and, if they operate close to maximum capacity, they limit the production of the subplants using their output. To help avoid such problems, Toyota Motors, which never uses only one machine of a kind, usually has two to three times the amount of machine capacity of other automotive companies.[2]

Exhibit 2–4 illustrates capacity utilization of an electronic manufacturing plant that has two families of printed circuit-card assemblies. Machine insertion has been split along product-grouping lines. The machines that sequence electronic components on a continuous roll, for later automated machine insertion, were installed in each subplant, resulting in low utilization of each machine. If only one sequencer had been available, it would have been put into a separate, small sequencer subplant, avoiding the cost of the second machine. Two machines were already available, however, and thus were used in the two machine-insertion subplants to maximize the synchronization of sequencing and insertion.

Some processes may use large amounts of raw materials common to a great number of items manufactured, and/or the items may have common usage in multiple product types. When this occurs, process specialization is likely to be more feasible than vertical integration. For example, consider the wire preparation operations in a factory using numerous inexpensive automatic machines. These machines process coils of wire by cutting them into lengths and stripping the ends. However, wire preparation for two product families requires few raw wires, and few completed wires, unique to either product family. Thus, inventory requirements for two separate wire preparation subplants would be more than those for

---

[2]Shigeo Shingo, a consultant responsible for Toyota's industrial engineering training, has written a book in which he compares the ratio of machines at Toyota with that at other companies and the true economics of investment in them. See *Study of Toyota Production System*, Japan Management Association, Tokyo, 1981.

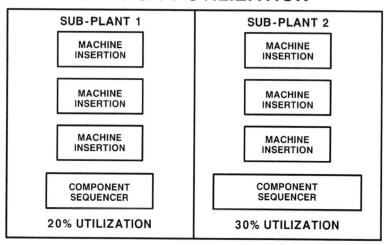

EXHIBIT 2–4

the single subplant. In this case, commonality of inventory is the important factor, not availability of equipment.

Often subplants can, and should be, temporarily organized around the location and structure of existing departments. This approach has the advantage of allowing many benefits of focus to be realized with minimal reorganization cost. The processes in Exhibit 2–5 have been temporarily reorganized into four subplants:

1. Inbound ingot and insert storage and die casting
2. Inbound coil and flat stock storage and punch press
3. Inbound plastic storage and injection molding
4. Machining and outbound storage

Long-range plans, however, should provide for further reorganization along routing lines or by product produced. In Exhibit 2–6, the machining processes have been moved into subplants for each of the basic manufacturing processes. Each subplant is now a complete miniature plant with areas for receiving and storage, processing and shipping (outbound storage). The end result of reorganizing most factories is a layout of not just subplants but of two, three, or more clusters of related subplants. In the factory layout illustrated in Exhibit 2–7, there are three clusters of subplants:

TEMPORARY ROUTING FLOW

Based on
Original
Departments
INBOUND
STORAGE
PUNCH
PRESS
SUB-PLANT 2
SUB-PLANT 1
INBOUND
STORAGE
DIE CAST
MACHINING
OUTBOUND
STORAGE
INJECTION
MOLDING
SUB-PLANT 4
SUB-PLANT 3
INBOUND
STORAGE

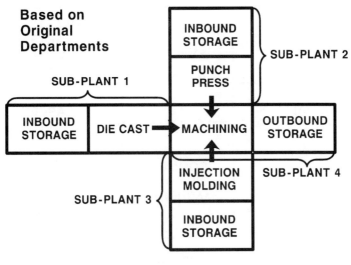

EXHIBIT 2–5

ROUTING FLOW
NEW SUB-PLANT ORGANIZATION

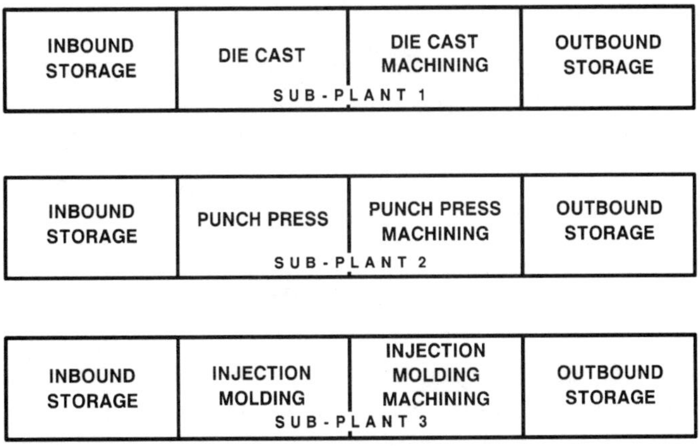

INBOUND
STORAGE
DIE CAST
DIE CAST
MACHINING
OUTBOUND
STORAGE
SUB-PLANT 1
INBOUND
STORAGE
PUNCH PRESS
PUNCH PRESS
MACHINING
OUTBOUND
STORAGE
SUB-PLANT 2
INBOUND
STORAGE
INJECTION
MOLDING
INJECTION
MOLDING
MACHINING
OUTBOUND
STORAGE
SUB-PLANT 3

EXHIBIT 2–6

PRODUCT / PROCESS CLUSTERS

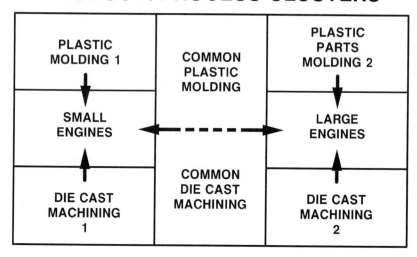

EXHIBIT 2-7

1. The final assembly subplant for small engines, and the subplants for plastic molded parts and machined die cast components unique to small engines
2. The final assembly subplant for large engines, and the subplants for plastic molded parts and machined die cast components unique to large engines
3. Subplants for plastic molding machines and die cast machining equipment used to make components common to both small and large engines

In this layout, all machines of the same type are in close proximity. Thus, if requirements for one subplant decrease and those for another increase, machines can be reassigned from one subplant to another without moving them.

MATERIAL MANAGEMENT

When factories were new and smaller, the process of receiving, storing, and issuing materials was simple and inexpensive. As materials and components were received, they were immediately taken to and stored in the vicinity of the process in which they were used. Thus, machine operators and assemblers found materials close at hand; they could actually see every material used, monitor availability, and give advanced warning of potential shortages. As factories grew, the number of materials and components increased, requiring large numbers of staff to maintain inventory records, and to order materials. Records of on-hand inventory became inaccurate because of the factory's size and complexity. It was no longer practical for an employee to personally check the actual status of inventory in relation to its use in production.

At this point, most factories concluded that it was necessary to develop a separate function for materials storage. To guard against workers taking materials from storage without formal withdrawal transactions, walls or fences were constructed between the new storage area and production facilities. Computer systems were developed to process material receipt and issue transactions. Production could no longer continue manufacturing items using materials stored in the vicinity, but had to request them from the stockroom. Thus, total inventory investment rose sharply, as additional time was now required to receive material into the storage facility, stock it, and then issue it for manufacture. In addition, a small army of personnel (and related costs) was added to the business: storeroom managers; data processing transaction entry clerks; systems and data processing development, operations, and system maintenance people; storeroom employees; and fork-lift drivers to transport materials from receiving areas to production areas.

The organization of focused subplants provides a basis for returning to the simple, low-cost methods and procedures of materials management in the small factory. Exhibit 2–8 provides a conceptual example of how large manufacturing plants are being reorganized into subplants for productivity improvement. Here a large factory has been divided into four subplants, each with its own receiving, inbound storage, and outbound storage areas for parts, sub-assemblies, or assemblies waiting to be used by other subplants in the factory. Unlike Japan, other countries have special problems to resolve with this type of reorganization. First, there is a need for a secure receiving and storage area, as many items are subject to pilferage because of their value or high commonality of use. Until a better way of controlling theft is found, it may be necessary to include a centralized, locked storage area in the overall layout. Second, there is a temporary need for a common parts receiving and storage area. In Japan, there is no need for this. For example, if all four subplants in a Japanese factory require small amounts of a common fastener, trucks would deliver them in individual containers to the receiving dock of each subplant where they are needed. Near term, for western companies it will be diffi-

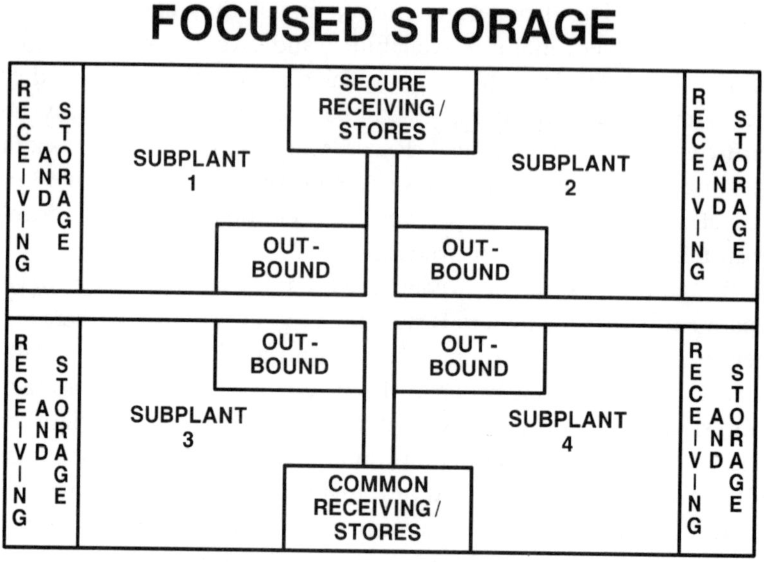

FOCUSED STORAGE

RECEIVING	STORAGE	SUBPLANT 1	SECURE RECEIVING/ STORES	SUBPLANT 2	RECEIVING	STORAGE
			OUT-BOUND	OUT-BOUND		
RECEIVING	STORAGE	OUT-BOUND SUBPLANT 3	OUT-BOUND COMMON RECEIVING/ STORES	SUBPLANT 4	RECEIVING	STORAGE

EXHIBIT 2-8

cult to negotiate such delivery arrangements with suppliers without incurring additional costs. For this reason, productivity improvement project teams are implementing receiving and storage areas for common-use materials. Eventually every company's target should be to receive all materials directly at the subplant where they are used, including even those items common to multiple subplants.

Centralization and specialization characterize the large out-of-focus factory. For example, materials management was created in the 1960s as a new organizational function and has remained popular to this day. Exhibit 2-9, a partial organization chart, depicts the traditional philosophy of materials management. Since materials comprise 60 percent or more of product cost, and constitute most of the inventory investment, an organization dedicated to controlling and managing all aspects of materials procurement, storage, handling, and transport should produce the best operating results. The only shortcoming of this organizational form is that responsibility for total performance is split between plant operations and materials management. Neither organization can individually control operating results. For example, if material is procured on schedule but plant operations produce later than scheduled, inventories will exceed target. If purchasing lowers material costs at the expense of reducing quality, total factory expenditures may increase. If materials management schedules (or achieves) late material deliveries, plant operations may not

TRADITIONAL MATERIALS MANAGEMENT

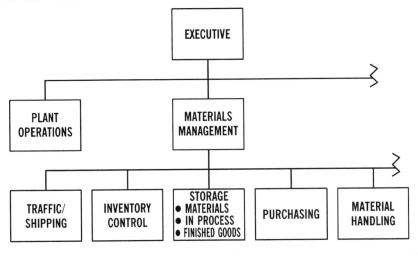

EXHIBIT 2-9

be able to produce on schedule, thus incurring cost penalties such as overtime and unplanned setups. It is often argued that the executive level has responsibility for every aspect of performance. Although theoretically this is correct, seasoned professionals understand that better control and coordination of materials and production rest at much lower organizational levels. Establishing focused subplants for factory operations is part of virtually every productivity improvement project. Less dynamic progress has been made in reorganizing staff functions and integrating them into the subplant. Every manufacturing organization, however, must have a totally focused organization as one of its long-term goals. Exhibit 2–10 shows how the focused materials management functions can be organized within the subplant. This organization, however, does not necessarily eliminate the continuing need for the materials management organization itself. Responsibility for storage of materials and work in process should obviously be moved into the subplant organization. By contrast, when finished goods are stocked on the factory site, materials management will usually continue to have centralized responsibility for their storage facility. One reason for this is that most shipments to customers will still include a mixture of products produced in several different subplants. Thus, a single storage and shipping facility will be necessary for efficient filling, of customer orders. For most companies, finished goods storage—and traffic and shipping functions—will remain in the materials management organization.

FOCUSED MATERIALS MANAGEMENT

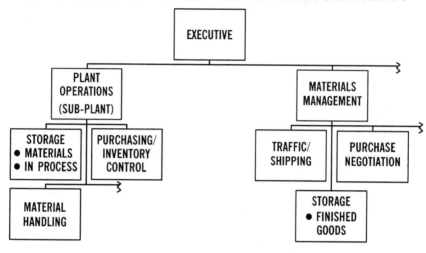

EXHIBIT 2–10

In many materials organizations, responsibilities for inventory control and purchasing are separate. (Exhibit 2–10 combines these tasks.) In companies now organized for centralized materials management, uniting the two responsibilities can simplify and speed the production process. At the subplant level, there will rarely be need for more than one person per subplant or multiple subplants to perform the combined inventory control/purchasing function. The central materials management organization can be expected to retain some purchasing functions (e.g., purchase negotiation of items common to many factories and/or subplants). As an initial and temporary step towards decentralization, purchasing functions related to order placement, shipment expediting, and communications might be transferred to the subplants, while responsibility for purchase negotiations would be temporarily retained by central materials management. As discussed in the chapters on productivity systems (Chapter 8), purchase orders should be recognized as obsolete vehicles for communicating requirements between manufacturers and suppliers. Thus, the purchasing function in the subplant will eventually be responsible for schedule communication, not for order placement.

Exhibit 2–10 did not include production control in either the materials management or subplant organizations, and the reason for this omission is important. When new productivity systems are implemented, the need for production control virtually disappears. The CONBON (kanban in Japan) system (described in the chapter on productivity systems) is the chief tool now replacing production control jobs. For example, Harley-Davidson Motor Co. in Milwaukee has eliminated more than 85 percent of its production control positions. As previously noted, some of the most successful Japanese manufacturers have 90 percent fewer office personnel than their Western counterparts. But Harley-Davidson and other leading-edge Western companies have shown that in some office areas equally substantial reductions are possible outside of Japan.

Throughout this chapter, illustrations depict the focused subplant organization. Exhibit 2–11, for instance, gives an overview of the organizational structure of an entire plant or plant site. Personnel and finance (shown in the chart) are the two staff functions that will probably continue to be necessary to support subplants and clusters of subplants. Other probabilities are tool making, systems, data processing, and building maintenance functions.

As previously discussed, the ideal subplant may average 30 employees, with several subplants having even fewer. The largest subplants shown in Exhibit 2–11 are managed by one supervisor; the smaller subplants are managed by lead people, who are usually direct workers and who have slightly greater responsibilities than other direct labor employees. In small factories, all subplants report directly to the plant manager, keeping in mind that an important business objective in designing the focused organization is limiting the number of organizational levels, not increas-

FOCUSED PLANT ORGANIZATION

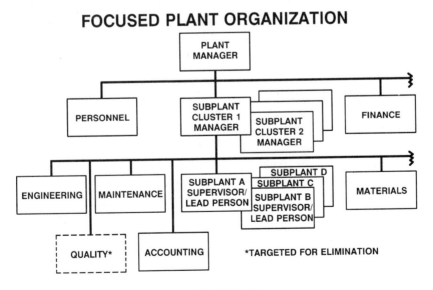

EXHIBIT 2-11

ing them. The illustration above also shows clusters of several subplants under a single manager. One manager is appropriate for approximately every 100 subplant employees, per shift. In most organizations, engineering, maintenance, quality, and materials are functions that should report to the cluster manager. If the workload warrants, these functions could report to the subplant supervisor. This, however, is not usually the case. Exhibit 2–11 also indicates that the quality function reports to the cluster manager. However, the ultimate goal of process design is to eliminate the need for quality control personnel.

MAINTENANCE FOCUS

Normally, the factory maintenance organization is centralized. To the extent practical, it should be decentralized for the same reasons that materials management functions should be moved into the subplant. When large maintenance organizations are broken into smaller entities, they become more manageable and can provide a higher quality of service. In a typical maintenance organization, there are centralized locations for tool benches, and for work areas and components used by maintenance employees who spend large portions of their time in various factory locations. With a central maintenance organization, there are several problems that arise. First, due to plantwide responsibility, supervision of maintenance employees is very difficult. Second, it is extremely hard to communicate dynamic changes in work priorities to maintenance employees in various remote plant locations. The following scenario demonstrates this problem:

> Maintenance workers have been assigned to repair two machines in two separate corners of the plant. Although these machines are down, currently no work is scheduled for them. While repairs are being made, the central maintenance department receives notice that a machine is down in a third area. This piece of equipment is critically needed for ongoing production; however, it will take time to locate and move the maintenance workers from the less important job to the vital one. Often work on the critical machine cannot even be started until repairs on the other equipment are completed.

A further disadvantage of centralized maintenance is the time that workers spend travelling to the repair site, then back to the maintenance department for special tools not included in tool kits. Once back at the repair site, they may again need to return to the centralized maintenance area for additional materials and spare parts to fix the dysfunctional equipment. In a centralized maintenance organization, one of a supervisor's most difficult jobs is setting proper priority in sequencing worker assignments throughout the shop. Supervisors answer to management of all operating departments in the plant. Normally, the maintenance workload is greater than can be immediately handled by available personnel. Time delays in completing previous projects and in repairing machines are not unusual.

Just as it is beneficial to reorganize the manufacturing plant from one large factory into more manageable subplants, it is also desirable to decentralize maintenance so that each subplant has one or more maintenance workers. They should have their own area with workbench and storage for tools uniquely required in the subplant. Although most of the maintenance organization should be decentralized, some shop activities and storage facilities still need to be centralized to house machines for low-volume repair of shop machine components. Low-volume work justifies a central location rather than several subplant areas. Also, supplies and component parts used by more than one subplant would continue to be stored in central storage.

In most factories, the maintenance manager reports directly to the plant manager, and this structure will not change in the factory of the future. He will still be responsible for workers who maintain the physical factory versus those who service equipment. In time, the people in plant maintenance will tend to be specialists—electricians, plumbers, carpenters, millwrights—and some may be mechanical/maintenance personnel.

DESIGN ENGINEERING FOCUS

To understand the potential for improvement achievable through focused design teams, it is essential to examine some of the problems of design engineering organizations. In Exhibit 2–12, a design engineer on one side of a wall has produced and passed his approved design (in the form of blueprints and specifications) to a manufacturing engineer on the other side. There, the engineer uses these blueprints and specifications to produce tooling specifications, manufacturing routings, process sheets, etc., and then passes his work over a second wall, where it is received by the manufacturing organization. Now that department is expected to produce high-quality, low-cost parts to the specifications developed by the engineers. Typically, manufacturing people have little or no input in the product or process design. In most companies that operate in this manner,

THE FIRST WALLS

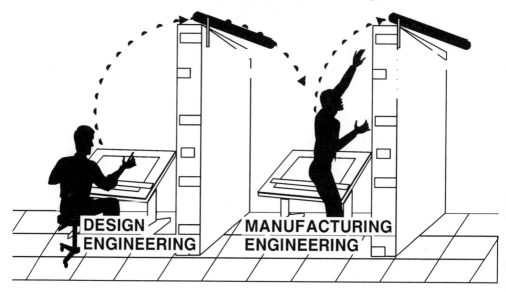

DESIGN ENGINEERING

MANUFACTURING ENGINEERING

EXHIBIT 2–12

the amount of person-to-person contact between design and process engineers may be limited to minutes per month. By contrast, contact in the world's best companies is minutes or hours per day.

Exhibit 2–13 shows the same design engineer tossing a set of identical blueprints over another wall into the quality-assurance department. Someone here then develops test and inspection procedures that he, in turn, passes over a wall to the manufacturing and inspection organizations. As before, these organizations are expected to produce low-cost products through a process developed by other organizations—a process in which they had little, if any, participation. Following these procedures, there is scant three-way communication among product designers, manufacturing engineers, and quality assurance personnel. To illustrate another problem of out-of-focus design teams, there is, say, a factory situated between an office building that houses manufacturing engineering and another building that houses quality-assurance. Both of these organizations are physically remote from the manufacturing processes for which they are responsible. In a similar vein, design engineering is located in a beautiful, wooded spot far from the manufacturing process. Ideally, the engineering organizations of the future (quality assurance, design engi-

THE NEXT WALLS

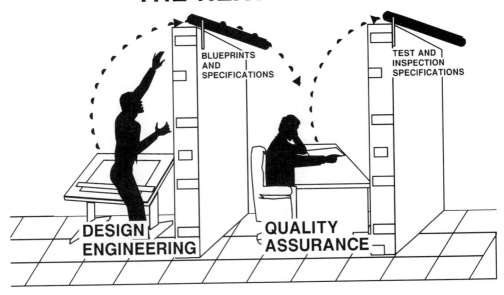

BLUEPRINTS
AND
SPECIFICATIONS

TEST AND
INSPECTION
SPECIFICATIONS

DESIGN
ENGINEERING

QUALITY
ASSURANCE

EXHIBIT 2-13

neering, manufacturing engineering) should be located within the factory itself, close to the production areas.

In most Western manufacturing organizations, design engineering departments tend to have relatively large staffs, but despite their size these are often not adequate for the amount of work required. In comparison to competitive organizations in the Orient, western organizations are often grossly understaffed. Clearly, the East recognizes the importance of design to the success of a manufacturing organization. Quality assurance is also understaffed in relation to the size of the job it performs. In recent years, quality-assurance people have been added. This move goes against the overall productivity improvement objectives of reducing the number of people and the complexity of the manufacturing operation. As previously stated, a key objective should be to eliminate the need for separate test and inspection of the manufactured products.

An additional problem of out-of-focus engineering organizations is their inability to adequately meet the workload. In such organizations, design engineers begin by developing a product and then passing it to manufacturing engineers, who create the manufacturing process, and to quality-assurance people, who design the test and inspection procedures. Next, the manufacturing organization puts the product into production, where it encounters quality, reliability, and performance problems that require the product be scrapped and reworked. All too often, production continues, leading to additional scrap and rework, with patchwork methods developed to salvage the product as designed. Eventually, though, the production problems result in a repeat of the design process—the product, process, and test and inspection specifications are reviewed and redesigned. Because of poor communication and the cohesiveness of the design team, additional problems will likely surface after the redesign process. It is no wonder why manufacturers in the West go through so many cycles before producing a product of reasonable performance and quality.

Many people refer to jobs performed after the initial product engineering effort as "product improvement" or "cost improvement" projects. But a more appropriate description is "error correction." If the design is right the first time, the wheel is round, not square, and overall design costs are sharply reduced. The presence of focused design teams, however, could assure the design job is accomplished properly at the start. When new and reorganized manufacturing plants are developed, large factories are divided into smaller focused subplants. Manufacturing companies should divide and organize product design teams to match the needs of these subplants. For example, based on the horsepower of its products, a plant can be divided into two subplants. The design team of each subplant could be composed of a team of design engineering, manufacturing engineering, and quality engineering specialists, who then would work together to develop and maintain the design of products and processes within their subplant.

When focused design teams are successfully implemented, many benefits can result. First, designers become multifunctional, just as they are in the Orient. Design engineers, quality engineers, and manufacturing engineers become interchangeable and can work in any of these areas as they have extensive training and experience in each. Focusing the design engineering organization reduces the amount of error-correction work. Thus, with fewer engineers, the same number of products can be designed and maintained, but this does not necessarily mean that the company will find it desirable to reduce the size of the engineering organization. When the results of using focused design teams are achieved, the engineering organization may then have enough personnel and time to meet the design requirements for new products and product enhancements. To improve manufacturing engineering organizations, it is important to add personnel capable of designing new and improved manufacturing processes. A majority of the manufacturing engineering organizations throughout the West are smaller than their counterparts in the East. But, unless the appropriate amount of engineering effort is available to focus more attention on designing less expensive, more efficient, and higher quality manufacturing processes, it will never be possible to compete with Oriental manufacturers. In the future, focused staffing will also make it possible to reduce the number of people needed in the quality engineering organization. This will be attained by eliminating inspection and paperwork preparation, and by introducing a manufacturing process that does away with the need to test and inspect. The quality-assurance person of the future will carry a quality engineering title.

THE PEOPLE AND THE SYSTEMS

If two companies implement exactly the same technical improvements in their factories and one achieves far superior performance, what are the reasons for this difference? Usually, this can be attributed to the amount of attention paid to the people and the systems. When changes in technical productivity are combined with corresponding organizational changes, and when the people responsible have continuous involvement in design and implementation, projects are more successfully implemented and organizations can more readily achieve continuous improvements. People in the new, focused organization (discussed further in Chapter 3) need more than just technical changes and focused organization. Unfortunately, many factory systems require large volumes of transaction reporting, focusing primarily on inventory and on direct labor efficiency reporting. They often fail to monitor meaningfully problem operations or period product costs. Therefore, people of the focused organization need new performance reporting methods, to minimize costly reporting of routine business transactions and to focus on simple and effective measures of performance that highlight problems and opportunities. These new types of systems are discussed in Chapter 8.

In summary, new highly productive machining, assembly, and process operations can be readily installed by reorganizing and modifying available equipment and automating those processes that produce a fast payback. Although physical reorganization has significant benefits, revising organizational responsibilities and authorities is the best permanent way to continuously improve operations. The focused subplant is the new organizational building block on which new styles of organization and management structures should be erected.

3

□□□

Future Vision:
The Plantwide Plan

THE LAYOUT AND FLOW of virtually every factory in the world, including the newest ones, are imperfect. Since these imperfections are often not minor, improvements in the layout and flow of an entire factory can dramatically increase its productivity. A tool for achieving this is the plantwide plan. In its simplest form, this plan is a layout for a single factory, which includes, to the extent practical, not only the ideal layout but also step-by-step strategies for the movement of individual processes from current locations to final target locations. In many companies, the plantwide plan needs to encompass several buildings on a single site, or even buildings on sites in other parts of the world. For most factories, creation of a visionary master layout plan can be wasted effort if management does not recognize the "living" nature of the plan. As needs change, it must be changed dynamically. For the master plan to be practical, it should be less detailed than the final layout of a machining or assembly process. Since the business itself changes constantly, the master plan needs to be dynamic and flexible. For example:

1. New products are developed and added to the product lines. Existing products are changed or dropped.
2. Product lines are added as a result of acquisitions or dropped because of divestitures.

3. Processes are altered to reflect product changes and process improvements.
4. Processes are added and eliminated as a result of changes in make or buy decisions.
5. Sales volumes change over time.

In factories with light, portable equipment, it may be practical to reorganize the factory to achieve the ideal master plan in a very short time and to subsequently change the factory layout each time the master plan changes. Most factories need several years, however, to rearrange all processes. In fact, the largest, most dynamically changing factories may never achieve their ideal layout because of the frequency of change and the high cost of moving large processes. In these factories, a master plan should be maintained and followed as the only means to maintain reasonable control over cost penalties associated with poor production flow.

A Siemens factory in West Germany, where Andersen Consulting did a productivity project in 1982, was the first factory outside Japan to develop this type of plantwide plan. This plan served as the roadmap for reorganization of facilities into a highly productive factory. At the Siemens factory, the products and processes were subject to rapid technological change. In the two years prior to the master planning project, the factory space that was rearranged due to these changes roughly equaled that of the total factory area. We, therefore, recommended, and management accepted, our strategy for reorganizing only those areas of the factory where technological change made reorganization necessary. Thus, the costs of reorganization were not incurred solely to achieve productivity improvement but were attributed mainly to the technological change. Since the productivity project was not charged with reorganization costs, payback of other project expenses was even faster than usual.

It was the plant manager who coined the term "future vision" to describe the product of plantwide planning. Pilot projects in his 3M plant in New Ulm, Minnesota, quickly demonstrated that only 50 percent of the existing factory space would be required after existing operations were reorganized into highly productive cells, subplants, and subplant clusters. Management recognition that factory space could be reduced by half triggered awareness of the urgent need to know where to locate revised processes. Management deemed it vital to have a plant layout that would avoid creating islands of manufacturing surrounded by large, unused, empty spaces, located in less than ideal locations within the plant. Similarly, it was important to locate component supplying and the using cells or subplants in close proximity, to reduce material transport costs and work-in-process inventory, and to improve employee communications.

With only the basic knowledge of the concepts of a plantwide master plan, it is understandable why most factories have less than ideal layouts. Exhibit 3–1 is a simplified diagram of the layout of one of the oldest and highest-volume plants in the world (various factory additions were constructed over several decades). This case mirrors the typical growth pattern of most companies. From the relatively haphazard pattern, it is obvious that there had never been a comprehensive master plan for systematically adding building modules to achieve a layout and production flow capable of superior productivity. As the exhibit illustrates, the travel paths of two component parts (1 and 2) from point of receipt, through various production processes, into final assembly and then to shipping are unreasonably long and complex. This flow pattern necessitates excessive people and forklift trucks. Worse still, the great distance between the various steps in the process causes poor-to-nonexistent communication between the receiving area and the supplying areas, thus resulting in substantially larger inventories and shortages than in plants with closely linked production steps.

In the typical chronology of change in a factory's layout, additions of odd size and shape are constructed. Moreover, as new and revised proc-

ILLOGICAL LENGTHY FLOW

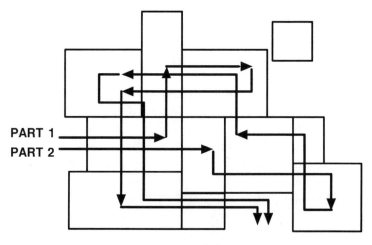

EXHIBIT 3–1

esses are haphazardly set down in any available space, the layout of each of the old and new factory blocks becomes less productive. Also, in numerous factories, many departments or workcenters within buildings or building additions are of varying sizes and irregular shapes because new and revised processes have been shoehorned into any available space.

Even new factory design and construction are influenced by the old layout. Often, inefficiencies of the old factory are repeated in the new. In small factories, the actual movement of *all* processes to their ideal locations may require only one or two years, or even less. In most large factories, designing and relocating *all* new and revised processes in the factory might require five, ten, or even more years. In fact, due to continual change, the master plan is most likely never achieved.

LAYOUT OBJECTIVES

The primary objective behind the development, achievement, and maintenance of a visionary layout is to increase or maintain profitability. Coincidentally, such a layout also improves quality, customer service, employee satisfaction, etc. The most important objectives of physical layouts of the future-vision factory are to:

1. Reorganize the factory into subplants. This new entrepreneurial organization is the most fundamental concept for achieving superior manufacturing status.

2. Provide maximum perimeter access for receiving and shipping materials, components, and products as close to each subplant as practical. The processes with the highest receiving and/or shipping volume are located in the areas of the factory with the most access to perimeter receiving/shipping.

3. Cluster all subplants that can be dedicated to a product or product family around the final process subplant for that product or product family. Thus, components and subassemblies produced in dedicated subplants will be transported a minimum distance to the final assembly subplant. More important, the proximity of user and supplier subplants facilitates communication between both, minimizing inventories and shortages.

4. Locate supplier subplants of common components in a central location. This minimizes the distance between the supplier subplant and all subplants that use components produced in it. The supplying subplant should be closest to the subplant that uses the highest

amount of output in terms of monetary value. Conversely, the supplier subplant should be located farthest from the lowest user in terms of value.

5. Minimize the size of the factory. When it is limited to a practical minimum, the costs of waste time and motion of workers can be reduced. Further, limiting space reduces capital costs for the plant and for conveyance or lift-truck equipment. Inventory is also limited by restricting plant space. If there is no space, it should be easier to avoid producing or procuring excess inventory. Finally, the smaller factory makes it easier for subplant teams to achieve cooperation and for the manager to supervise the operations.

6. Eliminate centralized storage of purchased and manufactured materials, components, and assemblies. The objective is to move storage operation responsibility into the focused subplant organization and into the subplant layout.

7. Minimize the amount of factory reorganization that will be made necessary by future change and growth.

8. Avoid locating offices or support services on factory perimeters. The best use of perimeter locations is for receiving and shipping, except when a portion of the perimeter has no potential for future use as an entry/exit point (for example, a side of the building abutting a river, another factory, or a steep grade).

9. Minimize the ratio of space occupied by formal factory aisles to the space occupied by production processes.

In many cases, it would be completely impractical to rearrange the factory to come closer to the optimum productivity potential of its existing building. This occurs when the costs of rearrangement would so greatly exceed the benefits that it would take years to recoup them. Other rearrangement problems include individual monuments—such as plating lines, paint lines, and other very large machines—that are deemed immovable; the loss of production while moving; the elaborate and costly utilities systems that tie the monument to its location; and deep, costly foundations and pits.

Although it may be inexpedient to ever plan moving to the ideal layout, every factory should develop such a layout, assuming that any monument could be moved to its most suitable location. This ideal but impractical plan can serve three useful purposes:

1. It eliminates the common problem of compromising ideals, too early, to accommodate assumed monuments. This precludes cost/benefit analysis to see if the monument is really a monument.

2. After the ideal layout is developed, the compromise suboptimal layout must be created. Its assumption must be that monuments remain in their existing locations indefinitely. But costs and benefits are examined, and suddenly some monuments are no longer considered to be such.

3. If monuments in the plan ever need major repair or rebuilding for other reasons, it may suddenly make moving the monument to its ideal location practical. Thus, the compromise should not entirely ignore the possibility of an eventual move to the ideal location.

LAYOUT CONSTRAINTS

New and reorganized layouts, developed to improve productivity, usually entail moving operations within existing factories. Some companies need to develop layouts for purchased or rented factory buildings, however, or even for new construction factories. Few have an opportunity to create a truly ideal factory layout. The reason is that both existing and new construction factories are subject to physical constraints that limit achievement of the ideal. In general, opportunity to achieve the most ideal layout is least restrictive when designing a new factory, somewhat more restrictive when planning the layout for a purchased or rented building, and most restricted in the case of reorganizing an existing factory, its equipment, and inventory. Following are some important factors that prevent establishing an ideal layout:

1. Pillars/posts directly supporting the roof or floor above, and walls between sections of the factory that cannot be removed without major construction to avoid roof collapse

2. Monuments, such as paint lines, transfer lines, automated storage and retrieval systems, or large machines requiring pits or foundations (moving costs or lost productive time may be prohibitive)

3. Ceiling height. Large machines and equipment may require especially high ceilings

4. Perimeter access obstructions

5. Multistory building

6. Location of utilities

7. Changes in floor level

8. Locations of large overhead cranes

9. Dimensions of building sections

10. Floor load limits

This list of constraints merely identifies some factors that may dictate which locations within a factory are best for a particular process, and those areas that may be unsuitable or impractical.

The master plan for one of several buildings that comprise Mark Control Corporation's Pacific Valve factory (Exhibit 3–2) clearly illustrate access constraints on the perimeter of the building. At that site, space occupied inside the factory was reduced by 44 percent, even though additional inside storage space was provided for approximately two acres of castings previously kept outside. The obstructions in the perimeter, indicated by Xs, consisted of another adjacent building, an electrical substation, and a number of very large silos. The Os, on another side of the building, indicate possible access from the outside; however, in this particular case, costs to accomplish modifications for access were great enough to prevent this option from being a short-term objective. The Xs (on right) between the main body of the building and the maintenance department indicate a barrier to access. In this area, there was a major difference in elevation between the two building parts, making it economically infeasible to move materials or work in process between them.

In every plantwide plan, identification of access barriers is vital to developing the ideal layout. Plant areas most remote from points of access are less desirable locations for manufacturing operations than areas adjacent to the exterior. The reason is simple: it costs less to move inventory

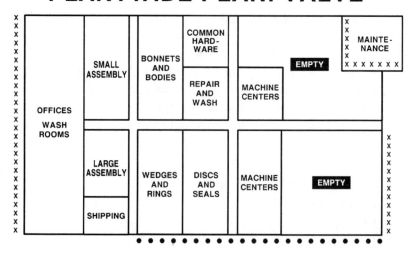

PLANTWIDE PLAN: VALVE

EXHIBIT 3–2

in and out of plants at points with easy access. Thus, areas with poor access, whether existing or potential, should be used for offices or left idle by the space compression of all manufacturing processes. The ideal master plan should always avoid scattering pockets of empty space about the factory, in favor of locating them together in one area. Subsequently, this vacant space may be used for new products, or sold or leased after constructing a barrier between the two sections.

After overall layout concepts are presented, large blocks of processes used in the layout should be enlarged, by themselves, to show the next level of detail. Exhibit 3–3, an enlargement of the valve factory machine center process block, shows that it consisted of two large, modern machine centers. However, at that time, the cost of moving the machine centers was quite high, more than the company was willing to pay in the foreseeable future. Although the then-current location of the machine centers (dotted lines) was less than ideal, and near-term relocation of the centers was not practical, an ideal location (solid lines) was identified. Because of the large cost of moving monument-size machining centers, a plan that assumed machines would eventually be moved to the ideal locations fit executive management's objectives. This minimized implementation expenditures, and made it possible to eventually move the machines when the expense was more feasible.

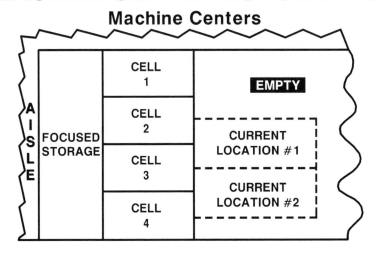

MACHINE CENTER MONUMENTS
Machine Centers

EXHIBIT 3-3

NEW LAYOUT CONCEPTS

Most traditional, generally accepted principles of plant layout and their evaluation criteria continue to be valid. In his book *Plant Layout and Material Handling*, James M. Apple[1] lists such criteria, and of these, we would change only two: straight-line flow and appropriate point-of-use storage. Straight-line flow has traditionally meant receipt of purchases at one end of the factory and shipment at the other. Fifty percent of material handling personnel and equipment cost involved in straight-line flow is usually wasted. Transport of material, for example, from receiving to processing would be a full container. On the trip back to receiving, the container would usually be empty. Second, in the ideal plant, point-of-receipt storage would always be appropriate, as it eliminates the costs of unnecessary transport and the added complexities of control associated with central receiving and storage.

Thus, in place of Apple's two criteria, we propose a single one: point-of-use receipt and storage and, where necessary, outbound storage. In the ideal situation, each process using a component from a supplying process would be directly linked, in perfect synchronization, with the using process. In reality, the majority of supplying processes in most companies will continue, indefinitely, to work on batches not directly linked to the consumption of the using process. Thus, it will remain necessary to decide whether to keep the resulting inventory in the user or the supplier area until immediately prior to its use. Usually, any inventory, except for the minimum necessary, should be kept in the supplier's outbound storage area.

Almost every plant layout is detailed, with the exact location of each piece of equipment specified and drawn to scale. This in itself may be one reason most companies are unable to dynamically update the master plan when business conditions change. The detail layout is, perhaps, too sizable and complex to develop and, subsequently, to maintain. A better method is to detail the relatively few actual changes that will be made in the short term, and to leave the majority of the layout in relatively large blocks for areas that will change in the long term.

Exhibit 3–4 illustrates the difference between the level of detail in the plant layout master plan and in the cells designed at a later stage. This plan calls for work centers of approximately 14 machines (a single process block) for which detailed layouts of cells or subplants can be developed at

[1]Apple, James M., *Plant Layout and Material Handling* (New York: John Wiley & Sons, 1977).

PROCESS BLOCKS

**MASTER PLAN
BLOCK**

**INDEPENDENT
CELL DESIGN**

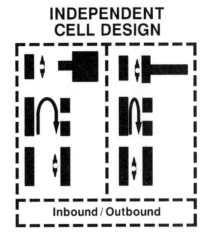

Inbound / Outbound

EXHIBIT 3–4

some future date. At this point, experienced personnel review the existing process and, without doing final layout work, estimate the reduced amount of space that will be required in the future layout. For most of the master plan, this block of space is the appropriate level of detail.

In the later design project, two designers working independently of the other might each lay out a cell (Exhibit 3–4). In the earlier stages of the project, a few rough designs may be produced for selected cells, lines, or subplants to demonstrate how space can be saved. However these do not yet make effective use of space—each rectangle shows the waste created by the irregular shapes and sizes of machines. In fact, both the master plan designs and the detail designs do not effectively utilize space. A later design-integrating step—*inter*dependent cell design—will improve use of cell space ever further. In all likelihood, the typical factory will require half as much space as expected. Developing a reasonable estimate for needed space for each process is, thus, a vital part of master planning. Timing the development of a plantwide plan is also critical. It is usually a mistake to start productivity improvement with a master plan. Unless the team responsible has had sufficient experience in reducing production, storage and office space, it will usually design plans that require the same or even more area than the existing layout. At best, inexperienced people will minimally cut space provided.

UNIFORM PROCESS MODULES

The building blocks of the ideal plant layout, as illustrated in Exhibit 3–5, are process modules designed with one common dimension, N. In this layout, an aisle system has been planned to service processes in the factory that should have a common dimension N (or a multiple of N). Assuming that N has been determined to be 50 feet and that the area required by each process is as follows, the target area dimensions would be:

	Area Required	*Target Dimensions*	
Process Type	(SQUARE FEET)	(N DEPTH)	(LENGTH)
Bench assembly	750	25'	30'
Large machining cell	3,750	50'	75'
Final assembly	20,000	100'	200'

One objective of the planned layout is to avoid extremely long, narrow processes. Thus, final assembly target dimensions are 100 feet ($2 \times N$) by 200 feet. Similarly, the smallest processes are a uniform fraction of N. For example, a simple bench assembly process requiring only 750 square feet would be planned to fit an area 25 feet ($\frac{1}{2} N$) by 30 feet.

UNIFORM PROCESS MODULES "N" DIMENSION

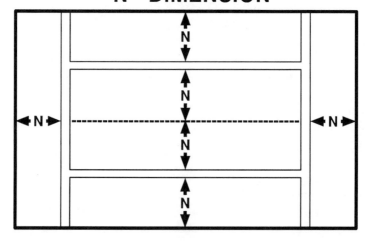

EXHIBIT 3–5

It may be fairly easy to visualize paper cutouts (or computer equivalents) for each process, to scale, that can be placed on the aisle layout. To develop the ideal layout, a multitude of alternatives can be tested by trial and error. When a process is eliminated, added, or changed, it is comparatively easy to test once again numerous layout alternatives to revise the target ideal. Even more important, uniform-size process blocks can be picked up from one area of the factory and put down in a new location without redesigning the process to fit an area of different dimensions.

Not all existing processes can be expected to fit the N dimension concept. This is because some, or perhaps all, of the equipment used in the factory is large and irregularly shaped. For example, most paint lines and plating facilities traditionally have been designed as straight-line flow processes, and their current equipment must be used indefinitely without modification. In these cases, process block sizes and shapes are, and must be, dictated by equipment dimensions. Sometimes, it *is* practical to influence the design of equipment used, such as changing paint lines from long, straight processes to relatively short ones. When this occurs, serpentine processes will usually simplify the job of overall plant layout and may even reduce total equipment cost. In summary, although uniform process module design best supports ideal plant layout, many factories include at least some equipment of irregular and/or large size. In these instances, uniform process modules may be less important to the design.

The chapters in this book on assembly and machining process design explain why the ideal process forms (or shapes) are serpentine or U-form. Based on the equipment used, or on the low volume of products and components produced, many factories have large blocks of processes that are not several operations linked together in lines, U-forms, or serpentines. Thus, the conceptual plant layout depicted in Exhibit 3–6 is close to the ideal since it consists only of multiple operation cells (or lines) in line, U-form, or serpentine shapes. In this exhibit, the largest cell (line) occupies a space for which one of the dimensions is $2 \times N$. Many processes have one dimension equal to N, while others occupy spaces that are fractions of N. The exhibit illustrates these important aspects of ideal plant layout:

1. Input and output ends of each process are organized to be closest to the plant aisle.
2. Every aisle serves processes on both its sides; thus, the ratio of aisle space to process space is higher than that of an aisle adjacent to a wall or a nonproductive facility, such as a tool repair shop.

UNIFORM PROCESS MODULES
SERPENTINE AND U-FORM PROCESSES

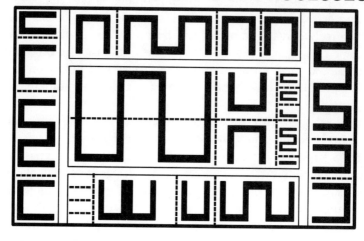

EXHIBIT 3-6

3. Serpentine and U-form shapes are fairly easy to compress and expand, like an accordion, to fit the N dimension.

AISLE SYSTEMS

Every structure—no matter what its size or complexity—is based on a framework. This framework, whether for an airplane, a ship, or a building, determines the structure's performance characteristics. For a factory layout, the framework is its aisle system, whose symmetry often indicates the quality of the factory layout itself. In fact, lack of aisle symmetry clearly points out the fact that processes are often designed in a wide variety of sizes and shapes. Such irregularities make it difficult to facilitate changes, and still maintain near optimal flow and productivity. In the future, if some processes are eliminated and others added, it could be difficult to find blocks of space that match the needed area exactly. Because of differences in size and shape of the processes, the sliding of processes back and forth to insert new ones could be impossible.

As seen in Exhibit 3-7, in order to best utilize aisle space, the aisle should service production areas of N depth on both sides of every aisle. Additionally, every aisle should originate at some point on the building's perimeter. The entry points for a rectangular building should be on its

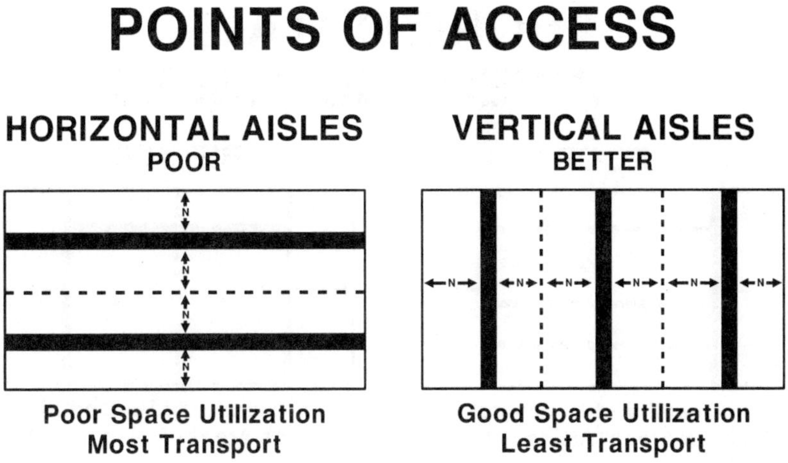

POINTS OF ACCESS

HORIZONTAL AISLES
POOR

VERTICAL AISLES
BETTER

Poor Space Utilization
Most Transport

Good Space Utilization
Least Transport

EXHIBIT 3-7

longer sides. As the exhibit shows, entry points on the shorter walls of the factory require more linear feet and total area than those on the longer sides. When entry is at the shorter side, the travel path from the entry to aisle midpoint is also longer. Aisles that originate on one side of the factory and end on the other are not adequate for most plants. These would be sufficient if all materials and components received at points of entry were used only by processes located adjacent to the aisles, or if items produced in these processes are not subsequently required by operations located on different aisles. Most factories, however, need and use connecting aisles to accommodate movement of materials between the main aisles.

If the ratio of factory space used for aisles to that used for production areas is to be near optimal, connecting aisles parallel to the longer sides of a factory should either total one or an even number. Exhibit 3-8 shows an odd number of connecting aisles, on the left. This provides one process area with two aisles, a higher ratio of aisle to process area than the example on the right. Here each process area is served by only one horizontal connecting aisle, which better utilizes factory space. The worst possible design is one which places an aisle next to the perimeter of an outside wall. This cuts the process area served by that aisle to one-half that of an aisle with processes on both sides. Additionally, travel distances and costs of processes on perimeter aisles are greater than those on interior aisles.

In many factories, aisle widths are exorbitant in comparison to their

HORIZONTAL CONNECTING AISLES

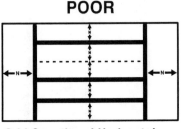

POOR	BETTER

Odd Quantity of Horizontal Process Areas / Aisles Is Bad

One Area Is Wastefully Served by Two Aisles

Even Quantity of Horizontal Process Areas / Aisles Is Better

Each Process Area Served by One Aisle

EXHIBIT 3–8

maximum needs—i.e., they are much wider than the size of material containers transported in them. Some large companies even have plant layout standards that dictate that their factories have aisles of specified, excessive widths. Some erroneous assumptions that lead to this wasteful use of space for aisles are as follows:

1. Lift-truck traffic must be very heavy since all purchases are received in one location and trucked to remote locations throughout the factory. Similarly, completed products are transported to a common central storage and/or shipping area.

2. The only economical way to move materials and components is in large containers that cannot be moved without a lift truck or hand-lift truck.

3. Every aisle corner must be wide enough to accommodate two lift trucks traveling in opposite directions and turning the corner at the same time. Thus, the width of the turn dictates the width of the entire aisle system.

4. At every point on the aisle, a forklift truck must have space to make a right-angle turn into the process area in order to pick up and set down skid-size containers.

5. Machine operators and assemblers who are located between their machines or lines and the aisle must have extra aisle space to protect them from stepping back into the path of a forklift.

6. Aisles must handle not only heavy lift-truck traffic, but also high volumes of people. All employees travel to and from their workstations in the aisle systems.

7. Aisle clearance for two lift trucks traveling in opposite directions must be very liberal to help avoid collisions.

8. In the future, the largest machines in the factory might need to be moved, or new, oversized machines might be brought in, so aisles must be wide enough to accommodate movement of such machines.

The new, ideal way of organizing factories into focused subplants drastically changes the functions of aisles. Since these subplants have their own receiving and storage facilities, much of the movement necessary in the old factory between receiving and central storage, and central storage and the process area is eliminated. At each manufacturing level, this also minimizes movement into and out of central storage and process areas. Also the ideal focused subplant can be, on average, half the size of the old factory. Therefore, the transport of materials within the subplant will be half as much as that in the old factory.

In Chapters 4 and 5 of this book, assembly and machining process design, we will explain in greater detail why small containers can be more economical than large containers. In addition, large and small containers can be designed for facile movement without the aid of manual life equipment or lift trucks. The ideal focused factory can eliminate 90 percent or more of the lift equipment required in the old factory, due to targeted focus, better container design, and other productivity-improvement techniques.

New interest in space conservation dictates new concepts of factory aisle design. Serving as a parallel is the design of modern interstate highways which now feature wide intersections. For most of their length, these highways are narrow, then become wider at intersections to provide space for exiting and entering. Likewise aisle design in factories should be carried out in the same way. Like an interstate, the number of exit and entry points on a factory aisle is strictly limited. When containers requiring lift equipment for movement are filled at a subplant along the aisle, they can be manually pushed into the aisle for pickup. Alternatively, a small pickup/putdown area for the entire subplant can be designed to occupy a small space adjacent to the aisle, eliminating extra space all along it. Like the interstate, the aisle need only accommodate turns at intersections and in pickup/putdown areas.

Additionally, one of the original features of modern, limited-access highways was to incorporate broad, grass divider strips between lanes of opposite direction. Strips reduced, but did not completely eliminate, the incidence of accidents. In urban areas where the cost of grass strips was prohibitive, barriers were built. At a fraction of the cost, they proved completely effective in preventing head-on collisions. In the case of factory aisle systems, the few workers who have workstations directly adjacent to the aisles could have low-cost barriers to protect them from accidents. The majority of employees in the ideal subplant, however, are automatically protected from traffic in the main aisles because focused storage is usually located between workstations and the aisles. Most workstations in U-form and serpentine lines are between line legs that are perpendicular to the aisle, as can be seen in Exhibit 3–6.

In the ideal focused subplant, employees should enter (and exit) directly into (or out of) the subplant from the closest outside access point. Much informal, secondary aisle space within the subplant is designed solely for people traffic; thus, internal aisles can be used to a minimum by people, and to a maximum for equipment.

In the past when traffic was minimal, cities designed and constructed streets and avenues that are typically too narrow to efficiently handle the volume of traffic today. Because properties adjacent to the streets are so valuable, it has been impractical to widen them. The solution has been to design one-way streets that move volumes of traffic at much higher speeds. Factory aisles can and should be designed likewise, as seen in Exhibit 3–9. Most of the traffic in this factory moves in two rectangular paths, each of which travels in opposing clockwise and counterclockwise directions. Component parts that must pass from one rectangle to the other are transferred at a set-down point indicated by the circle.

In the ideal focused factory, there will always be deliveries and pickups at each subplant on the route because of small, frequent lot production moved just-in-time to the next production process. Further, layout of the ideal factory locates supplier and user subplants in close proximity. Consequently, most traffic in the one-way system is picked up at one subplant and delivered to the next. In many cases, wheeled containers make it practical to manually push completed containers directly out of the supplying subplant into an adjacent or close subplant, without waiting for a lift truck. Finally, the aisle system is designed primarily for one-way traffic. Since there will, in reality, be only one or two lift trucks operating in a circuit, it will usually be practical to back up to make the next pickup or delivery if this results in the most productive use of the operator and the lift equipment.

When one-way aisle systems are adapted, extra aisle space required for protection against collisions between lift trucks traveling in opposite di-

ONE WAY AISLES

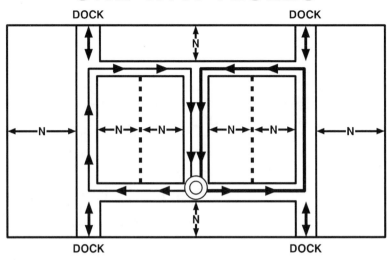

EXHIBIT 3-9

rections is eliminated. In many aisles, trucks pass one another in a minimal amount of time. With focused receiving and storage, and containers on wheels, the incidence of lift-truck collisions should be substantially reduced. If two-way aisle systems are still necessary, it would be more practical to have lift trucks slow down and pass with caution than to increase aisle size.

Finally, factories with extremely large machines rarely move them around; thus, the provision of wide aisles for this purpose is especially wasteful. The ideal layout, which consists of a U-form or serpentine line of machines, makes it difficult to reduce or increase the number of machines without relocating *all* machines. But since all machines must be moved if any machine is added, a new layout must be designed anyway. Additionally, most aisles are lined with in- and outbound storage areas that are reasonably simple to move temporarily, in those few instances when large machines need to be relocated.

A project team for Fabricacion de Electrodomesticos, S.A. (Fabrelec) in Basauri, Spain, faced the dual challenge of making its factory competitive with others in the European Common Market and doing so within the constraints of the illustrated five- and three-story buildings in Exhibit 3-10. Initially, the company thought that it would be necessary to use additional space on the second and third floors of the five-story refrigerator plant. The business plan to double capacity included the production

FIVE STORIES - BEFORE

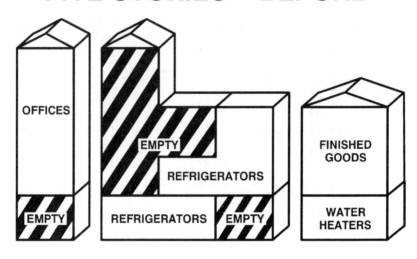

EXHIBIT 3–10

of previously purchased major components and the addition of a new frost-free refrigerator product line. As soon as the productivity improvement project team was organized, it encouraged management to adopt a new target: empty the building used for storage of finished goods and for manufacturing water heaters. As a result, the company could benefit by selling or renting the vacated building and also by eliminating routine loading of finished goods at the refrigerator plant, transporting the truckloads a few hundred yards to the finished goods warehouse and, unloading them there.

As Exhibit 3–11 shows, the objective of emptying the three-story finished goods warehouse/water heater plant was achieved, freeing up some 270,000 square feet of space for sale or for other new business growth. In this factory complex, there were fewer existing docks and potential shipping dock spaces in the refrigerator plant than in the finished goods warehouse. It was, therefore, necessary to develop a highly efficient system for sequencing warehouse picking, for lowering required refrigerators to shipping, and for rapidly filling and dispatching loaded trucks. To accomplish this end, one low-cost, continuous-flow elevator is used for each set of two docks (see Exhibit 3–12). The two docks make the loading of trucks a feasible, continuous operation. While one truck is loaded, another at the second dock can be sealed and pulled out. A new truck can then be spotted at the dock, while loading continues on

FIVE STORIES - AFTER

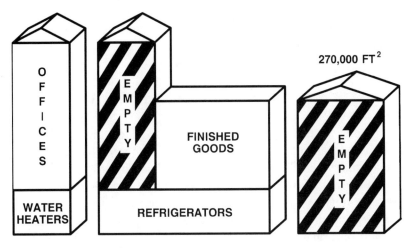

270,000 FT^2

EXHIBIT 3-11

the other. Space for the elevator system is severely limited in the dock area, however. Thus, second- and third-floor loads are merged in proper sequence on the second floor, and carried to the dock area by a single conveyor. The loading supervisor is then able to mix different products to optimize the use of space and distribution of products on trucks. The

FINISHED GOODS ELEVATORS

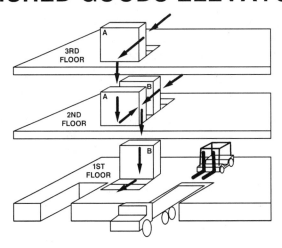

EXHIBIT 3-12

most encouraging message for companies with multistory buildings is that designers can greatly reduce most of the problems associated with them by providing adequate vertical transportation and focusing operations. When this occurs, the multistory building may be a lower-cost producer than the one-level factory.

PROXIMITY RANKING

In a complex manufacturing environment, the ideal master plan might encompass dozens of processes in multiple plants totaling more than a million square feet. Therefore, a definitive body of procedures is necessary to determine, as simply as possible, which processes need to be in close proximity. When, for example, suppliers and users of particular items are located in adjacent or nearby areas, there will be savings in the reduction of total inventories in both supplier and user subplants, and reduction of the costs of transporting components between suppliers and users. In most typical factories, the savings due to inventory reduction are several times greater than those due to decreased transport costs. Thus, processes should be located on the basis of their potential for reducing inventory. Rarely is there need to consider the volume and the cost of material transported as a criterion for determining where processes should be located in relation to one another. In a few cases, volume is only considered to break a tie between two processes with equal inventory savings potential, in terms of which should be located closest to the process using their products.

Increases in the total amount of inventory between suppliers and users can be exponential as the distance between them increases. This is illustrated by the following examples, which are based on a component used on the final assembly line at a rate of 20 per hour and produced at the supplying subplant at an equal rate.

1. When supplier and user subplants are directly linked, the target normally is to complete the component and deliver it to the assembler exactly when it is needed. Thus, theoretically, the inventory between processes could approach zero but will be considered, for purposes here, to be one piece.

2. When supplier and user are separated by an aisle, it becomes necessary to move a container of components from one to the other. The average inventory for both would be a minimum of half a container.

Since wheeled containers could be pushed from one side of the aisle to the other, the amount of transit is negligible. Thus, if each container holds a one-hour supply, inventory in it, between operations, would be 20 pieces. In this example, the few feet of distance across the aisle increased inventory by 2,000 percent.

3. When suppliers and users are at different ends of the plant, at least an hour can elapse between lift-truck trips and transit. Inventory between suppliers and users would constitute two containers totaling 40 pieces and would increase by 4,000 percent, compared to the one-piece inventory of hand-to-hand delivery.

4. When suppliers and users are in separate factories, a truck can make deliveries to users' docks once a day. Delivery from receiving point to point of use is also necessary. The inventory increase for ten containers totaling 200 pieces is 20,000 percent.

The method we use to rank proximity is based on the monetary value of the output of the subplant. The higher that value, the closer the placement of the supplier to the user. Although a more elaborate ranking model could be constructed to optimize inventory, this is seldom necessary. Since simplicity is of the utmost importance to increased productivity, in the majority of factories using proximity ranking, common sense was adequate to determine each subplant's position.

When proximity rating is done, big problems are first broken into smaller ones. As previously discussed, based on products or family of product groupings, clusters of subplants are laid out and then each subplant is ranked in comparison to the others in the cluster. Next, the multiple subplants involved in processing the same components are reviewed. These subplants should be grouped close together, while only the final subplant in the flow needs to be ranked in relation to other processes.

To the degree practical, one long-term objective of the plantwide plan is to isolate all vacant space. For example, the master plan for one typical job shop machining factory, seen in Exhibit 3–13, isolates vacated space on one end of the factory, as indicated by the diagonal black and white stripes. If and when additional businesses are acquired, this space could be more easily used than empty areas scattered throughout the factory. In the event that additional process capacity is required, it is rarely feasible to revise a cell, but usually necessary to add a new one. The large, vacant space can best accommodate new cells without rearranging several others. This example depicts achievements of such master plan ideals as common-size process blocks and efficient aisle systems; it also shows how

JOB SHOP MASTER PLAN

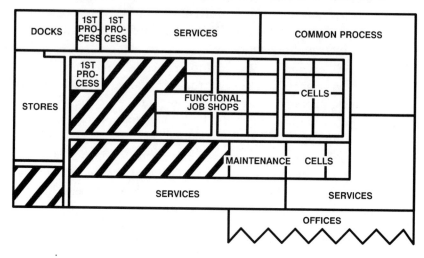

EXHIBIT 3–13

to compromise due to restraints imposed by monuments such as receiving docks in the only feasible location and large or costly common finishing processes installed on the other end of the plant.

ESTIMATING PROCESS SPACE REQUIREMENTS

Some managers and executives charged with responsibility for developing and maintaining plant layouts make a number of common mistakes, the most frequent being to prepare every layout in specific detail. There are many other problems too, such as allocating space for areas that are the same or greater than the existing layout. When detail design is completed, requirements for space are expected to be reduced by an average of 50 percent. Thus, a new layout with as much or more space than the old misses the point of productivity-oriented design. Also, often too much attention is paid to incorporating forecast requirements into the plan when future products have not yet been designed, let alone the processes that will produce them. And, as forecasts are never quite accurate and change frequently, a layout based on projections can be obsolete before it is even completed.

If change or growth occurs, a plantwide master plan with no provisions for these could cause considerable problems. Thus, growth and change must be practical components of any plan. In some cases, these factors could require cell or line changes. Those needing less space are not a problem. Changes requiring more area may be disruptive unless there is extra space in and around the cell or line. For this reason, the focused inbound/outbound storage area of a cell or line is usually designed with some surplus space. If space is provided for current inventory volumes in the focused inbound/outbound cell area, 70 to 90 percent of it will become available as a result of the project's inventory reduction. In many cases, it may be easy to see that when the capacity of planned cells or lines is fully utilized, the simple and logical remedy will be to develop a new cell or line rather than modify an existing one. When these instances occur, and when new products necessitate new processes, the new cells and lines can be easily placed in empty areas of the factory. These can be created by compressing the space occupied, or by locating them in a new plant or plant addition.

In numerous companies, the majority of processes have capacity for much higher volumes of production. For example, factories with single shifts have the potential to increase their output by 200 percent by operating three shifts. If, instead of having one 40-hour shift, three seven-day shifts are worked, the theoretical capacity would be 168 hours, or a 400 percent increase. By adding shifts and days-per-week worked, most processes have the potential for large capacity increases. Therefore, the addition of capacity should be limited to those processes operating closest to theoretical capacity only.

Most companies have relatively short-range plans to procure and install new factory machines, cells, and lines. Plantwide master plan project teams should become familiar with these short-range plans and should include them in the master plan. To the extent that some companies have longer-range plans, these are usually so vague that there is little point in trying to incorporate them in the master plan layout. Too much space has typically been provided for ill-defined future products.

Plantwide planning teams should always review existing long-range plans and forecasts. By doing so, they can judge the feasibility of translating future requirements into loads for existing and planned machines, cells, and lines. In those few cases when projection is highly accurate and future product design and new processes are well known, the forecast should be the basis for calculating required capacity. In most instances, however, forecasts will be less than accurate. Further, new and revised product and process designs have not yet and will not be invented until shortly before production start-up. In reality, management cannot expect to accurately forecast market demand or market share, which products and components will be produced, or which machines and lines will be operated. Thus, the most efficient way to provide for future growth and change is to allow for extra space and process capacity. For example, if a company would like to increase capacity by as much as 50 percent, and if every process has the equipment or space to place new equipment required to reach this goal, capacity problems will be minimal in the foreseeable future.

As previously noted, potential increase in capacity by increasing the hours worked per week may be enough to cover more than a 50 percent increase for most processes. Management can then focus its attention on the few processes for which this great a capacity increase is not possible without new equipment.

Before any work on plant layout can be started, it is necessary to know approximately how much space will be required for each process, assuming that before every process is rearranged, a new and detailed area design will reduce the space required. On most plantwide master plan projects, process space requirements should be based on various levels of detail or on minimal analysis and design, as follows:

1. The project team has previously or concurrently developed either initial design (Phase I) or detail design (Phase II) layouts for some processes. Space requirements defined in these phases are used as the layout requirements for the master plan.

2. In a few selected process areas, each team member is assigned responsibility for developing an abbreviated initial design. The purpose of this design—which is even less detailed than the initial (Phase I) design—is to demonstrate specifically how utilization of space can be improved in the area.

3. In most process areas, every project team member estimates the amount of space required. The approximate average of these estimates is the space allotted in the master plan.

While steps are taken to develop estimates of space savings, it is important to remember that the degree of accuracy per process block is not of major importance because precise space requirements are developed later, during detail design. Some original estimates will be high, others low. Since most of the pluses and minuses are minor and usually offset each other, the total space estimate is usually reasonably accurate. The master plan itself must be continually updated. Often, after the detail design of a block has been completed, the actual size of the block differs from the original estimate. In estimates for focused storage, space is allowed for changes or estimate errors.

At the start of a space estimating project, team members are each assigned responsibility for estimates in a particular factory area. Each responsible team member then conducts a limited review of the processes in his or her area and leads the entire team on a working tour. During the tour, the individual responsible explains the process, describes anticipated process or volume changes, and highlights opportunities for better space utilization. This person also advises the other team members of potential changes that might affect space requirements and of any other factors that might result in space savings. At this point, all members record their space savings estimates independently, and individual estimates are then summarized on the worksheet. Team members with the most experience tend to estimate more accurately than less experienced ones do, and they come closer to estimates developed by other experienced individuals. When estimates among team members are widely diverse, the team should return to the assigned area, discuss each of the estimates, and then prepare revised projections. This action usually narrows the range of the estimates, as well as informs and trains the project team.

ESTIMATING FOCUSED STORAGE SPACE REQUIREMENTS

In most factories, future requirements for focused storage space should be much less than those for today. This is because storage for existing inventories rarely takes up more than half the cubic volume of space available. In the long term, these inventories can be reduced by as much as 90 percent or more. Obviously, lower levels of inventory require smaller amounts of space for storage. In a very short time after implementing newly designed assembly and machining processes, work-in-process inventories can also be reduced by about 90 percent. The reduction of purchased item inventories, however, might take years to accomplish. When focused storage for purchases is implemented, it is necessary to plan for storing existing inventories and not for the reduced levels expected in two or more years.

Productivity improvement project teams must work to reduce wasted space in new layouts—even though space should be provided for future changes, such as an increase in the required volume or new and/or bigger machines or workstations. In fact, storage requirements are greater in earlier years than in later ones. As inventory is reduced, the space freed up can provide a planned allowance for future changes in the master plan, or even for alterations in subsequent detail designs.

As in the case of process design, it is usually impractical and unnecessary to detail focused storage space requirements for each process block in the master plan plant layout. Total factory space needs, including process and storage, provide a plantwide ratio of "storage to process space" that can be used to prorate storage space to each process block. An example of this procedure follows:

Line Item	Square Feet
1. Process areas	190,000
2. Focused storage (long term)	10,000
3. Total combined process and storage	200,000
4. Allowance for future change (20 percent of line 3)	40,000
5. Storage of existing inventory	100,000

Existing inventory requires 100,000 square feet of storage, double the total storage of focused inventory (10,000) plus the allowance for future change (40,000). Therefore, each process block storage space provided will be 52 percent of the process area (100,000 ÷ 190,000), since the area required for present inventory will be much more than required for future change, after inventory is reduced. If the existing inventory required only 30,000 square feet, the provision for a storage area would have been 26 percent (10,000 + 40,000 ÷ 190,000). In this case, the larger of the allowance for future change, 40,000, is used rather than the amount of space required for existing levels of inventory.

Uniformly increasing the size of every process block by the percentage of storage space required does not accurately reflect storage needs. Some areas will require more storage than others. Nevertheless, it is reasonable to add the allowance to every block to ensure that space provisions of the total master plan are acceptably accurate. Detail design will more closely identify the specific storage space requirements for each area. Setting the allowance for change should be done simply and rapidly. In a factory that has had little history of changes to processes, a 5 percent allowance would be appropriate. An extremely volatile factory would warrant perhaps 20 percent, while an average plant might use 10 percent. In most cases, storage space for existing inventories would be more than adequate to cover the allowance for change.

BUILDING LOCATION EVALUATION

Plantwide master plan projects (as previously mentioned) may encompass existing and potential sites anywhere in the world. This section, however, assumes that the scope of a project encompasses only a single building, or perhaps multiple buildings on one site. When evaluating various areas of a building or comparing one building to another, a crucial issue becomes which areas of the building (or which building) can be used to produce which products with the highest level of profitability. Further, different processes can operate more economically in some locations within the plant than in others. Some require higher ceilings due to equipment size and the size of the items produced. Others need large volumes of purchased materials or components. These processes can be operated most economically when their locations are closest to the best points of access from outside the factory. Processes requiring inordinate use of expensive utilities, such as electricity, water, and waste water disposal, often cannot be moved to factory areas where the utilities are unavailable or inadequate. The costs of extending the utilities to another factory area may be prohibitively high.

Clearly, large, open, unobstructed areas are easiest to use. They can provide the best environment for achieving near-optimal utilization and for closer proximity between suppliers' and users' subplants. Historically, some factories have evolved into a series of connected, contiguous buildings. Such arrangements, however, may present several obstacles to efficient layout because shared walls between two buildings may be load-bearing, and also floors and ceilings of different buildings may occur at uneven levels. These factors make it impractical to design a layout in which one (or more) processes span the common wall. Most likely, the wall cannot be economically removed, and a large step or drop-off at the dividing point makes design of efficient continuous flow processes difficult. When all other things are equal, given a small and a large building, or a building section, the one with the greatest amount of unobstructed space will produce the best results.

In general, factory walls, partitions, and fences are inhibitors to achieving and maintaining an ideal layout. Further, they are barriers to free-flowing communication between supplier and user processes. By reducing opportunities to interdependently lay out cells on both their sides, walls prevent achieving near-optimal space utilization. Walls, however, are sometimes unavoidable. For example, if a factory has dirty processes as well as processes that require a clean environment, walls will be necessary to separate the two types.

Exhibit 3–14 depicts a layout of two machining cells. At left, the designs were independently created by two designers. The layout, at right, shows the space improvements from integrating separately created cells into a single design, with irregular boundaries. This illustration highlights how a factory layout with walls can result in poorer space utilization than one that is open. To help the master plan designer present this information to executive management and operating personnel, one or more simple, approximate, to-scale sketches should be prepared. The main objectives are to:

1. Identify existing and potential perimeter locations where there are (or could be) points of access into the factory
2. Identify the portions of the factory perimeter where access from the outside is either impossible or completely impractical
3. Readily understand the various elevations of floor and ceiling, if they exist
4. Identify where utilities are (and are not) available
5. Identify the comparative sizes of unobstructed areas of different buildings and/or building sections

FINAL LAYOUT

INDEPENDENT CELL DESIGN

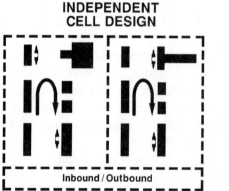

Inbound / Outbound

INTERDEPENDENT DESIGN

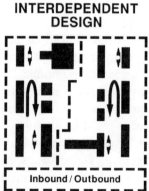

Inbound / Outbound

EXHIBIT 3–14

6. Know the locations of large equipment, which is unlikely to be moved because of prohibitive costs
7. Identify load-bearing interior walls and those that are not
8. Identify, in a complex building, the distance from the building section being evaluated to the closest point of access from outside
9. Identify building locations with existing and potential overhead cranes
10. Identify load-bearing capacities of floors in various areas, highlighting those requiring extensive repair

To help identify target sites for different processes, a matrix of the comparative value of different locations should be prepared for each building or building site. This matrix should include a ranked evaluation of various areas (bays) in a building. The lowest total rating would represent the best location for the most productive operations. This matrix and the to-scale sketches, however, are not adequate for decision support. For this reason, the designer should prepare a second visual that contains specifics for each area, such as square feet, ceiling height, etc. Finally, if shortcomings in key areas, such as utilities unavailability, necessitate large expenditures to use the space, an analysis of costs versus benefits would be required. As a general rule, when a building or building site has many bays or sections and numerous product subplants or subplant clusters, the highest-volume products, by value, are obviously assigned the best locations. The exception would be if some characteristic of the product process, like size, renders it impossible to use one area of the factory, or makes another ideal.

MULTIPLE-SHIFT PRODUCTIVITY

Sometimes a factory operates with fewer (or more) shifts than it should, or has imbalances in shift levels between different subplants. In these cases, operating the entire factory with the same, appropriate shifts creates greater gain in profitability than any other single productivity-improvement technique. Determining the number of shifts required to meet normal market demand is an important issue that can have significant effects on total factory productivity. For a few process plants, the decision is simple. Capital investment in factories like paper mills, plywood plants, and chemical plants is so high that these factories should run seven days a week, 24 hours per day. Also, the nature of some process plants (or process operations) is such that a seven-day-week, three-shift operation is necessary or desirable. For example, steel mills, foundries, and heat-treatment facilities are operations in which the cost of capital investment is a large factor in determining the number of shifts; but equally, or more, important is the expense of shutting down and restarting operations of this nature. If furnaces and melting processes are involved, shutdown and start-up are very expensive.

In most instances, factories whose processes do not require a high capital investment or around-the-clock operation should be planned as either one- or two-shift plants. Imbalances in the number of shifts operated in different subplants (departments) of a factory, however, can seriously reduce overall productivity. For example, in a factory with three interrelated subplants, extra inventory buffers are required when subplants have a different number of shifts. Components and/or assemblies flow from subplant A into subplant B and then to subplant C. Subplants A and C work one shift, while subplant B works two. Subplant A needs to build up at least an eight-hour work buffer in order to make enough work available for subplant B to keep it operating on the second shift, during which subplant A is idle. Similarly, subplant B works the second shift, while subplant C is idle. A buffer of at least eight hours of work will build up between subplants B and C.

When a plant is designed and/or managed as a uniform two-shift factory, the capital investment in plant and equipment could be up to 50 percent less than that of a factory designed and/or operated for one shift, producing an equal volume of products. When two companies manufacture the same product with the same level of market demand, the one designed and operated as a two-shift factory should always be able to produce products at lower costs than the one-shift plant. When every subplant of a factory operates a uniform number of shifts, the buffer inventory between each one can be reduced to a minimum.

A majority of low- to medium-volume assembly factories, worldwide, operate one shift and must solve a problem unique to assembly in order to gain some of the benefits of multiple-shift operations. The problem is that the shortest, practical assembly cycle times are also the most labor-productive in terms of hours required to assemble a product. If an assembly line produces 100 units per day on one shift, a cycle time of five minutes per worker per unit would be increased to more than 10 minutes per worker per unit by changing to two shifts that produce 50 units each. The degree of added complexity for longer cycle time and extra wasted motion would probably cause a 10 to 20 percent drop in productivity.

When machining departments of a factory work two shifts and final assembly works one, the inventory between machining and assembly must equal no less than one full shift of machining output. If, however, there are two assembly lines, each operated on different shifts, the inventory between machining and assembly could be reduced by as much as half. Moreover, if assemblers on both shifts could be trained to move from one line to the other during each shift, the inventory between machining and assembly could be cut even further.

Before reorganization of Fabrelec's (Fabricacion de Electrodomesticos, S.A.) refrigerator factory in Basauri, Spain, foaming operations were performed on three shifts and final assembly on two. The shift imbalance required refrigerators to be moved from a continuous-flow foam process to storage, then from storage to final assembly. The penalty was not only the extra labor required to move refrigerators individually, back and forth between storage or the space needed to store them, but also an unacceptable level of defects. The unusually high number of flaws (small scratches and dents) was a direct result of additional handling between two portions of the process and stores. By installing additional foaming equipment, it was possible to balance operations in the Fabrelec plant. The swap of capital tied up in buffer inventory to capital for the new equipment was about even. It was of greater importance that large improvements in material handling and reduced expenses for defect repair gave an immediate payback.

An auto assembly plant that Andersen Consulting worked with in Argentina also had an imbalance between shifts. All employees on body and final assembly lines worked one shift, and employees on the paint line worked two. This forced the factory to carry a buffer of hundreds of automobiles on expensive and complex overhead conveyors. To eliminate most of the overhead buffer stock, some body and final assembly lines could be scheduled on each shift.

When other practical considerations do not dictate three shifts, plants should most often be designed as two- rather than three-shift plants. Given lunch times and breaks, without considering downtime for maintenance repair, 21 hours or less normally can be worked in a three-shift plant. The gain from adding a third shift is five hours, from 16 hours of work per day to 21. This production improvement costs an amount equal to an additional eight hours per day. In factories operating three shifts and achieving only 21 hours of production, it is practical to raise capacity by more than 14 percent by increasing production hours to 24. Factories working at full, three-shift capacity, and capable of selling any increase in output, should design relief procedures for manning equipment during the absence of their normal operating crews, thus keeping the plant in operation 24 hours. When a factory is designed and operated for three shifts, weekends are the only time available to meet urgent new market demands or to recover from time lost due to repair. A factory designed for one or two shifts can achieve flexibility of capacity by working overtime any day of the week, or by temporarily adding shifts. This greatly increases its customer-service level and speeds recovery from unusual downtime.

COST/BENEFIT ANALYSIS

Any improvement project should produce both tangible and intangible results. Since businessmen recognize that the purpose of being in business is to generate profit, intangible benefits are properly considered as bonuses provided by the project, which is undertaken with the objective of increasing profitability. Every company has its own forms and procedures for requesting and authorizing projects. Few, however, have disciplines for tracking estimated and actual costs and benefits during the design and implementation stages. The standard methodology for productivity improvement used in the case examples in this book includes preparation of pro forma financial representations of the effect of planned and actual results. The pro forma statements most meaningful to top executives are balance sheets, operating statements, and cash flow statements.

Productivity teams should review and understand company accounts and base current and projected costs and profits on recent operating results and balance sheet information. Some project teams have attempted to estimate future results based on future sales forecasts and budgets. Usually, they find they have a full-time job just trying to update projections to correspond to the latest forecasts. The problem is simple: every forecast is inaccurate; thus, each is subject to frequent change. It is reasonable to expect projections of costs and benefits, based on an initial base period, at the end of each phase of a project, including the implementation phase. In cases where existing operations are reorganized, management should expect project teams to pay back the costs of design and installation in 12 months or less of operation. When the project permits design and installation of a new plant and major equipment purchases, payback in two to three years of operation is a reasonable management-directed target.

OFFICE LOCATION IDEALS

Focused manufacturing ideals call for the movement of office and other support functions into the subplants to which they directly relate, as outlined in Chapter 2. There are numerous such functions, however, that will continue to operate as centralized services. But the question is where should both types of offices and facilities be located. Factory services (such as plant maintenance, tool crib, tool repair, supplies stores, test laboratory, credit union, and cafeteria) are often located around the perimeter of the building. When they are located adjacent to exterior walls, factory productivity is reduced because they limit the opportunities for direct points of material receipts for subplants.

Offices related to focused subplants should be in the subplants themselves, or adjacent to them. A large office block in the center of the factory, however, may cause supervisors and other service providers to be too remote from the operations they service, or may interfere with the otherwise logical flow of production and communications between subplants on opposite sides of the offices. Therefore, in many factories, it may be best to locate offices in mezzanines above or near the processes supported. Although the most ideal locations for support functions are in closest proximity to the subplant, offices should not be placed where they would interfere with the flow of production.

PUTTING IT ALL TOGETHER

An earlier example, the Fabrelec five-story refrigerator plant, demonstrates the blending of all elements of a plantwide plan. The existing factory plant, shown in Exhibit 3–15, presented an array of obstacles to efficient layout. For instance, the factory abutted a river on one side and several buildings on two others. Therefore, potential entry and exit were limited to less than one-third of the perimeter of the building. The paint line, large enough for refrigerators, was unquestionably a monument that was too costly to move. It was also located where it did not interfere with entry/exit to the building and did not separate different processes, thus causing lengthy transport from processes on one side of the paint line to those on the other. As previously discussed, the company business plan involved adding more component manufacturing and a new product line and doubling its capacity overall. The new factory layout (depicted in Exhibit 3–16) compressed all existing operation space. For example, all

REFRIGERATOR PLANT - BEFORE

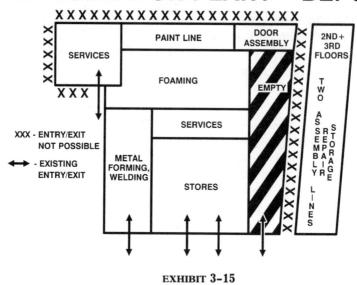

EXHIBIT 3-15

REFRIGERATOR PLANT - AFTER

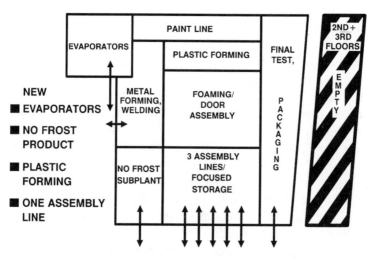

EXHIBIT 3-16

three new assembly lines and their related focused storage are now located in the area that was previously used only for storage. Assembly, user of the most components purchased from other suppliers, is adjacent to the area with access to the greatest number of docks.

New receiving points have been provided for metal forming and welding processes that use large steel coils and for new evaporator subplants. An existing entry, previously used to receive steel coils, now receives all components and materials needed by the independent subplant for the new product line, frost-free refrigerators. The mainline flow of the largest items is almost continuous. It starts with metal forming and welding, moves into the paint line, and out to the foaming process. From foaming, the process flows in and out of final assembly lines. Completed refrigerators are then conveyed to finished goods warehouse areas on the second and third floors. The evaporator, made in its own subplant, is not as large or expensive as the components of the mainline flow. Thus, it is located fairly far from assembly. By contrast, the new plastic forming area, used to form very large inner liners, is located as close as possible to its next point of use.

To sum up, most factories around the world have illogical and lengthy process flows that interfere with the achievement of superior productivity. Worse, few of these factories have plans for systematically rearranging the plant layout to eventually achieve process flows and manufacturing costs that are even close to perfect. Every factory must develop, maintain, and follow a plantwide master plan to ultimately attain the objective of being the superior manufacturer.

4

□□□

Assembly Process Design

BRINGING THE OPERATION of the assembly process up to superior manufacturing levels is akin to discovering the proverbial pot of gold at the end of the rainbow. Some opportunities for improvement are directly or indirectly related to assembly, such as reduction of investment in purchased and manufactured component inventory, and in work-in-process and finished goods inventory; as well as reduction in factory space and payroll. These reductions in assembly are often significantly higher than those for the same categories in other parts of the factory. Typically, stocks of components and finished goods are the biggest portion of inventory; space reductions of 80 percent are common; and assembly employs more people than other departments. If executive management wants substantial gains in profitability, it can usually expect the assembly department to generate greater benefits than other factory areas and probably with relatively low capital investment.

Unlocking the improvement potentials of the assembly process, however, entails understanding and agreeing with some simple premises. For example:

1. The area occupied by the existing assembly line is more than required. Excess space around the process fills with unnecessary inventory, causes wasted time and motion, requires greater plant and equipment investment, and inhibits team spirit.
2. The sizes of containers used at the assembly line require the area to be larger than necessary. Big containers also increase the time and

motion involved in taking something from (or putting something into) a container.

3. Employees' capacity to excel at manufacturing tasks is underutilized in terms of quality and quantity. Physical process design inhibits teamwork and team spirit since the distance between workers is too great.

4. In numerous cases, tools, fixtures, and low-cost automation are not used to improve assembly jobs in terms of the time required for the operation, the quality of assembly, and worker comfort.

5. Component shortages frequently interfere with producing the schedule.

6. A bureaucracy of support organizations adds time and cost to the assembly business.

CONTAINERS

It is highly probable that the importance of container design is still one of the least-understood aspects of productivity improvement. Without a doubt, the containers are one of the essential building blocks of better manufacturing, but their chief shortcomings are they are too large and require packaging material and labor. It is imperative to understand that every container is too big, unless, of course, there is no container at all.

Decidedly, container size can have a great effect on inventory investment. For example, consider an item received in containers of 100 units each, then processed at a machine where each completed unit is put into another container capable of holding 100. In this instance, the minimum work-in-process average investment and throughput time would be 100 units, 50 each in both inbound and outbound containers. By reducing the container size to 10 units, lead time into and out of the machine operation and inventory in process would be lowered by 90 percent. In this example, only one operation was performed. If the item required 10 machining operations, the savings in inventory units would be 900 rather than 90. Thus, container size has an even greater effect on inventory and lead time when items manufactured require numerous operations.

In addition, large containers cause two types of wasted time and motion. The first, excessive reaching, is illustrated in Exhibit 4-1. In this case, the factory worker removes large, heavy completed parts from the machine and bends and stretches to put them into the outbound container. He then turns to the inbound container, bends and stretches to

POOREST PRODUCTIVITY

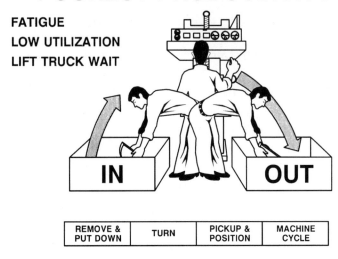

FATIGUE
LOW UTILIZATION
LIFT TRUCK WAIT

REMOVE & PUT DOWN	TURN	PICKUP & POSITION	MACHINE CYCLE

EXHIBIT 4-1

pick up the next part, and positions it in the machine, which he then starts. As an example, at Harley-Davidson's machine shop, the average operation using large containers wasted up to 75 percent of the machine's potential cutting time. Using the smallest possible containers and placing them at machine height improves machine utilization while reducing operator fatigue. Even further improvement can be realized by eliminating the idle time operators spend waiting for forklift trucks to remove full boxes of completed items and bring the next container to be processed. With the use of a short conveyor that brings parts to the process and takes them to the next one, or by putting wheels on the container, this idle time can be reduced. As for replacing human operators with robots, it is a fact that most robot cells duplicate the mistakes of manual operations. Thus, the robot often travels the same distance previously moved by the operator, wasting both costly machine and robot capacity.

A vendor productivity team in the Xerox, Resende, R.J., Brazil, plant worked with Metalurgica Jardím, its supplier of a sorter tray subassembly, to design the wheeled, self-packaging container in Exhibit 4-2. It is used at the last supplier's operation, eliminating the cost of labor and materials required for cardboard packaging since the container is designed to protect the contents without cardboard dividers. The wheels on the container permit it to be rolled from the last operation, adjacent to the supplier's shipping dock, onto a truck. Then it subsequently is rolled off the truck

XEROX TRAY CONTAINER

EXHIBIT 4-2

to the point of assembly at the Xerox factory. With wheels on the container, there is no need for a forklift.

The second type of wasted time and motion caused by large containers is excessive walk time (illustrated in Exhibit 4-3). In this example of a motorcycle assembly line, enormous containers beside the line hold large components such as tires, wheels, and handlebars. These large boxes dictate the length of the conveyor. It is easy to see that assemblers must make multiple trips between the large containers behind the line and the motorcycles being assembled. The long line, caused by the large containers, results in there being more motorcycles on the line than workers to assemble them. And any unit in work-in-process not being worked on is excess inventory. In Exhibit 4-4, container size has been reduced and the containers have been redesigned for easy access from the front. Making this adjustment eliminates the walk time, although workers must still turn to get each required part. Line length is reduced, to the minimum needed when the number of units on the line is equal to the number of assemblers on it. This is especially important to achieve flexibility in changing the output/manning of the line. When required volume on a line with distant workstations is cut in half, a company likes to reduce the number of assemblers by the same amount. Because assembly stations are far from one another, it is either impractical or more expensive for

LINE STORAGE - - BAD

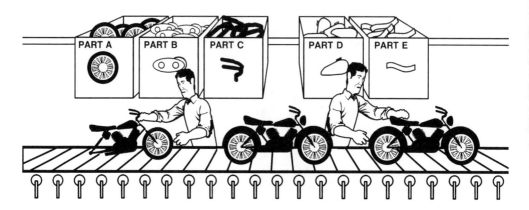

EXHIBIT 4-3

one operator to man two stations since the assembler would spend added time walking from one station to the other.

As demonstrated, reducing container size lessens the amount of time wasted in walking, turning, and reaching. Many factories use containers that add unnecessary labor and material to both packaging and opening

LINE STORAGE — GOOD
DROP FRONT CONTAINERS

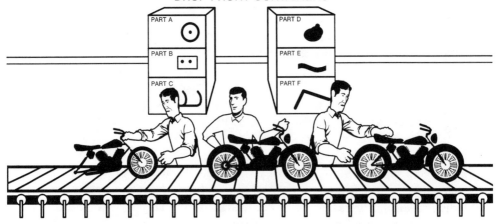

EXHIBIT 4-4

packages. Perhaps most of the containers used in a majority of factories are cardboard cartons, requiring suppliers to expend labor to assemble them, as well as the internal dividers and layer separators that cushion carton contents and protect them from damage caused by jostling or rough handling during transit.

When received at the using factory, the carton or package must be disassembled, either at a receiving or storage point or on the line as part of the assembly job. The materials used in packaging—cartons, internal dividers, cardboard sheets, tape, and banding—do not add value to the product produced but add labor and material costs. Frequently, packaging material is scrapped by the factory after the contents are used. A superior design is a self-packaging container, which is constructed as a turnaround container and returned empty to the supplier, filled, and then delivered again to the using factory. Such a container saves on packaging material costs since it has built-in damage protection and, if necessary, internal partitions. The container eliminates packaging/unpacking labor because of its permanent, turnaround design.

Manufacturing executives usually quickly understand the advantages of smaller, self-packaging containers. Additionally, they recognize the need to implement their use if it is practical to pay back the cost of different containers. Individuals responsible for implementing the use of smaller containers should understand the answers to these questions:

1. We have 10,000 containers in the factory, and our suppliers have the same amount. How can we afford to replace 20,000 containers?

Answer: Inventories of items in containers will be reduced by as much as 90 percent or more. Thus, the potential number of replacement containers should equal hundreds, in the low thousands, or even none.

2. Even 2,000 containers are costly; how can we and our suppliers afford even 2,000 new containers?

Answer: Although the container size used for each component will be reduced, most factories already utilize three or more different-sized containers. Thus, many items can simply be stored in existing, smaller containers.

3. If all container sizes are reduced, the number received and handled will increase. Will this cause an upsurge in material handling cost?

Answer: Improved factory layouts will reduce internal material travel distances by 80 to 90 percent. Thus, even if the number of processed containers increases, material handling costs should decrease. As Exhibit 4–5 illustrates, the forklift truck, moving several small containers

MATERIAL TRANSPORT

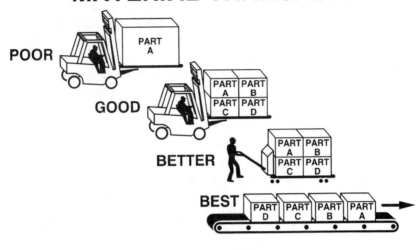

EXHIBIT 4-5

(each of different part numbers), can haul the same cubic volume of parts as it can when it moves a single container full of a single item. Even better, if the material handler is equipped with a handcart that permits him to manually move the same volume, an expensive forklift truck can be eliminated. Until something better is invented, a very short conveyor connecting the point of supply and that of use is best. This would eliminate the forklift truck and most of the material handling personnel.

4. Many of our suppliers are thousands of miles away; how can we expect to receive reusable self-packaging containers from them?

Answer: In the short term, it probably will not be practical to receive reusable self-packaging containers from distant suppliers. The short-term objective of every manager should be to develop more local sources of supply and eventually have only local sources.

5. After we use as many old containers as possible, downsize those used for most parts, and reduce inventory by 90 percent, what if the cost of the new superior container is prohibitive?

Answer: The purpose of superior manufacturing is to be the world's best. This means having both the lowest labor and material costs and the lowest investment in equipment. Container designs, like everything else, should be cost justifiable. If they are not cost effective, a different, less costly design or solution should be developed.

6. Will advocating self-packaging containers lead to the development of custom-designed containers for every part number? How could we afford this?

Answer: Because each container designed must be cost justified, the factory will be able to afford new container designs. In general, however, large numbers of components can be expected to be stored in one of several standard-size containers. The range of standard sizes is three to nine for a company that needs to downsize the size of each component to near optimum.

7. Is there a mathematical model available for calculating the size of containers that should be used? Is it based on opposing costs of time, motion, and inventory investment versus material handling cost?

Answer: At one time, we avidly pursued the mathematical solutions of manufacturing optimums, but experience has led to a change in emphasis as follows:

- Use the simplest and fastest possible method for reaching a decision. The answer may not be perfect, but the improvement is significant enough not to delay implementation.
- Instead of balancing opposing costs, continuously invent methods for reducing and even eliminating them. This gets rid of the need for the model.

8. We have many self-packaging containers now. Admittedly, they are larger than they probably should be. Is it necessary to scrap them?

Answer: A company should always consider the possibility of modifying existing containers. Surprisingly, it is frequently feasible to cut one into two or more containers.

At this juncture, the facts and experience indicate that smaller, reusable, self-packaging containers are a vital ingredient of superior manufacturing. However, smaller, better containers are not good enough. The best conceivable case eliminates containers from the manufacturing process altogether.

TIME AND MOTION

The greatest factory improvements in productivity usually are not made in direct labor since this element of manufacturing represents only 5 to 10 percent of total costs. Nevertheless, direct labor cost improvement is not inconsequential. Thus, most productivity projects have as an objective the reduction of direct labor. The principles and practice of time and motion study and improved productivity were established by pioneers like Frederick Taylor and Frank Gilbreth in the early 1900s. Regardless of their shining examples of achievements in productivity improvement, something went awry between then and now because many opportunities still abound for improving these areas, the reasons for this being:

1. Pioneers in the field were honored men of education. Today, responsibility for time and motion in companies (where it exists) has relatively low stature and requires little advanced education.

2. Time and motion study employees mainly address establishing standards. Very little effort is spent on process design to reduce the required time and motion. This is probably due to a lack of education and training necessary to equip the practitioners for this more important aspect of time and motion.

3. Too much emphasis was placed on developing standards for pay incentives, measuring performance, and balancing the workload on a line. This led to a detailed and often complex set of forms, calculations, and measurements that were too costly to develop and maintain, and even costlier to use.

Frank Gilbreth pioneered the use of film to capture the motions, reaches, and travel distances of a job. The best use of the information gained was to develop improved methods. Over time, however, filming became primarily associated with establishing performance standards, with and without incentive pay. Labor union members eventually rebelled against this practice because it came to represent programs designed to squeeze the maximum possible physical performance from employees.

For capturing information about any operation studied, the modern video camera is a superb tool. Productivity teams at Andersen Consulting film both direct and indirect operations in assembly, setup, machining, stores, and office operations as a prerequisite to improved design. In the vast majority of factories in which taping was done, union resistance has not been problematic, in part, because we promised, when asked, that the film would not be used to set performance standards.

The superior techniques of time and motion analysis start with an understanding of three entirely new concepts. First, the position of a workstation does not need to be fixed. In fact, the boundaries of responsibility should be dynamically flexible in response to the status of work performed by adjacent workers. (This concept is more fully explained later in this chapter.) Second, crude estimates of operation times are all that is required to roughly balance a line. And, third, people are not standard. If superior productivity is to be achieved, work should be assigned based on individual ability.

In terms of increasing factory productivity, unnecessary time and motion probably still offer the most important opportunities for improvement. For example, one of several labor-reducing ideas of the Theurer, Inc., productivity improvement project team related to assembling a truck trailer and is illustrated in Exhibit 4–6. For assembly of large sides to floor cross-members of the trailer, two people were initially required— one to carry cross-members from a skid several feet to the trailer, and a second to receive each cross-member over the top of the trailer side. By installing an overhead wheeled trolley on which the low skid of cross-members was placed, a single assembler could then push the trolley along the trailer as it progresses, taking the cross-members from the trolley. Thus, one person was eliminated. This example illustrates, first, that productivity improvements can be based on simple, low-cost ideas; and, second, that many of these concepts apply equally to small and large products (wheeled carts or trolleys, for example). This innovation (and all other simple ideas) resulted in a total reduction of 25 percent of the man-hours required per trailer produced. By paying attention to productive time and motion, many factories have already reduced the potential for additional large gains in direct (value-added) activities. By contrast,

TRAILER FLOOR ASSEMBLY

BEFORE   **AFTER**

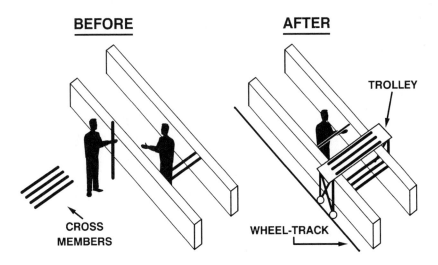

TROLLEY

CROSS
MEMBERS

WHEEL-TRACK

EXHIBIT 4–6

numerous indirect (non-value-added) activities have been widely regarded as necessary evils, and little attention has been focused on eliminating them and increasing the productivity of those activities that must be performed.

Not all wasted motion involves walking or reaching long distances; however, since inadequate attention is paid to absolute minimization of movement, most factories have numerous opportunities for improvement. For example, the productivity improvement project team of a low-volume precision assembly plant was able to reduce assembly labor by 25 percent. A large percentage of the reduction came from minimizing the distances assemblers had to reach to pick up assembly components. As seen in Exhibit 4–7, the parts trays at the front of the working surface and on the first shelf of the assembly bench helped to produce minimum reaches. Angled shelves are now used to hold larger components and to replenish line supplies of parts from the opposite side of the station. An adjustable-position magnifying glass, suspended from the bench, freed the assembler's hands and could be swung aside when not required. Exhibit 4–8 illustrates the replenishment of line stocks. When an assembler empties a container, he puts it in a slide which moves the container to the other side of the bench by gravity. At the same time, he changes the light switch from green to red. The red light signals the material handler in this area (or in the adjacent focused storage area) to come to the station

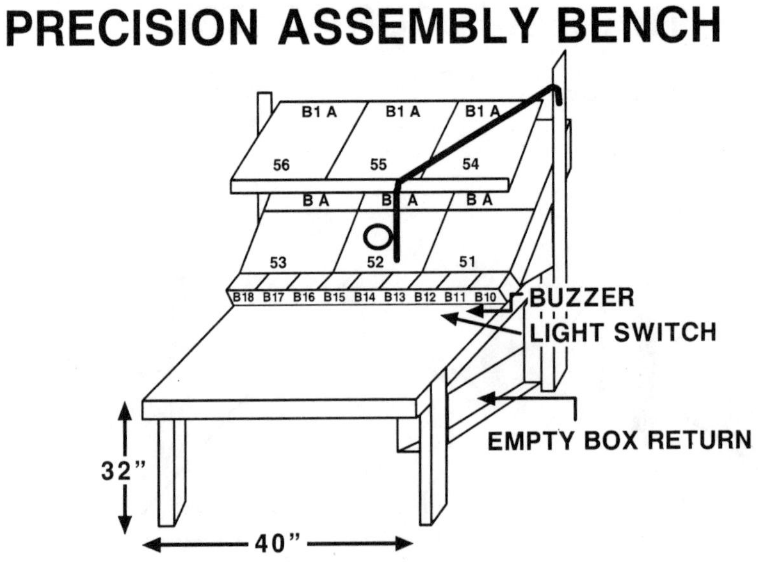

PRECISION ASSEMBLY BENCH

EXHIBIT 4–7

ASSEMBLY BENCH REPLENISHMENT

EXHIBIT 4–8

to replenish one or more parts. When any problems threaten the assembler's ability to continue working, he uses a combination of the red light and a buzzer to call for assistance.

NUMBER OF LINES

At the start of a project involving the design of new, superior assembly lines, the main issues to consider are whether the present number of assembly lines is right, and if there should be more or fewer lines. To make such decisions, the following points need to be taken into account:

1. Fewer lines to produce the same number of products will permit the cycle time to be reduced. This is usually accompanied by productivity gains through simplified, shorter, individual assembly operations and the subsequent reduction of wasted time and motion in the shorter operations. Conversely, splitting one line into two will clearly lengthen the cycle time for each product; and this is likely to reduce productivity.

2. If two products or product families produced on two different as-

sembly lines have a high percentage of common components, combining them into one might not cause the number of containers on the combined line to be significantly more than on either or both of the two lines. If there is little commonality of components, there will be more containers on the combined line than on either of the two separate lines. This will increase both the size of the line and wasted time and motion involved in walking to and/or reaching for components. It may be feasible to remove containers for components of one product or family and bring new containers for the next when changing from assembling one product to another. Although this avoids large numbers of containers in the line, it would cost extra for material handling at each line changeover.

3. When the sizes of the products in two families of products are substantially different, transport equipment, tools, and fixtures applicable to each are different. Combining lines for two different product sizes will complicate the line and add capital cost.

4. Combining two lines into one would appear to have potential for reducing the space occupied by as much as half. Actual reductions may be less or even insignificant if there are either many different test equipment, fixtures, or tools; or if the combined line is much larger due to the need to store more components on the line.

5. Simplicity of design and operation is a primary objective of a productivity project. Designing of a combined line for two product families will be more complex, as will several management aspects of the combined operations. Conversely, if the cycle time is halved on the combined line, each individual operation may be simpler.

In sum, the disadvantage is that it could be difficult to objectively evaluate whether the number of lines should be increased, decreased, or left the same. To evaluate accurately would require a heavily detailed design and cost/benefit analysis of the two alternatives, nearly doubling the design effort. The advantage is, however, that it is rarely worthwhile to change the number of lines because common sense or detailed study has set them at levels lengthy re-analysis would only reverify. Simply stated, in most cases, it is not worth the effort to evaluate changes in the number of lines applicable. (There are always exceptions to the rule. One, where the number of lines was successfully changed, is reported later in this chapter in the section entitled "In-line and Parallel Subassembly.") With minimal study, experienced productivity improvement specialists should be able to determine if there is a reasonable possibility that the number of lines might change. If so, more detailed evaluation should be performed.

ASSEMBLY-LINE SHAPE

Throughout the world, the majority of assembly lines in use are straight and long. Of the various shapes possible, however, a straight line is the least desirable. Where applicable, the serpentine line is the most preferable shape. Exhibit 4–9 illustrates the serpentine assembly line and the focused receiving/storage areas around it. When a factory uses a straight, long assembly line on which pallets or other types of carriers are used, it is necessary to build conveyors for the pallets or carriers to return them to the start of the line. With a serpentine line, the distance and cost of returning pallets are often substantially less. In many factories, it is important that supervisors and material handlers be able to expeditiously move from one side of the line to the other. If necessary, breaks should be provided in the serpentine line to provide easy passage from one side to the other. The same is true for straight, long lines. The major advantages of the superior assembly line are cultural rather than tangible, like reduced motion. For instance, the serpentine line brings all employees on it into reasonably close proximity. This physical nearness creates a bond that promotes teamwork.

In typical low- and medium-volume auto assembly plants with long final assembly lines, the employees on one end never meet the people at

MODEL ASSEMBLY LAYOUT

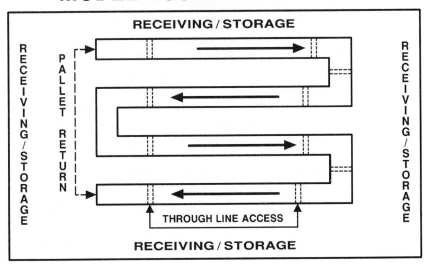

EXHIBIT 4–9

the other. Among the workers at the end of the assembly process are the inspectors. Their chief responsibility is to identify defects, repaired at the end of the line, and to prepare daily summaries of their findings. The defect summary report is distributed to assembly supervisors, and sometimes causes the supervisor to discuss problems with assemblers; however, most defects usually are not continuous or even frequent occurrences. Thus, assemblers often find it impossible to respond to defects in one or more vehicles produced the previous day in terms of identifying ways to eliminate them in the future.

When serpentine lines are installed, defects are reduced and eventually eliminated. At such time, inspection is also eliminated. The burden of producing and responding to ineffective inspection reports is substituted as quickly as possible by direct conversations between inspector and assemblers. Shortened distances between the two facilitate this direct communication. In those instances where the inspector detects a defect caused by assembler error, it is practical to stop the line and shout correction instructions to everyone on the line. This enables the entire team to immediately work on correcting the defects between inspection and the point of assembly where the error originated. Quality defects often drop by 75 percent or more, simply as a result of converting assembly to a serpentine form.

Management and supervision of the compact serpentine line are also easier. Often, the sheer length of the straight, long line necessitates multiple supervisors. Where this occurs, no single supervisor is directly responsible for the entire line. By contrast, the serpentine line, which usually occupies up to 80 percent less space, can often be supervised by one individual who can view the entire area from any point on the line and travel from point to point in seconds. Proponents of mechanized assembly conveyance, however, have readily identified one important drawback of the serpentine form—the corners. Equipment for turning corners on a mechanized line can be substantially more expensive than that for a straight line. Regardless of the cost, for several reasons, the serpentine line is still a better choice:

1. It is easy to develop and change a layout in which all process blocks, such as the assembly line, are compact rectangles. People who have worked on plant layouts can readily understand the difficulty of designing an optimal flow, when everything else must be arranged around straight, long lines that occupy narrow and long strips of the factory.

2. The serpentine line form is often superior to the straight, long line because the ratio of major aisle space to process space is usually better. The straight line often has major aisles on each side for its entire length. By contrast, the serpentine line usually has aisles on two or three sides of its perimeter.

3. Where transport on the line is automated, the straight line is frequently so long that existing buildings are not big enough to hold them. Thus, in most factories, the line already has, and must continue to have, corners. In the past, the exterior or interior walls dictated where the corners were placed in the line. The new serpentine line has no more or fewer corners than the straight line or any other alternative line layout.

4. Usual mechanical solutions for turning corners on a line are more elaborate, thus more costly than necessary. Simpler, less costly alternatives must be either found or invented.

To focus all material handling of inbound and outbound components and products, the ends of several serpentine (or U-form) lines are usually along one or both sides of a common aisle. As mentioned in Chapter 3, the five-story Fabricacion de Electrodomesticos, S.A. (Fabrelec) refrigerator plant was designed with three assembly lines for three families of products. Large refrigerator cabinets, insulated with foam in an adjacent area, required transport to the lines, and completed refrigerators needed to be transported to the common test and packaging area. An early layout that used straight assembly lines and two sets of conveyors, to and from them, became a complex and expensive maze of overhead conveyors. Both to-and-from conveyor systems required that hardware travel back and forth from the line and return empty to foaming or assembly. Changing the relatively short, straight assembly lines to U-forms (as shown in Exhibit 4–10) enabled a single conveyor to take cabinets to the line, pick up and deliver completed refrigerators to test, and return to the foam pickup area. This design sharply reduced the amount of travel, the complexity of the maze of conveyors, and the cost of the total conveyance system.

Often it is not possible to locate two or three sequential processes in close proximity. In these cases, when the items produced are very large, conveyors will eliminate the alternative costs of material handling and transport. Also not all products can be conveyed at ground level. Some must be conveyed overhead. This is especially true when the conveyor system must pass through an area that people and material handling must

FABRELEC OVERHEAD CONVEYANCE

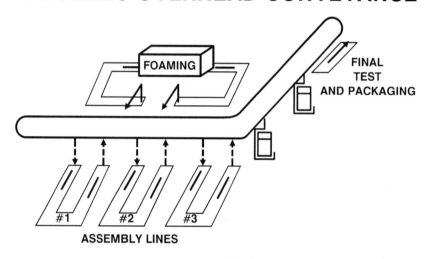

ASSEMBLY LINES

EXHIBIT 4-10

cross. When conveyors are used to transport items for less than minimal distances, overhead conveyors improve utilization of the floor space below.

One final point is that not all products require a long final assembly line. Many manufacturing plants assemble small products with relatively few components—products like locks, automobile jacks, and office furniture. These factories have assembly operations consisting of a few assemblers. In the case of a one- or two-man assembly facility, the shape of the line should almost certainly be straight. For a line with two to eight assembly positions, a straight, L-shaped, or U-form is likely to be applicable. Lines with nine or more positions make it feasible to consider the serpentine line. As a practical minimum, the serpentine and U-form lines tend to have five positions for each line leg.

Not all assembly lines are simple serpentine or U-form since complex products change size and shape in the process of assembly. One project team even designed a line of roughly U-form shape but with different paths of travel for various products. Before creating this line, production flowed to numerous unlinked workstations scattered in the same general area of the factory. Some of them were unique to each of the product families, while others were common to each. The business volume of the two families did not support two complete assembly lines. Therefore, a single line was designed to combine the workstations of both families to achieve continuous flow and to take advantage of the combined volumes of both product families.

The single line required significantly less work in process than the previous independently located workstations. In the past, products were produced simultaneously on independent workstations, then queued up for their turn on common facilities. Thus, there were always some of both products in process. With a single line, assemblers work on the same product family at the same time, thus reducing work-in-process inventory and manufacturing lead time.

IN-LINE AND PARALLEL SUBASSEMBLY

Carried to the ultimate, superior manufacturing would eliminate independent subassembly processes. Ideally, in-house subassemblies would be produced in a network of assembly lines working to achieve a single finished product production schedule. Few factories will be able to change from present subassembly methods to ideal networks in the short term. Most, however, can substantially increase the amount of subassembly work performed in line and in linked parallel subassembly. Exhibit 4–11

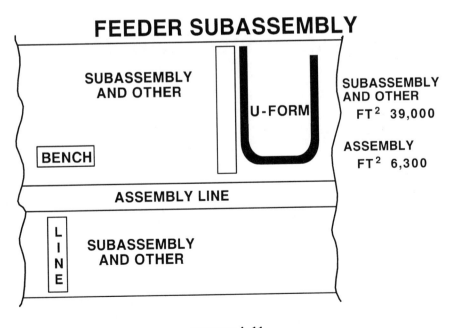

EXHIBIT 4–11

shows a small segment of an assembly line surrounded by various types of subassembly facilities, including benches, small lines, and even a U-form conveyor assembly line. This example of subassembly perpendicular to the main line demonstrates how *not* to organize subassembly. As illustrated, in this factory, the area occupied by subassembly, empty space, and inventory was more than six times larger than the area occupied by the main assembly line itself. In this case, subassembly facilities were placed as close as possible to points on the assembly line where they were used. Little attention was paid to the wasted space that resulted from the perpendicular measurement of the longest subassembly facility on both sides of the line. In fact, this space was filled with inventory ordered from component storage long before it was needed for assembly or subassembly. The situation in this factory was made even worse by not directly linking subassembly processes to the main assembly line. Tens and hundreds of subassemblies were built far in advance of being used in assembly. Thus, inventories of both components and subassemblies were substantially higher than those required for superior manufacturing.

Designing subassembly processes to be perpendicular to final assembly is often a bad practice. It is usually better to either produce in line or on a parallel line. In Exhibit 4–12, four subassemblies are manufactured on

PARALLEL SUBASSEMBLY

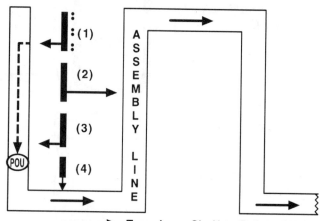

- - - ► :Travels on Shelf to Point of Use
(1) (2) (3) (4) Subassembly Lines & Benches

EXHIBIT 4–12

a line between, and parallel to, two legs of the main assembly line. Three of the subassemblies shown can be fed directly from the subassembly line to the point of use, either by hand or by very short conveyor. The numbers of subassemblies used on two legs of the main assembly line are almost never equal the space available for assembling them directly between the two legs. Further, two or more subassemblies are often required at approximately the same point. Therefore, something must be done to facilitate movement of subassemblies from a parallel subassembly location fairly distant from the point of use to this point. In the illustration, the solution was to place the subassembly on the conveyor pallet or on the product on the conveyor, and to let it ride to the point of assembly.

Incidentally, by designing extra space in the main assembly line pallet for conveying subassemblies to their destination, a working surface was provided for producing the smallest subassemblies on the main assembly line. In all of the subassembly lines highlighted, the lines would ideally be designed with enough space for only one unit of the subassembly between the subassembly line and the main assembly line. This achievement represents the ultimate in just-in-time, subassembly inventory when it is feasible.

Subassemblies for the humidifier tube used for oxygen breathed by medical patients were assembled in the general vicinity of the main assembly line at the Kenmex plant (Tijuana, Mexico). Although this provided better control than subassemblies manufactured in widely separated areas, it still resulted in excess supplies of subassemblies, which tended to fill the areas around the processes, as shown in Exhibit 4–13. Before redesign, the entire process occupied 3,128 square feet.

The Kenmex plant represents an exception to the general rule that the number of assembly lines in use before redesign and the number after are usually the same. Before redesign, Kenmex assembled tubes for adults and children in the same line, although those for children required more subassemblies. The combined line was thus larger and more complex than necessary. This not only caused it to be longer and bigger than needed, but also made it more difficult to reasonably balance work performed by each employee on the line. The result was poor balance, which wasted a great deal of labor.

After redesign, the humidifier tube subplant required only 1,216 square feet of space, approximately 61 percent less than previously needed. This reduction was possible even though separate adult and pediatric assembly lines were developed. In the adult assembly line (shown in Exhibit 4–14), subassemblies were designed to be manufactured in line. The pediatric subassembly stations were placed on both sides of the

HUMIDIFIER TUBE - BEFORE

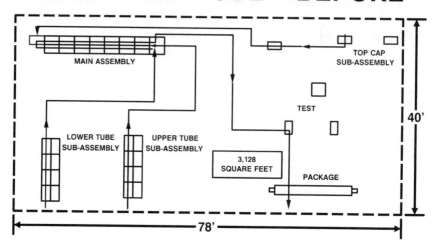

EXHIBIT 4–13

line in an interesting irregular pattern of flow within a line of fairly uniform shape.

Subassemblies are not the only components that should be produced in, or as close as possible to, the final assembly line. The Messier-Hispano-Bugatti productivity improvement project team in Molsheim,

HUMIDIFIER TUBE - FINAL

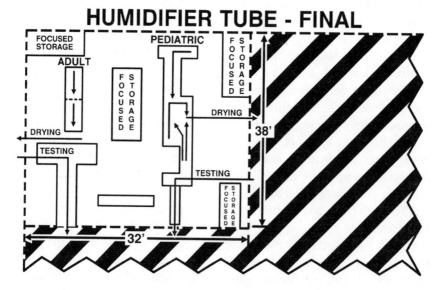

EXHIBIT 4–14

France, achieved a 75 percent reduction of work-in-process inventory and manufacturing lead time by changing from functional manufacturing to a product-oriented organization. The partial factory plant shown in Exhibit 4–15 highlights buildings on the site used to produce components and assembly landing gears for the Airbus. Typically, these separate buildings supplied components for several different products. Conflicting priorities and the difficulties of communicating among the buildings caused excessive work-in-process inventory and, at the same time, frequent late production of components. Now all the machining, subassembly, and final assembly processes used to make the Airbus landing gear have been moved to the single building highlighted in Exhibit 4–16. This became possible when a new design for process and storage reduced space by more than 50 percent. With production of the product and its components under one roof, it became relatively simple to coordinate final assembly schedules and component schedules, virtually eliminating work-in-process inventory.

COOPERATIVE RECOVERY

Cooperative recovery can be a powerful method for increasing the productivity of a team of workers responsible for a machine line or portion

FUNCTIONAL ORGANIZATION - BEFORE

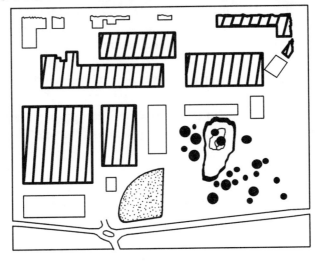

EXHIBIT 4-15

PRODUCT ORGANIZATION - AFTER

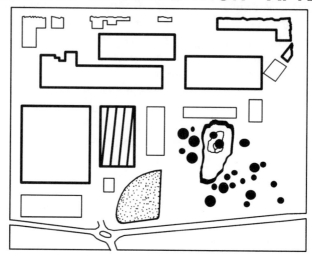

EXHIBIT 4-16

of a line of machines, or an assembly line. Several of the concepts of cooperative recovery are:

1. Instead of developing costly detailed labor standards for individual workers, estimates of required labor are developed for each operation. Work along the line is roughly balanced among all teams. On a short line, there may be only one team, whose members cooperatively apportion the work assigned to their team among themselves. This assignment is based on the natural speed of the individuals. Fine-tuning the amount of work assigned to each worker may be done by trial and error over several hours or even days of production.

2. When one operator in the line is done earlier than the others, he helps the assemblers in adjacent positions complete their required tasks.

3. A primary objective of cooperative recovery is to best utilize the natural speed of each operator by assigning tasks equal to the assembler's ability. Thus, a worker is expected to perform according to his ability rather than to a theoretical standard calculated for each operation.

4. An operator does not constantly need to help others complete their tasks, except when cycle times are long and variable. The coopera-

tive recovery applies primarily to exceptions, when some type of problem slows down one of the operators in a team. When assignments are not well balanced, the operators are expected to permanently shift some responsibility from the overloaded assembler to one with less work.

5. Group (team) discipline and motivation are always automatic. On one hand, operators inclined to do less than their natural ability permits are disciplined by the group. On the other, the team organization fosters a game/sporting spirit that causes operators to routinely enjoy working at a faster-than-normal pace. The phenomenon of speed cannot yet be precalculated based on a presumed pace, as time and motion can. Therefore, target improvement goals should also include an assumption that pace will increase by an unknown percentage as a result of team motivation.

The principles of cooperative recovery are based on the idea that almost all operation standards include errors or imperfections. In factories, most practitioners of labor standard development accept this premise based on the evidence that actual performance and standard performance usually differ. Further, the differences from standard vary each time the operation is performed.

It seems self-evident that perfect (or near-perfect) balance between operators cannot be achieved. One important reason is that people for whom the standard is developed are not uniform, but have variable natural speeds, which, in a large group, vary as much as 25 to 50 percent. In addition, their capability (speed) will differ from day to day, and from hour to hour. Only cooperative recovery can routinely and systematically compensate for these variations. By balancing work assignments to operator capability, the highest level of productivity may be achieved.

Cooperative recovery, however, is not always applicable. Several factors that influence its use are:

1. *Time required to complete task.* Cooperative recovery is most applicable when the total time of each operation is high. For example, it is easy to understand that if each operation requires only 10 seconds, it would not be practical for one operator to assist another.

2. *Type of task.* Assembly work includes both assembly of components and other nonassembly tasks, such as test. It is simple for one operator to assist another in assembly of components since the components and required tools can easily be handled by either assembler. For workstations like test, where the unit being produced is typically plugged into a large piece of equipment, it can be more difficult or

even impractical for anyone to help the tester when he falls behind schedule.

3. *Location of workstations.* If the distances between workstations cannot be short, cooperative recovery will not be as applicable. The time required for an assembler to move to a different workstation to assist another operator may be greater than the amount of time he could work to help the other assembler.

4. *Special needs.* If the operation requires special materials and/or tools that cannot be simultaneously used by both operators, the potential for cooperative recovery is reduced.

All around the world, superior manufacturers have adopted the use of Toyota Motor's andon—the concept of making production problems visible. In its simplest form, andon consists of placing one or more colored lights above assembly-line stations and machines. Some of the more common uses of andon are to signal that the machine or assembly station requires repair, to signal that the workstation is (or is about to be) out of required materials or components, or to signal a defect in either the unit being produced or its components. A following example, based on an indexed assembly line, shows how andon can be utilized to support cooperative recovery. It is important to this example to understand the difference between an indexed line versus a continuous motion line. An indexed line is one on which the assembler presses a button to start the conveyor to move a completed unit on to the succeeding workstation, and to bring a new unit forward. The continuously moving conveyor, on the other hand, causes wasted time and motion, since it is necessary for an operator to move back and forth between the starting and end points of the assigned assembly zone. Further, although it enforces a pace of work, the conveyor either moves at the pace of the slowest worker or else causes assemblers to miss operations if it moves faster than their natural pace. In contrast, by supporting each assembler working at his own natural pace, the indexed line permits the reduction of wasted time and motion. Operators do not have to work at the speed of the slowest assembler. The indexed line also sharply reduces instances of missed operations on a continuous line moving faster than the speed of the slowest assemblers.

Here is an example of the use of andon to support cooperative recovery, starting with all assemblers working on their units.

The yellow lights over each workstation are on, indicating operators are busy working on their assembly tasks. After the first worker finishes his task, he turns his yellow light off and his green light on. When all three workers are done with their assignments and have

PROBLEM SOLUTION

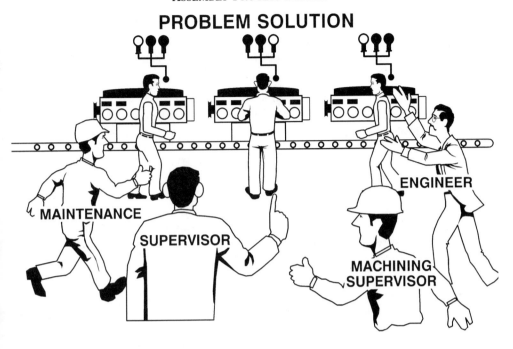

EXHIBIT 4-17

turned their green lights on, the conveyor indexes all units being worked on forward to the next station. If only two of the three workers complete their tasks and the third still has work left to do, the two are trained to help their teammate catch up. The red light is used to call for help when a major problem occurs. It means that the line must halt until a stopgap solution permits it to restart, or until a permanent solution is found to ensure the problem will not recur. The red light signals not only team workers, but also calls the supervisor, maintenance/repair person, and methods engineer.

ASSEMBLY-LINE LENGTH

Longer than necessary assembly lines penalize the profitability of their companies. As contrasted to lines of the minimum practical length, long lines are costlier in the following ways:

1. Excessive space on the line permits the line to hold more work-in-process units than just the units being worked on. This increases

the inventory investment and the time required to assemble each unit.

2. The investment in plant and equipment is larger than necessary.
3. Supervision is costlier since the area is larger.
4. Liberal use of space on and around the line causes workers to walk and reach more, cutting the amount of time they can spend on assembly.

After a fast walkthrough of an assembly line, we are frequently able to suggest that the length of the line can be reduced by 50 percent or more, based on our observations. To reach such quick conclusions, we estimate the ratio of the number of workers on the line to the sum of units in process on it. Since a basic ideal target is one unit per worker, if there are three units on the line per worker, the reduction potential would be 66 percent. When we tour a factory manufacturing larger assemblies like tractors or refrigerators, we also estimate a reasonable average number of employees who could (and should) simultaneously work on the same unit, since its size would permit this. When we see an assembly line with people working on only one side, while work needs to be done on both sides, we automatically visualize a new line with workers on two sides. There is often vocal and logical opposition, however, to the notion of an assembly design where the number of units is one per assembler. This arrangement can be seen in Exhibit 4-18.

WORK IN PROCESS IDEAL

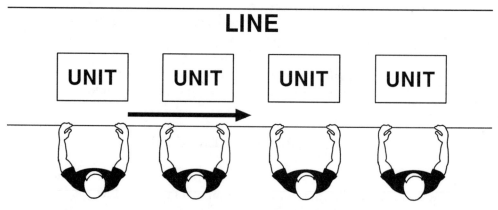

LINE

| UNIT | UNIT | UNIT | UNIT |

Number of People = Number of Units!

EXHIBIT 4-18

While the optimum work-in-process level, from the standpoint of investment and lead time, would be one unit (or less) for every operator in the machine or assembly line, there is some basis for including additional units. This is illustrated in Exhibit 4–19, which shows buffer stock between operations as an alternative to cooperative recovery. As can be seen in the exhibit, the use of buffer stock may reduce the opportunity for cooperative recovery since it forces each workstation to be farther from its neighbors. Cooperative recovery entails one worker assisting another to complete his work. This usually requires that the helper use the parts and tools of the worker being aided. Thus, the concept is not as practical when stations are far apart, as when they are side by side.

The reason for buffer stock is to provide for the contingency that one operator may finish his work sooner than the next or prior station. Since there are, theoretically, buffer units past the station and empty buffers ahead of it, operators should, ideally, be able to move the completed unit into the next empty buffer and take one out of the inbound buffer to continue work. Doing so should reduce lost work time by workers waiting for adjacent operators to complete their tasks and offers the potential for lowering lost time when the inbound buffer has a unit in process and the outbound buffer space is empty. The buffer provides some improvement for small disturbances. Large disturbances are generally greater than the work in buffers; thus, these problems are not addressed by the use of buffers.

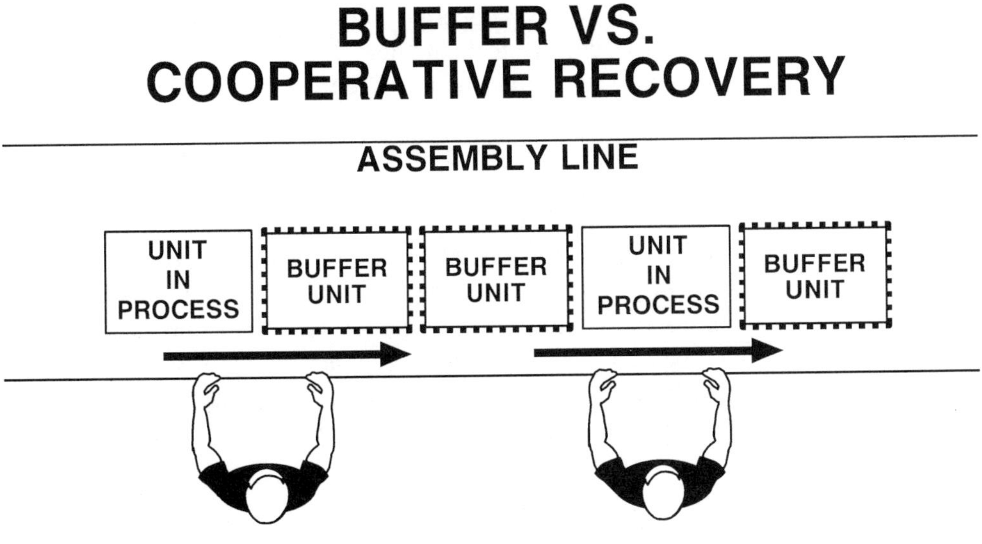

BUFFER VS. COOPERATIVE RECOVERY

ASSEMBLY LINE

EXHIBIT 4-19

Mathematically, assuming standard people work at a regular pace, it is true that a line should perform better with a buffer than without it. Fortunately, people are not standard and do not work at a fixed pace. Thus, every assembly plant has the opportunity of unlocking the potential of employee teams working together, cooperatively, to maintain production schedules without buffers. It can thereby tap the potential of lowering plant and equipment investment, reducing inventory investment, and cutting lead time.

As well, the buffer technique does not address opportunities for reducing line imbalance caused by the use of theoretical standards for nonstandard people. The line, regardless of buffers, must operate at the speed of the slowest worker in it. Thus, the inbound buffers of these slower people will often be full, and the outbound buffers will usually be empty. The penalties of buffer stocks are higher work-in-process investment, corresponding longer lead time, and a longer line, resulting in greater costs and space required. The final, and perhaps greatest, penalty is that buffer use tends to discourage development of solutions to small and large disturbances.

Cooperative recovery, where applicable, not only addresses small disturbances but also provides the potential for accomplishing near-perfect line balance. It is very important to note that permanent solutions to recurring problems may be achieved when cooperative recovery is practiced. The buffer, on the other hand, often masks problems. Neither the use of buffer stock in the machining line nor in the assembly line addresses large problems; however, cooperative recovery has none of the penalties inherent in the buffer stock method. In summary, there are three ways to help reduce idle time: the use of buffer stock, cooperative recovery, and a combination of both.

As a rule of thumb, longer cycle times are usually best for cooperative recovery and shorter cycle times for buffer stock. Permanent reassignment of work elements from one operator to another for balancing work with assembler speed can be accomplished in combination with buffer stock. By using only a small buffer between each of several cooperative recovery teams of operators along a machine (or assembly) line, buffer stock penalties can be minimized. A typical team of assemblers would be five to ten operators. Thus, the typical line, with team buffer, would include one buffer unit for every five to ten workers.

The concept of cooperative recovery has been one of the most difficult superior manufacturing techniques for manufacturing companies to accept and use. Many experienced executives find it hard to discard practices of decades to take a radically new tack. Others are unable to face the responsibility of working with factory employees to train them to adopt teamwork procedures. Still others have real problems with restrictions in union contracts and/or adversary relationships with union and/or rank and file members. The best companies find it comparatively easy to change and experience large productivity gains. Thus, whether or not this new technique will work depends on if and when the company is able to do what is inevitably necessary to achieve implementation.

CONVEYANCE/TRANSPORT

The cost, time, and physical effort of moving a product from one assembly station to another offer significant opportunities for potential productivity improvement. As in all areas of manufacturing, a company striving to become a superior manufacturer must carefully minimize both payroll costs and investment in equipment. The assembly-line designer has numerous alternatives for conveying units from one workstation to another; among them are:

1. No transport, assembly in place
2. Transport from one assembly station to another with overhead crane
3. Manual movement
4. Manual movement on conveyor
5. Mechanized conveyor, with manual indexing from station to station
6. Mechanized conveyor, with continuous motion

In general, the mode of movement from station to station is determined by the size of the product, the volume of production, and the number of workstations required. The smallest production assembled and those of lowest volume are generally transported manually. The highest volume and physically largest products are most often moved by mechanized means. Products that are very large are usually moved by crane or assembled in place, without movement. Somewhere between low and high volume is a break-even point, where the costs of mechanized conveyance and manual conveyance are about equal. Fortunately, in most situations, the volumes of production fall between the two extremes, which makes it easy to decide on the degree of transport mechanization applicable. In those few cases where whether or not to mechanize transport is a question, careful thought must be given to its answer.

Andersen Consulting has worked with automobile factory assembly lines producing a wide range of volumes, including plants producing 1,

7, 100, and 1,000 vehicles per shift. Movement on the line producing one unit per shift was manual, while it was mechanical on the lines producing 100 and 1,000. The payroll and fringe costs of manual movement in the plant producing one automobile per shift were approximately $9,000 per year. Those costs would have been $2.9 million annually moving 100 cars per day manually. The reason that manual movement costs in the factory producing 100 cars per day is not simply 100 times greater than the costs for the plant producing one car may not be readily apparent. The expense of manual movement increases by a factor of 322 due to the increased length of the process. Each car must be moved farther. Based on approximate operating costs (including depreciation and interest related to the extra plant and equipment required to move automobiles mechanically), the approximate break-even point at which mechanized conveyance in the plant producing 100 is warranted would be $2.9 million per year. If the transport equipment is less expensive, the investment in it would reduce total costs.

The assembly designer must be aware that there are a wide variety of possible conveyance alternatives that do the same job. The cost range of these can be quite broad. For example, in designing an assembly line using a manual conveyor for a medium-volume photocopy machine, two alternatives considered were: (1) conventional heavy metal rollers and (2) small nylon rollers in light metal tracks. The difference in cost of the two was about 20 to 1. Few manufacturing companies are large enough to have specialists familiar with every variety of conveyance available and capable of designing the detailed system required, except for the simplest of systems. Ultimately, purchasers of all but the simplest systems depend on the manufacturers of the system equipment to design and produce the equipment used. Nevertheless, the assembly designer on the productivity team must direct a comprehensive search for alternative types of conveyance equipment to narrow the field to the few suppliers with equipment and expertise to provide superior systems. Once a conveyance equipment supplier is chosen, the specifications he produces must be controlled. Most suppliers are not accustomed to customers who demand superior, low-cost systems. Indeed, many of the largest volume producers are quick to accept that a modern factory must have miles of high-cost conveyors. Therefore, the conveyance supplier is often accustomed to supplying complex, high-cost systems for applications for which simple, low-cost systems would be better.

For example, recently at Fabrelec in Basauri, Spain, we worked on a design project for refrigerator assembly line. All conveyor suppliers wanted the company to install the expensive equipment being used by most of Fabrelec's competitors on their newest assembly lines. This meant placing a conveyor buffer of refrigerators ahead of each assembly station, a separate side station for working in the refrigerator, and another buffer after the workstation. Every new assembly station would have equipment with which the operator could raise, lower, and rotate the refrigerator. However, the waste involved in using such equipment would have been considerable. For one, extra work in process, inventory investment, and plant and equipment costs would have been incurred to hold larger queues prior to each station. For another, unnecessarily complex and costly equipment would have been required to shuttle refrigerators from the main line to the workstation and to raise, lower, and rotate the refrigerator. Since the majority of work performed on each refrigerator was in the same height zones, we lowered the floor in relation to the line height in one area to the height required by work done on the bottom part of the refrigerator. Since both sides of the assembly line were used, rather than a single side as recommended by the equipment manufacturer, it was not necessary to rotate the refrigerator.

Another means of conveyance—driverless vehicles—has become increasingly popular for transporting products and components around a factory and for carrying products from one assembly or test station to another. Although this approach can be beneficial, it frequently entails greater cost and complexity than should be necessary. Rubbermaid, for example, uses driverless vehicles and trains of cars to carry finished products from production lines to a receipt point in its finished goods warehouse. The disadvantage of most such systems is low speed and volume of movement. Rubbermaid's system of moving trains, not just a single load, of material solved these problems and is an excellent example of how payroll and fringe costs can be eliminated by making a nominal investment in equipment. The amount of product moved in the train is impressive.

The use of driverless vehicles in a television factory, as a substitute for a conveyor line, was not as impressive. Other conveyance systems can be designed to do the same job, at a considerably lower cost. In most cases, automated movement does not address the real problem: the plant layout is poor, necessitating material over greater than necessary distances. The best solution is to revise the layout to eliminate most of the necessity for transport.

CYCLE TIME

The planned cycle time of an assembly process is the single foundation upon which the structure of the assembly line will be based. Cycle time can best be determined by establishing the target maximum quantity of the product to be manufactured per shift. Once an assembly process is constructed to reach that target, smaller quantities can be produced; however, doing so will result in some probable loss of productivity brought about by either changing the number of people assigned or by reducing hours per shift or shifts per week. Producing quantities greater than the target maximum for the line is unlikely to be practical, except by having employees work overtime or physically changing the line. As an illustration of cycle time expressed as units per shift, consider a line on which the target production per shift is 225 and the number of productive minutes per shift is 450. In this case, it will be necessary to produce one product every two minutes. The required cycle time is therefore two minutes. Next, if the total minutes of work per unit of production is 100, the number of assemblers will be 100 divided by two minutes of cycle time, or 50.

In its drive to become a superior manufacturer, setting a company's target cycle time can be one of the most important decisions it makes. All other things being equal, those with the highest volume, thus shortest cycle time, will be the most productive; however, to target a cycle time that is too short can have disastrous results. For example, if a line is designed to produce high volume, but marketing can sell only a small percentage of the capacity, this company will have higher than necessary plant and equipment costs. Even worse, the line will be designed for many more workers than are actually required. Lower sales levels can only be met by cutting the number of people in the line, thus forcing most workers to walk back and forth to multiple assembly stations to do their work. Walking from station to station, however, wastes time that could be better used on production.

The approximate curve of productivity illustrated in Exhibit 4–20 shows that worker efficiency (productivity) generally decreases as cycle time increases. Its peak is generally highest when cycle time is somewhat less than two minutes. At some point between zero and two, a decrease in productivity occurs because of the mental and physical demands of very short, repetitive tasks. Productivity drops further due to the potential for increasing the ratio of nonproductive time required to move units produced into and out of the workstation to the amount of productive work (see Exhibit 4–21). In the top bar, an example of a long cycle time, a worker starts by picking up the next unit to be assembled and moving it into the work location. This is nonproductive time as compared to the time spent on the next portion of the job, assembly, which increases the value of the product. The bar ends with the worker moving the completed

CYCLE / EFFICIENCY CURVE

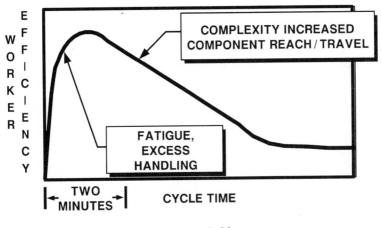

EXHIBIT 4-20

unit out of the workstation and putting it down. In this long cycle, 65 percent of the time is assembly time. On a long line, every employee might thus be working productively 65 percent of the time, compared to the lower bar. This bar illustrates the change in ratio of productive to nonproductive time resulting from increasing the number of assemblers on the line. The amount of time each assembler works productively is now reduced to 35 percent.

HANDLING TIME TRADEOFF

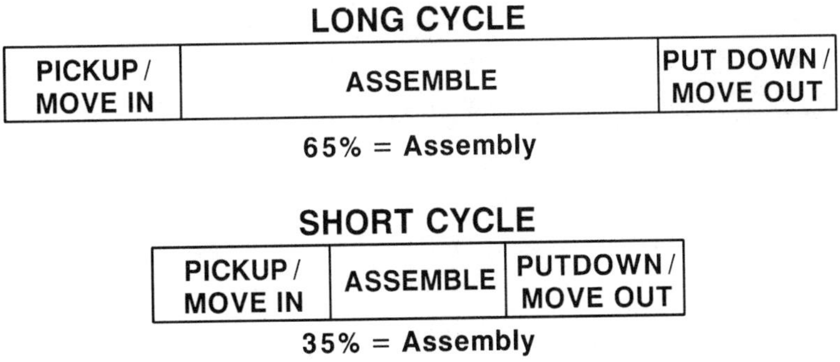

LONG CYCLE

PICKUP / MOVE IN	ASSEMBLE	PUT DOWN / MOVE OUT

65% = Assembly

SHORT CYCLE

PICKUP / MOVE IN	ASSEMBLE	PUTDOWN / MOVE OUT

35% = Assembly

EXHIBIT 4-21

As this example shows, at some point the decreased ratio of productive assembly to nonproductive movement might more than offset any increase in productivity. Thus, it is necessary to find some way to reduce or eliminate nonproductive movement. The usual way is to automate the movement, as shown in Exhibit 4–22. The cycle starts with the automatic advance (continuous motion line or indexed line) of the next and completed unit. While the units are advancing, the assembler is not idle. Rather, he picks up the next components and/or tools to be used. This assembly preparatory work completely overlaps the automatic advance; therefore, the amount of nonproductive work is almost zero. After the cycle is completed, the assembler may press the automatic advance button, perhaps a foot pedal (in the case of an index line), to repeat the cycle.

When Henry Ford changed assembly methods from complete assembly by a small team to an automobile assembly line, man-hours per vehicle dropped by 80 percent. The workers' productivity was increased by 500 percent not only by reducing wasted time and motion but also by simplifying each worker's job. The Ford sales organization was able to sell as many cars as the company could produce, and therefore, had no trouble sustaining the 500 percent productivity gain. Many manufacturers, however, will not be able to increase sales to such a degree. Thus, they will need fewer workers, each of whom will need more time to walk and reach and will have a more complex job. In summary, if more workers are added to shorten the cycle time, thus improving efficiency, more products will be produced. If there is not enough product demand to support more workers, their ranks need to be cut to the number that can produce only

AUTOMATED ADVANCE OVERLAP

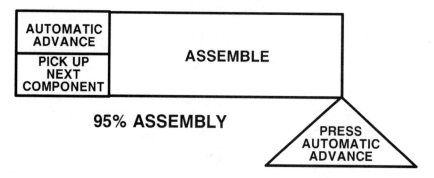

EXHIBIT 4-22

the requisite amount and no more. Yet doing so lowers the productivity of each worker by increasing the cycle time.

How is it possible to break the vicious circle? Consider the following example: Two assembly lines for two different products are each manned with one team of 10 assemblers that produces 20 units per week on each line. The line of 10 versus five workers in the past doubles productivity. Each assembly line can now produce one week's demand in half the time, 20 hours. But how can each line work only 20 hours per week? If each is operated half the time, four hours per day or two and a half days per week, moving one team of 10 assemblers from one line to another would reduce the number of workers needed to produce the same volume of units from 20 to 10. Thus, the circle is broken by reducing the number of workers and by moving one assembly team from one line to the other.

ASSEMBLY AUTOMATION

In numerous factories and portions of factories around the world, human labor is no longer required to assemble or to machine products and components. This trend should continue, but probably at a much slower pace. As yet, the increase of automation has not accelerated to the point that massive numbers of workers have been displaced. In fact, most automation projects tend to be justified more by intangible benefits than by solid contributions to improved profitability. Some of the intangible reasons for automation include:

1. Staying abreast with technological developments
2. Improving the quality of products and components produced
3. Providing flexibility in the process to permit it to produce a wider range of products and even to adapt to entirely new products

From the standpoint of top management, however, investments in areas other than factory automation may often be best. That is because direct labor is seldom more than 10 percent of the total costs of manufacturing and may be an even lower percentage of the sales price. As a result, automation of complex assembly lines, such as automobile final assembly, is not something to expect in the immediate future. Part of the reason is that some operations require simple automation, more complex operations need special purpose automation, and complex/variable operations require general purpose flexible automation, such as robotics. Also there are some operations for which automation is not now economically feasible.

One of the best articles[1] about superior manufacturing published in recent years describes General Motor's relatively new Hamtranck, Michigan, plant as containing as many robots as are ever seen in a factory. Nonetheless, the plant is barely competitive with the joint Toyota/GM plant in Fremont, California, that uses little automation but lots of superior manufacturing operations and management techniques. The reasons that GM had not yet been able to achieve superior manufacturing performance in the automated factory are probably the same as those for most automation disappointments. These include:

1. The product is not designed for automation, and the factory automation project did not include a new or modified design suitable for automation.

2. The manufacturing process prior to automation was far from ideal. The process could have been improved and simplified.

3. Automation is erroneously designed to imitate human performance. Instead of approaching the overall job from an automated standpoint, robots and machines were programmed to do the same series of human tasks, using the same methods and working in the same environment. Robots and machines are not humans and should be used to perform work in other ways and in different environments. For example, humans spraying paint should always stand as far back from the target area as possible to minimize breathing the fumes. A robot, by contrast, can stand nearer and move all around the target area. Being closer to the target improves the quality of the coating and reduces the amount of paint required.

4. Automation is applied, across the board, not only to those operations for which it is quite applicable but also to those that could be performed manually with better cost and quality results.

5. Automation is used to help live with problems rather than to work on the problems themselves. For instance, one automobile stamping plant spent several million dollars on vision automation to automate inspection of large stampings such as hoods and fenders. Flaws in the steel coils received from the mills were the primary cause of defects. Therefore, the best solution would be to work with the supplier to improve the process at the mill, thus eliminating the source problem.

6. Automation investment has been misdirected to activities that add no value to the product. As an illustration, material transport (giving

[1]"Factory of the Future." *Economist,* May 30, 1987, pp. S1–S18.

parts a tour around the plant), storage, or inspection should not be automated; they should be eliminated.

The vast majority of products are not designed for the best use of automation or even for optimum manual assembly. In the 1970s, the Society of Manufacturing Engineers[2] expressed the opinion that product design affects costs far more than any process design, whether automated or not. Later in the early 1980s, the automation project at IBM's Lexington, Kentucky, plant and Xerox's middle-range copier projects received widespread publicity.[3] In both cases, new product designs were simplified by reducing the number of components by 50 to 65 percent. Both IBM and Xerox considered revision of product design to be a prerequisite for successful automation.

To help comprehend the applicability of automation to assembly operations, it is useful to understand the major components of automation. Exhibit 4–23 graphically illustrates the four most basic elements of automated assembly, including conveyance of the main assembly to and through each process, the conveyance of components to the process, and the process that adds components and tests the assembly. The last compo-

ASSEMBLY AUTOMATION ELEMENTS

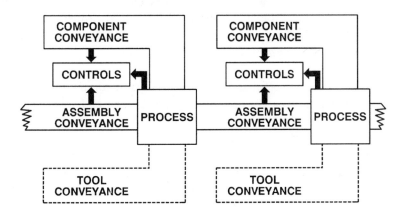

EXHIBIT 4–23

[2]Dallas, Daniel B., ed. *Tool and Manufacturing Engineers Handbook* (McGraw-Hill Book Co., 1976).
[3]"How to Streamline Operations," *The Journal of Business Strategy,* Fall 1987, pp. 32–36.

nent—the controls—applies to all of the other elements. The controls should not only regulate the normal operations of every element but also monitor each of them and stop processing when there are operating or quality problems. Tool conveyance (illustrated with dotted lines) is less frequently a part of automated assembly, and more often a part of automated machining. It conveys the various tools required by different operations within the process for one product in and out of the process, or may change all tools in the process when switching from one product to another by moving the tools between tool storage and the process. Some form of automation might be applied to one, more, or all of these basic automation elements. In fact, the economics of manual procedures versus automated procedures should usually dictate a different mixture of approaches for different assembly lines and stations.

Since the dawn of the industrial age, mankind has envisioned robots, capable of functioning exactly like humans. In the last two decades, the development of the practical industrial robot has led to a dream-like vision of manufacturing flexibility. In this illusion, a crew of robots can assemble any type of product assigned to it. Thus, as products evolve technologically and as customer demands shift from product to product, it is deemed possible to switch rapidly from one product to another. In practice, however, this type of flexibility is not, and perhaps may never be, possible. The reason is simple. Different types of products require varied kinds of automation, and some types of products must wait for the day when dream robots are available and economical. The real job of designing applicable automation involves selecting the proper economical mix of manual operations, tools, special purpose machines, and flexible automation for each element of the assembly facility being designed and constructed.

One of the most powerful and practical lessons in automation economics is the dishwashing case problem developed by Daniel E. Whitney[4] for robotics students. When most students review the motions of a person washing dishes and then automate the process, he explains, it soon develops into a complex and costly design. All different sizes and shapes of dishes would have to be delivered on a pallet to permit the robot to know where and how to pick up each item to be washed. The alternative would be a vision system and programming to distinguish the various pieces. Two robots would then be able to apply the dishcloth. One would hold and turn the piece over, while the other would wash. Additional special

[4]Daniel E. Whitney, "Real Robots Do Need Jigs." *Harvard Business Review,* May–June 1986, pp. 110–116.

automation would have to be applied to more complex problems, such as washing the insides of deep, narrow objects, like glasses, and scouring pots and pans with thick accumulations of baked- and burned-on residues. It is easy to see that almost every automation design developed would cost hundreds of thousands of dollars. The climax comes when Mr. Whitney calls his students' attention to the fact that automatic dishwashers cost only a few hundred dollars and are already available.

This example may understate the real dilemma. The most interesting issues may be how much human effort and costs will be reduced and what the quality will be. Owners of dishwashers know that for quality results, fine china and crystal are washed separately from pots and pans and that burned-on messes require separation from everyday dishes. The sorting and inserting of items into the dishwasher and the reverse extractions from it rarely require less manual effort than manual washing. Worse yet, the dishwasher usually is below the counter, thus necessitating a lot of bending, stretching, and reaching. Finally, the quality resulting from automation is lower than the quality of manual washing. Pieces frequently require rewashing, dishes are almost always spotty, and the harshness of the temperature, the water blast, and the detergent erode glass and fine china surfaces over time. Dishwashers are best used after meals for large groups. Large batches of homogeneous items can then be processed with no more, and probably less, effort than a batch of different sizes, shapes, materials, and conditions of food adhesion.

Although dishwashers may not save labor and produce lower quality results, they do make sense! They improve the quality of life by eliminating the need to put one's hands into hot, often unpleasant water. In the same view, automation in the factory is, and should be, employed in situations where cost justification is marginal, but where its use eliminates uncomfortable, hard, and hazardous jobs. The dishwasher example vividly illustrates how the concept of work should change when the process is automated. Changes include a move from one-at-a-time to batch processing, from manual scrubbing of surfaces to power spray, from hot to super hot water, and from an open to a sealed chamber environment.

Although Toyota Motor Co. is probably the best automobile manufacturer in the world, it is still less than perfect. For example, for years, Toyota's robot body welding lines have been used to depict how mistakes are made in designing an automated process. Video films of these lines show robots standing side by side for hundreds of feet in lines that could, perhaps, be as much as half the length. Thus, the amount of factory space required to house them could also be cut in half. The mistake here is that robot placement determines the length of the line. Robots stand along the line, just as though they were humans, but they are bigger than people and perhaps occupy even more space. Robots do not need to stand on the floor; they can also "stand" on the ceiling. If some were suspended from overhead, while others stood on the floor, the density of robots might be doubled. Further reductions could be achieved by having some robots work in pits underneath the car. This could also reduce the cost of equipment in the line used to turn the vehicle on its side for bottom welding.

Automation does not necessarily imply robotics. Partial automation may be achieved by adding power conveyors and power tools to a manual assembly process. Special and general purpose assembly machines should be thought of as automated assembly lines and vice versa. These machines are just collections of conveyance devices, processes, and controllers. The term "transfer line" is most frequently applied to machines and lines of machines with automatic conveyance devices that carry objects from station to station or machine to machine. Yet, the assembly machine is also just another form of transfer line, although usually smaller. The most avid proponents of flexibility, especially manufacturers of robotic types of equipment, say that transfer lines and special purpose machines (and, by definition, assembly machines) are relics of the past since they are inflexible. This means that when products produced on these machines are discontinued, those replacing them will require entirely new machines. Presumably, with little or no new investment, robotic type processes should have the capability of producing both the old and new products. In reality, transfer machines are now and will be in the future a practical necessity. Factors to consider are that:

1. Some products are subject to little or infrequent change. Thus, investments in specially designed, less-than-flexible equipment are warranted. Notable examples of these types of products include those of highest demand such as foods, beverages, personal grooming products, clothing, building products, bearings, hardware, and gaskets.

2. Rapid technological or styling changes do *not* necessarily benefit the customer. In the automotive industry, major styling changes have always added greater costs to the product. The consumer may benefit most from a system designed to produce the same product, or the same product with minor modifications, for as many years as possible.

3. Transfer machines, developed for the highest volume products, seem to be expensive. If their cost is prorated to the volume of pro-

duction, however, it is usually an insignificant percentage of product cost.

4. The life expectancy of transfer machines is usually not much different than the projected life of the product produced. Thus, the equipment should be about ready to be replaced at the same time that the product is replaced.

5. Transfer lines, specially designed for a product, continue to cost less per unit than more flexible equipment.

6. When designing the transfer line or machine, consideration should be given to whether or not flexible features could be part of the design.

Every process design project should recognize and pursue opportunities for automation of assembly operations, but not at the expense of economics. Special emphasis should be placed on simplification of product and process before making any costly investment in automation. In general, the criteria that most favor automation are product simplicity, high-volume demand, and small product size. The opposite criteria favor manual and low-cost automation methods of assembly.

The benefits of improving the assembly process are among the greatest in the factory. Chief among them are large inventories on the line and in centralized storage. Focusing storage of assembly materials at the assembly line (discussed in greater detail in Chapter 6) is one easy way to gain better control of component inventories. Smaller, portable containers also help to reduce space, inventory, and wasted time and motion. Yet, the number of workers, components assembled, and variety of products may also require a bigger project team than other simpler areas.

Automation, particularly if low cost, should be applied to the simplest assembly tasks to reduce manufacturing costs and increase quality. The day of the fully automated plant is, however, still in the distant future for most factories.

5

□□□

Machining Process Design

AS IN ALL FACTORY AREAS, machining operations represent an opportunity for considerable improvement. But typically, it involves numerous and complex problems. Both machine operators and indirect personnel spend relatively little time on keeping machines cycling and too much time on performing tasks and motions that add little value to the product being machined, or simply waste time standing idle. The amount of inventory in process, in units, is usually hundreds of times greater than the number of machines being used. Also machines break down frequently, causing a need for large inventories of machined items to provide a supply while machines are out of order. Defective items are often produced, which requires sorting of good production from bad, reworking and scrapping some items. As in the case of machine downtime, anticipation of defective production necessitates larger inventories of materials and machined items to provide a supply sufficient to replace those items, when they are produced. Because planning and scheduling systems are designed to support large inventories of work-in-process and machined items, lead times from raw material to the customer delivery are too long. Ideally, customers would like delivery of their orders a few days after placing them, since they know that this rapid service should be provided by the superior manufacturer. However, the factory unfortunately requires several weeks. In addition, setup costs, incurred when a machine is changed from running one item to producing another, are high. As a result, production lot sizes must be relatively large. That means, for instance, when component requirements are produced in lot sizes of one month, a factory's flexibility for changing schedules is reduced.

The first step toward solution of these problems is to rearrange the equipment used to machine and finish each family of manufactured items into a new layout called a cell. Before rearrangement, the machines, processes, and workbenches used for each family are located in diverse, widely separated areas of the factory, necessitating parts to be moved great distances between each operation performed. The new layout typically results in the following magnitude of performance improvement:

90 percent	Manufacturing lead-time reduction
90 percent	Work-in-process inventory reduction
90 percent	Lift-truck reduction
75 percent	Machine downtime reduction
75 percent	Defect reduction
50 percent	Plant occupied reduction
30–50 percent	Personnel productivity improvement

While personnel productivity improvement has averaged 30 percent, in some cases it has been as high as 50 percent or more. Cells can be arranged to permit operators to run multiple machines, especially when machine cycle times are long. In these cases, the number of machines operated by one person should increase dramatically. Savings can be even greater when simplification enables the elimination of operators through the use of low-cost, "put and place" automation. Robots are designed to perform any task for which they are programmed, thus have a high degree of flexibility but a cost in tens of thousands of dollars. Put-and-place automation, by contrast, uses mechanisms which would, for example, pick up parts to be machined from a fixed location in a conveyor and move the parts into the machining position. Subsequently, another put-and-place device would move completed parts out of the machine and onto an outbound conveyor, always placing the completed parts in exactly the same position on the conveyor. The cost of this simple automation alternative is usually hundreds of dollars.

Unfortunately, management in many factories has been able to identify only a few cells or none at all and have therefore concluded that opportunities for improvement are either limited or else do not exist. In fact, even factories with no potential to use cells can use other organizations that will produce similar but slightly smaller improvements. Since these other forms of layout are often applicable, understanding them is fundamental to reorganizing for superior manufacturing. The four possible organizations and forms of machine groupings are:

1. Functional departments (or workcenters)
2. Subplant job shop
3. Semicells
4. Cells

Where applicable, cell organization is the most productive; the functional organization the least. Yet, the functional organization is still most relevant for some cases.

FUNCTIONAL DEPARTMENTS

Exhibit 5–1 shows a simplified example of a factory organized into functional departments, in which each generic type of machine is grouped together. For example, all saws, regardless of their size (and therefore, capacity), are placed together in one department. All lathes are put together in a second department, etc. In this example, the number of machines and employees is considered large enough to warrant calling each grouping a department. Usually the department has a manager, supervisor, or foreman. When there are few machines in each grouping, it is

FUNCTIONAL DEPARTMENTS

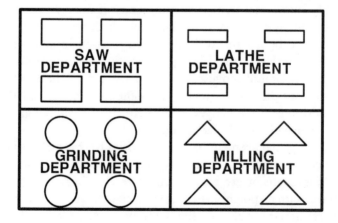

EXHIBIT 5-1

common to place several of the smaller ones, called workcenters, under a department manager, supervisor, or foreman. In the past, there have been strong, logical arguments in favor of functional groupings, including:

1. Machines are quite complex, and each type requires months, and even years, to master. Grouping machines of one type makes it possible to minimize the complexity of the jobs performed by specialists assigned only to this machine type.

2. The similar sizes and shapes of comparable machine types make it simpler to arrange large numbers of them into smaller physical spaces. (Those familiar with automatic lathe and screw machine layouts will readily understand this argument.)

3. Some types of machines characteristically produce completed products and components. Since these so-called "one-operation-routing" machines do not need to be grouped with other machines, cells are not applicable.

Machines, and the tools and fixtures used with them, should not be complex, but should be designed for ease of operation, maintenance, and changeover. The productivity improvement team is responsible for physical changes in equipment and tools, and/or methods that simplify operations. Properly designed, machine operations should be simple, primarily requiring the operator to load items to be machined and unload items when completed. There are several added costs and other disadvantages of functional versus cell organization. For example:

1. Each machine requires a scheduled queue (backlog of work awaiting machining), leading to excessive work-in-process inventory and longer than necessary manufacturing lead time. Jobs usually travel from machine to machine in large containers, one production order or lot at a time. Subsequent steps are not carried out on the first piece in the lot until all prior operations have been completed for the last piece. Thus, although the labor performed on a single item may be seconds or minutes per piece, it may take days or weeks to process the lot through the factory. The first piece becomes available only at that time.

2. Different jobs that could use similar or identical setups can rarely be grouped to save setup time: the reason being the complexity of scheduling parts with similar setups to arrive at a machine at the same time.

3. Some machines do not fully use the worker's time while operations are in process.

4. Each part travels several hundred feet, incurring material handling costs that are much higher than necessary.

5. Worker mobility and job satisfaction are limited by specialization.

In general, functional groupings of similar types of machines are rarely necessary; however, they continue to be applicable for one-operation-routing machines and for situations where there are virtually no families of items requiring operations on a common set of machines. Sometimes, it makes sense to move some machines into high-volume cells and to organize all other machines—typically machines used for low-volume production—into smaller, easier to manage functional layouts. This arrangement could be viewed as a temporary expedient, to focus on cells of highest profit potential. However, the remaining low-volume machines would eventually be analyzed for cell, semicell, and subplant job-shop organization potential.

CELL: FUNDAMENTAL FACTORY OF THE FUTURE

In Exhibit 5-2, one of each type of machine required to completely process a group of parts has been grouped together in a U-form cell in the sequence in which operations are performed. Parts machined in this cell flow continuously from one operation to the next, either one or a few at a time. Thus, the amount of time elapsed between the start of the first and last operations is approximately the same as the total machining and handling time for one piece. This difference, flowing production versus moving an entire lot from one operation to another, is the reason that production lead time is typically 90 percent lower in a cell than in a functionally organized factory. With this organization, safety stocks of completed items and inbound queues of waiting jobs can be maintained at minimal levels. Thus, the inbound/outbound storage area of the cell is minimal. In the functional grouping of machines, there is one operator per machine. This results in high machine utilization but poor use of the operator's time since he has little productive work to do while the machine is cycling. In the cell grouping, the cell is most often manned with 50 to 70 percent fewer operators than machines. Moreover, the machines are located in close proximity to permit the operator to attend several at once with minimal wasted time and motion.

The machine cell concept makes as much sense in the smaller, lower vol-

CELL

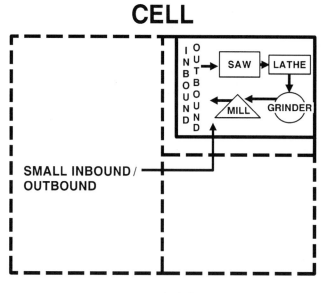

EXHIBIT 5-2

ume factories, as it does in the largest, highest volume plants. The Dumore Corporation proved this in its 45,000 square-foot Mauston (Wisconsin) plant that once housed groups of functional machines, organized roughly in lines of flow, as illustrated in Exhibit 5-3. The flow and the machines depicted in this example are used for producing armatures, one of several components Dumore uses for the electric motor it manufactures. As is normally the case, large queues of work in process between each machine caused excessive lead times. Consequently, quality problems were usually detected late, when nothing could be done to correct them, and sometimes too late to avoid scrapping an entire production lot. To help avoid this costly waste, the Dumore project team designed and implemented armature cells, one of which is shown in Exhibit 5-4. The benefits achieved included a decrease in space, work-in-process inventory reduction, and a 75 percent decline in the costs of quality defects. Good cell design includes not only organization of machines but also focused stores for each cell or for groups of cells, where parts and materials are common to several cells. Dumore's new plant layout included several cells and focused stores for fields, armatures, and assembly components. The combined production and storage area required was 50 percent less than previously needed.

Many early efforts to create cells were unsuccessful because machine

FUNCTIONAL LAYOUT - BEFORE

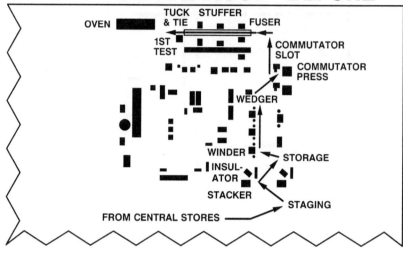

EXHIBIT 5-3

ARMATURE CELL

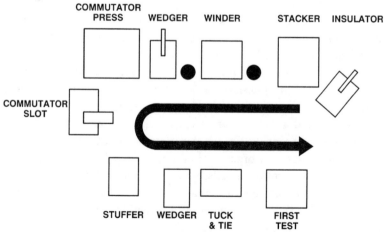

EXHIBIT 5-4

CELL LAYOUT - AFTER

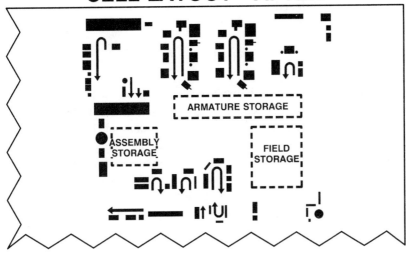

ARMATURE STORAGE

ASSEMBLY STORAGE

FIELD STORAGE

EXHIBIT 5-5

setup times were not reduced. As a result, large production lots were forced through the cell, causing excessive inventories and long lead times. A second reason for failure was inordinate machine downtime in the cell. When one machine broke down, all machines were stopped. For successful cell operation, it is critical to decrease setup time (as described in Chapter 7) and to reduce machine downtime. In summary, some of the major benefits of the cell are:

1. Drastic reduction of work-in-process lead time.
2. Cross-training of workers to perform operations on multiple processes in the cell. This gives the employee greater job satisfaction and enhances his skill base, making it easier to transfer him to another cell with similar processes.
3. Cells can be manned with a variable number of operators on different shifts. Thus, cell capacity has the flexibility to meet changing levels of requirements with appropriate levels of production.
4. Inventory is reduced at least the same proportion as work-in-process lead time. Since lead time is much shorter, just-in-case stock of completed items can also be drastically reduced.
5. Setup times and costs are decreased by running items of similar setup needs in the same cell.

6. The number of containers required and material handling costs are drastically reduced.

SEMICELL

The semicell, Exhibit 5–6, is usually composed of a set of machines for performing all operations needed to produce a group of parts. Often, the semicell has one machine of each type. It has many of the characteristics of the cell, but there are differences. First, is that the various parts produced in the same semicell must be machined in various different sequences of operation. By contrast, all parts in the cell flow through it in the same sequence. Second, since semicell parts do not flow continuously, the focused inbound storage area is larger than that in the cell. Some parts move back and forth between machines and focused storage. This is necessary when one operation is completed and the next machine in the flow is still being used for another part. When a group of parts clearly requires a common set of machines, the semicell is a logical grouping. Additionally, it is appropriate when the requirements of the group of parts warrant dedicating the capacity of the machines to the group. The semicell is appropriate when the routing sequence of the machined parts

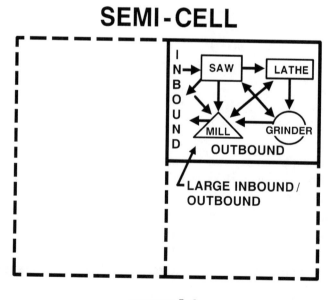

SEMI-CELL

EXHIBIT 5-6

varies greatly from one part to another, or when there is a large variation in the cycle time of each machine.

SUBPLANT JOB SHOPS

Almost every factory, including those in which some cells can be developed, has machines that do not fit into cells. They can be reorganized from functional departments into subplant job shops like those shown in Exhibit 5–7. In this illustration, some types and quantities of machines previously seen in four functional departments have been reorganized into two subplant job shops: one for subsea, oil rig products and a second for onshore, oil rig products. To provide logical flow for most items, the machines are arranged in the most typical sequence of operations. Each of the subplant job shops has many of the desirable management characteristics of focused subplants. For one, each subplant is under the management of an individual who has responsibility and authority for every facet of the required operations. And, for another, the total number of machines is limited to a quantity low enough to ensure that the person responsible can manage the subplant by personal knowledge and by direct, frequent observation.

Subplant job shops can be organized when there are products or component parts that can be gathered together for production on a group of

SUB-PLANT JOB SHOPS

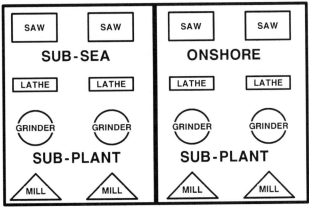

EXHIBIT 5–7

machines. This grouping is desirable when it is not feasible to use the machines in cells or semicells, for example, when:

1. The parts machined have a large variety of routing sequences that make it impractical to develop cells because no cell would have enough parts to justify dedicating the machines to their production.
2. The number of parts machined is unusually high, and the required volume of each part is very low. This usually occurs in combination with extreme routing variability.
3. There is inadequate time and budget to create cells. Therefore, cells are developed for the highest volume parts of similar routings. All other machines are organized into subplant job shops.

GROUP TECHNOLOGY

Group technology is most often described as coding the characteristics and dimensions of manufactured parts in order to group items with similar process requirements. The coding, when analyzed, permits the identification of a group to which a cell may be applicable. However, Andersen Consulting's experience in more than 400 factories around the world has shown that it is not necessary to code parts in order to identify opportunities for cells. The *process matrix* approach described in this chapter can do the job faster. In fact, of the two types of tools available, the code might be likened to a tack hammer: It is a slow, inefficient tool for a big task. By contrast, the process matrix approach that we use is more like a sledgehammer: It rapidly breaks a big job into small, manageable segments.

This and other sections make reference to the Harley-Davidson Motor Company case study. One part of this project included analysis of the gear and sprocket machining department to determine if cells could be developed. Exhibit 5–8 depicts the simplified layout and flow of that department and illustrates old machining techniques. The flow in this department was excessively long, caused by typical groups of functionally similar machines: chuckers, hobs, lathes, shavers, etc. Today, new cells have been developed through an easy-to-understand comparison of the machines with the parts processed on each.

The resulting matrix, seen in Exhibit 5–9, was created as a by-product of knowledge gained while performing a setup reduction project in the department. A prior consultant spent six months coding and analyzing codes of gears and sprockets, and concluded that the variety of shapes

TYPICAL FLOW - BEFORE

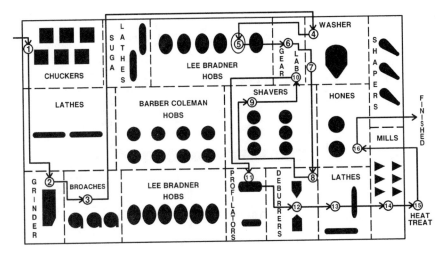

EXHIBIT 5-8

and sizes was too complex for cells. By contrast, it took Andersen Consulting's setup reduction project team only a few days to develop the matrix necessary to identify the machines needed to form cells and to subsequently develop the specific layout. The cells are illustrated in Exhibit 5–10, while the layout is shown in Exhibit 5–11. The new layout resulted

GROUP TECHNOLOGY MATRIX

PART NUMBER	WORK CENTER / MACHINE					
	CHUCKER	BROACH	L.B. HOB	B.C. HOB	WASH/TRIM	SHAVER
20	X	X	X			X
21	X	X	X		X	X
24	X	X	X	X	X	X
25	X	X	X		X	X
28	X	X	X		X	X
29	X	X	X		X	X
30	X	X	X		X	X

EXHIBIT 5-9

U-FORM LINES

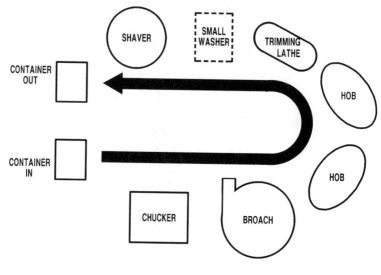

EXHIBIT 5-10

GEAR / SPROCKET DEPARTMENT - AFTER

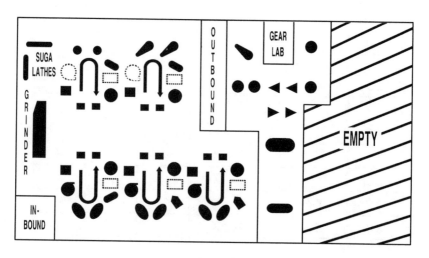

EXHIBIT 5-11

in the usual benefits of 90 percent reduction of work-in-process inventory and lead time, with additional savings in areas such as labor and defects. Today, the amount of material handling within the cells in the Harley-Davidson case is almost zero. All movement into and out of the cells is focused around the aisle between them.

By contrast, linear material handling requires traveling back and forth from one process to another, making it unproductive when one of the trips is made with a full load of materials and the return trip is made with none. In the U-form material example, illustrated in Exhibit 5–12, material handling follows a repetitive circular route in which all movement is focused around a single aisle. In fact, if containers on wheels are used, the cell operator can push containers from one cell to another, moving only a few feet.

Most companies need to quickly implement improvements in operations to begin paying back the costs of productivity-improvement projects and to make progress towards retaining or increasing market share through superior manufacturing. Therefore, it is vital to find ways to rapidly complete the definition of cells, semicells, and subplant job shops. Usually the "old hands" in the factory know the main flows of the process quite well. Thus, discussing these flows with them may be the fastest, simplest way to begin to develop cells. This is especially true because in most instances the highest volume, most expensive machined

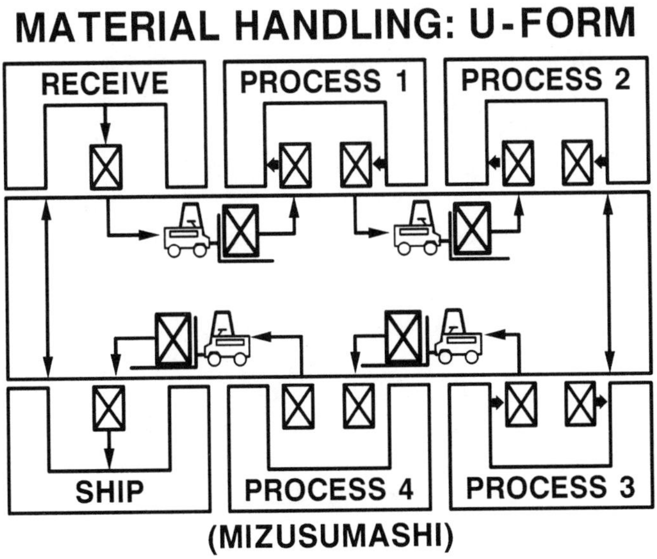

MATERIAL HANDLING: U-FORM

(MIZUSUMASHI)

EXHIBIT 5–12

items are the easiest to understand and the most promising prospects for cell machining.

The fastest way to design and implement new cells is to use the machines presently used as the basis for design, rather than studying each part to determine if its operations should be shifted to a more economical machine. Rerouting a job from one machine to another may often require modification of corresponding tools and fixtures. This further delays the implementation of the cell and increases its costs.

To develop new cells, it is sometimes (but not often) necessary to reroute operations of certain jobs to machines other than those specified by current routing. Rerouting should normally be avoided to reduce the time and effort required. It is necessary, however, when existing routings do not indicate a specific machine, when the machine specified in existing routings is seldom the lowest cost alternative, and when the machine specified in existing routings is seldom the machine used to produce the part.

CELL BACKUP

When a manufacturing company contemplates organizing machine cells, it naturally worries about two critical questions:

1. What will happen to the business if a machine in the cell breaks down and is out of operation indefinitely?

2. What will happen if the mix of products sold varies dynamically, therefore causing requirements of components to have peaks and valleys of demand? Since this is usually the case, machines in one of two similar cells might often be overloaded, while those in the second cell might, at the same time, have excess capacity. How can a manufacturer be assured that machines in every cell will have the capacity required for different levels of product mix demand?

The answer is that every ideal cell should have a backup. The work will then be offloaded from one cell to another, by exception, when imbalances require this to be done. Unfortunately, not everyone understands these concepts. As a result, numerous companies do excessive detailed work to select a group of parts that will almost exactly utilize the capacity of machines in the cell. Further, inordinate amounts of time are spent dealing with a machine breakdown in the cell that could stop production for hours or even days. In most factories, this kind of detail and concern is unnecessary since the best design will provide a backup cell or backup machines for most items produced. Some of the potential problems of cell machine utilization are purely hypothetical in most job-shop machining factories. In these, the majority of cells rarely operate at, or close to, full utilization—three shifts per day, seven days a week. Typical cells are usually found to need to operate on one of the following: a fraction of one shift, one shift and a fraction of another, two shifts and a fraction of another, and three shifts plus occasional overtime. The reason most cells should run fractional shifts every day is because factory products are not sold at a fixed rate equal to the capacity of plant processes. In fact, quite the contrary is true. A variety of uncontrollable external factors cause variable rates of demand on a factory. Not only are there weather changes caused by seasonality, but also economic cycles, increasing and decreasing demand, variability in the number of consumers in various age groups (due to varying birth rates over the years), shifts in shares of market from one manufacturer to another, and holidays and vacation periods. All of these factors contribute to the irregular demand of most products.

Exhibit 5-13 illustrates two similar cells purposely organized side by side. Each has a saw, lathe, grinder, and mill. The purpose of designing a plan in which similar cells are side by side is to provide a practical way to balance the load between the cells. Parts 1 and 2 can only be produced in the first cell. Parts 5 and 7 can only be done in the second. However, parts 3, 4, 5, and 6 can be completed in either cell. These part numbers

SIMILAR CELL PLANNING

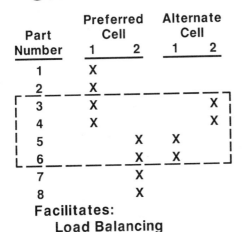

Part Number	Preferred Cell 1	Preferred Cell 2	Alternate Cell 1	Alternate Cell 2
1	X			
2	X			
3	X			X
4	X			X
5		X	X	
6		X	X	
7		X		
8		X		

Facilitates:
Load Balancing
Downtime Backup

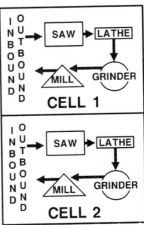

CELL 1

CELL 2

EXHIBIT 5-13

can easily be shifted from one cell to the other when loads in them are out of balance. Thus when large disturbances (such as machine downtime) occur, some of the cell load can be moved to the similar cell. The design and installation of similar cells simplify or eliminate the need to calculate long-range loads for machines in a cell. In fact, it is usually impractical to compute future loads because:

1. It is impossible to forecast accurately future demand of products, the components of which are machined in the cell.
2. Future products and components have not even been designed.
3. Existing machine time standards are inaccurate.
4. The factory does not have meaningful data on current and theoretically achievable maximum machine utilization.
5. The mix of loads between cells will vary from time to time. Therefore, some cells might be idle, while others will not have enough capacity for the load.

If cells are designed with backups, detailed capacity analysis of each is not critical. That is because selected jobs should be routinely shifted to other cells in response to load fluctuations.

SINGLE MACHINE CELLS

In some factories, numerous individual machines can be operated as cells or even like the smallest of focused subplants. Where this is possible, the speed and low cost of implementation and the fact that benefits can rapidly be achieved make development of single machine cells an attractive management target. Consider, for example, a small press center, one of several in the punch press department. It contains four identical small presses. A remote raw material storeroom causes material issued to the presses to be transported a long distance. Because the stockroom stores materials for every department in the factory, finding the required material often requires location control records. The die storage area is also large and complex. Since it contains all dies used by the entire punch press department, locating a specific die can be problematic. Additionally, although the die storage area is not as remote as raw material storage, it is still not convenient for quick access to machines that use it. In this workcenter, jobs are run on the machine that is available at the moment. Thus, the quality of the parts produced varies as a result of slight dimensional differences of the presumably identical machines. Because of these differences, adjustments made during setup vary slightly for each machine.

One important benefit of single machine cells is specialization. All operators of a given machine, regardless of shift, can concentrate on producing a specific, smaller group of parts that is always assigned to them. This concept is critical to quality improvement. Although four machines can theoretically be the same, there are always minute differences that make setup of a part different from one machine to another. By designating a group of parts to be run on one machine, and almost always using it, it is possible to perpetually repeat the correct setup without adjustments for machine uniqueness. Since adjustments may be done improperly or inaccurately, one important source of problems of quality can be avoided.

In many companies, the computer database can be used to provide data like those found on the "Workcenter Where Used" report (including raw material and die information). These are likely to be the major criteria for grouping parts to be run on each machine. For example, if aluminum and brass are the two types of raw material used, they might be one way to establish groups of parts for each press. One press could run all aluminum parts and the other, all brass parts. If two presses were required for aluminum parts, one could run parts made from size one and another, all parts made from sizes two and three. Die information could also be vital if die sizes vary. Dies of the same approximate size should be used on the same machine to help minimize setup time and cost. (If machines from other areas of the factory can be added to these single machine cells to create more conventional cells, the results are even better.) Each machine is assigned specific part numbers to produce. The dies for the parts assigned to each machine are kept at the machine. Raw material, when received, is delivered directly to the storage area adjacent to the machine that produces the parts made from it.

There are several tangible advantages of assigning specific part numbers to designated machines in single machine cells. For one, this new cell substantially reduces wasted time and motion spent traveling to and from raw material stores and the die storage area. Second, there is the additional benefit of enabling a machine operator to specialize in a limited group of items produced.

When we discuss assigning specific part numbers to designated machines, experienced manufacturing people almost always exclaim that this would be impractical since requirements for different items produced fluctuate widely over time. Thus, to make such assignments would continuously result in some machines with overload and others with inadequate load. One of the most important reasons for designing similar cells is to be able to routinely shift some load from one cell to another, *by exception*. The longest-running items are those used to level major load imbalances from one cell to another. Shifting one long-running job from an overloaded cell to one with available capacity is easier than shifting several smaller jobs and ensures that the most jobs possible will be produced on the assigned machine rather than on another machine. This is vitally important to minimize problems of setup adjustment and quality defects resulting from dimensional differences among machines.

MACHINE UTILIZATION

To best comprehend machine capacity utilization in the cell, it is helpful to understand some basic facts about machine capacity, utilization, and load. It is also helpful to see the fallacy of certain myths about utilization and capacity, such as:

1. Cycle times, thus capacities of machines in a cell, are/can be balanced.
2. Machine capacity in the factory is/can be fully utilized.
3. Long-range machine load can be accurately/meaningfully forecast.

Why are these only myths?

1. In most factories around the world, machines are utilized considerably less than 100 percent and should be.
2. Machine capacities of almost any factory are not and cannot be balanced in terms of every machine in a group of machines performing required operations for each part in the same amount of time. This is due to two basic facts. First, different machines have different feeds and speeds, and second, various part numbers require different machining times for each operation.
3. Long-range machine load cannot be forecast. Manufacturers, worldwide, have become increasingly aware of the impossibility of forecasting future demand. Since machine loads consist of varying loads for different products, it is even less possible to accurately forecast future loads. For this reason, most manufacturers either plan for excess capacity to meet peak demands or ration capacity to customers in periods of high demand.

These general observations hold true in most cases, but there are some rare exceptions. Some processes call for such large-scale investment in machines and equipment that profitability will require operating as close to 100 percent capacity as possible. Notable examples include paper, textiles, and plastic molding—in fact, most types of process manufacturing. These products require equipment that can be purchased from manufacturers who supply everyone in the same industry. Since everyone has, or can have, the same equipment, competition is usually fierce, and profit margins are paper-thin. Thus, the degree of equipment use can make the difference between profit and loss. The competitive conditions in other industries besides process manufacturing may also force companies to use equipment at near-full capacity. Industries specializing in such products as bearings, fasteners, and gaskets can be counted among the few examples. Again, such manufacturing requirements are not typical.

In the majority of job-shop operations around the world, the circumstances are different. For example:

1. Numerous existing machines have capacities far in excess of any foreseeable requirements.

2. The portion of product cost due to machine depreciation is quite low. In many cases, operations are performed on equipment that has been fully depreciated.

3. In the marketplace, demand is subject to cyclical peaks and valleys, to seasonality, and to overall increase or decrease trends. Manufacturers and their suppliers have little option but to vary their output operations to match market requirements. Types of manufacturing subject to variations in demand include: automobiles; appliances; soft goods, such as clothing; agricultural, transportation, construction, and recreational equipment; and machine tools. It seems obvious that these products have trend, seasonal, and cyclical demand. They are listed only to show that the number of factories with variable requirements is much greater than those with relatively stable demand. During most of the business cycle, these plants operate well below their peak potential capacity.

When demand exists or can be generated, increased utilization of existing machines can be expected to improve profitability. The majority of factories, however, are producing as much as the market demands and less than the maximum possible. Even in plants producing to full capacity on some machines, large numbers of others are operating at less than total capacity. Thus, increasing the hours machines produce, by raising hours utilized, can pay off only if demand exceeds existing levels of production.

Many manufacturing executives, managers, and engineers spend much more time than warranted determining whether machines in a cell can be fully utilized. Some have even rejected organization of machines into cells because they realize that cell utilization can be quite low. They make this decision before properly evaluating the following factors:

1. The importance of significantly reduced manufacturing lead time, thus improved customer service, sales, and margins, through cell organization.
2. Whether or not *real* utilization in the cell is better or worse than in the existing factory.
3. Whatever demand exists or is likely to be developed for more capacity than the cell provides.

It is important to understand these issues in order to quickly conclude whether or not cells are feasible and how much attention, if any, must be paid to full utilization as a requirement. Misunderstanding may seriously delay cell installation and even cause cells not to be developed.

Exhibit 5–14 illustrates the actual load and utilization of four machines in the functional department layout, as 4, 40, 20, and 8 hours per week. These four machines, coincidentally, could be extracted and reorganized into a cell and used to produce exactly the same items as previously machined. Exhibit 5–15 shows the cell constructed to produce the same

DEPARTMENT MACHINE UTILIZATION

HOURS PER WEEK

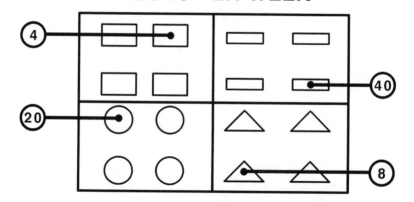

EXHIBIT 5–14

CELL MACHINE UTILIZATION
MINUTES PER PIECE

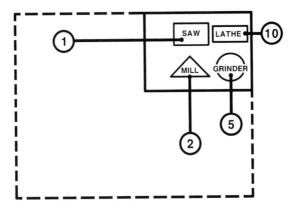

EXHIBIT 5-15

family of parts, using the same machines. For a given part number, the machining minutes per piece average 1, 10, 2 and 5. Manufacturing technicians and some executives look at this apparently gross imbalance of load and worry about the poor machine utilization. Obviously, all four machines will need to operate at the speed of the slowest one.

What is commonly forgotten is that the operating cell will probably be manned by only one operator instead of four. Also typically forgotten is the fact that the functional department weekly load of 4, 40, 8, and 20 hours is exactly the same ratio of utilization as the cell load of 1, 10, 2 and 5 minutes. Thus, utilization in the cell would be almost the same as in the functional department. The actual utilization of the 10-minute cycle time machine in the cell might be slightly less than in the functional department since the single operator might be attending another machine in the cell when the 10-minute cycle ends.

Manufacturing executives must establish ambitious, but realistic, targets against which to evaluate the viability of a cell's potential capacity. For example, they must plan what to do if the load in each cell increases by 50 or 100 percent in the future. This does not necessarily mean designing the cell to handle the increase since greater load could be managed in any of several ways, including:

1. Designing the cell with space for selected additional machines that would be required given a specified level of increase.

2. Planning to install another, perhaps duplicate cell if necessary.

3. Offloading some of the load to other similar cells.

When reviewing two representative part numbers, as illustrated in Exhibit 5-16, it is apparent why machine capacities usually are not and cannot be balanced. The two parts, jobs 1 and 2, require different amounts of material to be removed by the lathe operation, as indicated by the external dotted lines. This process requires 30 seconds for job 1 and 10 seconds for job 2. Both jobs require drilling a hole partially through the center of the cylinder. The hole drilled for job 2 is much deeper than that for job 1. Thus, the job 1 hole requires 5 seconds to drill, compared to 15 seconds for the job 2 hole. Note that the relative amount of load for job 1 is highest in lathe, lowest in drill. The reverse is true on job 2. These simple cases are the rule, not the exception, in the majority of cells and potential cells. Additionally, no one could predict the machine load effect of a yet undesigned new part number.

The fact that most factories have few machines utilized at 100 percent of real capacity is an important factor in simplifying the work required to calculate loads by machine within a cell. The majority of machines in all cells can be expected to have insignificant capacity limitations. For instance, in one factory we considered to be fairly representative, some 800 machines were manned daily, approximately as follows:

CAPACITY BALANCE PROBLEM

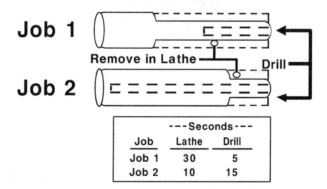

| | ---Seconds--- | |
Job	Lathe	Drill
Job 1	30	5
Job 2	10	15

Next New Design?

EXHIBIT 5-16

500 machines:	less than one-half shift
300 machines:	more than one-half shift
200 machines:	more than one shift (200 out of the 300 above)
50 machines:	more than two shifts (50 out of the 200 above)
10 machines:	more than three shifts (10 out of the 50 above)

In this case, any detailed comparison of the adequacy of total available machine capacity could be limited to the 50 machines currently approaching it, i.e., the last two groups listed.

MACHINE CELL BALANCING

The routine of developing detailed standards for every machine operation is deeply entrenched in management practice. These former standards were originally developed for two purposes:

1. To motivate increased productivity by providing a basis for paying incentives for production in excess of standard and for nonincentive measurement and evaluation of work performed versus standard
2. To provide a standard labor cost basis for pricing products and maintaining inventory accounts for work in process

In terms of motivating individuals and small groups to increase production, standard systems have produced desired results. When properly administered, they have been an effective foundation for cost and inventory accounting. These systems made sense when factories consisted of thousands of independent machine operators with no direct links to other operators or machines. In fact, when machining operations consist of large groups of independent machine operators, these systems still apply. For many superior manufacturers, however, their day is over.

Standard systems have yielded significant benefits, but not without corresponding costs. For example, the administration of standard systems for pay, performance evaluation, standards development and maintenance, pricing, cost accounting, and inventory accounting adds a significant amount of non-value-added costs to manufacturing organizations. In addition, standard systems have not been well accepted by organized labor, but have been a frequent cause of poor labor relations, union grievances, and strikes. Over the years, numerous contract negotiations have involved elimination of the use of incentive standards. Further, standards, in the main, have usually been set at levels far below a reasonable pace for the average worker. This is evidenced by the fact that average production in factories covered by incentive systems is 25 percent higher than standard, while the pace of workers is still typically well below the maximum achievable. "Loose" standards have evolved because unions and individual employees have fought for decades for the easiest possible standards.

The new manufacturing organization, the focused subplant, and the cell transform the world of machining. Worldwide, hundreds or thousands of individual machine operations have been replaced by far fewer "lines" of machines and/or groups of machines organized by product lines. Measuring the activities of each individual within a line is a waste of time and effort since line output is limited by either the slowest worker in it or the one with the most amount of work to perform. If motivating incentives are to be instituted, they should be applied on a group, rather than individual, basis. For this reason, managers are becoming increasingly interested in cooperative recovery concepts similar to those already discussed in Chapter 4, "Assembly Process Design." When applied to machine cells, cooperative recovery involves a team of employees, working together cooperatively, to produce jointly the total required product. Each worker on the team does as much work as he reasonably can, not just the work formally defined as his responsibility.

Cooperative recovery concepts apply as much or more to machine cells. Following is an illustration of how operators should work on two different jobs machined in one cell. Assume that operator time per machine for each job is nominal and somewhat less than machine cycle time and that the two jobs require the following approximate cycle times.

		Cycle Time in Seconds	
		JOB 1	JOB 2
Machine 1		10	8
Machine 2		9	---9---
Machine 3		---8---	6
Machine 4		9	5
Machine 5		10	4
	TOTAL	46	32

Conventional line-balancing theory assumes that an operator can only man a fixed, whole number of machines—one, two, three, four, etc. In this case, the first operator would probably run machines 1 and 2 for 19 seconds, while the second would operate machines 3, 4, and 5 for 27 seconds, thus wasting 8 seconds of the first operator's time. With cooperative recovery, both operators would share responsibility for machine 3. In the first cycle, the first operator would operate machine 3; in the second cycle, the second operator would do so, and so on. The dotted line indicates the machine number shared cooperatively. For job 2, the first operator would operate machine 1 and share responsibility for machine 2 with the second operator. In this example, operator assignments are determined by approximate, rather than precise, cycle times. This point is repeated to emphasize the potential savings of simple approximations versus formal standard development.

Although items machined in the U-form cell should usually flow around the U, in one leg and out the other, worker assignments should not necessarily be sequential operations. This would waste some operator time and require more space in the center of the cell, for two operators, back to back, as illustrated in Exhibit 5–17. A better arrangement would be to put operations on both legs of the U. This would permit locating machine workplaces directly opposite those on the other leg of the U. As Exhibit 5–18 demonstrates, the result is two workers operating four geographically close machines. Thus, travel between machines can be minimized. In the prior illustration, the worker might need to walk back and forth between the first and last machines in a straight line. This

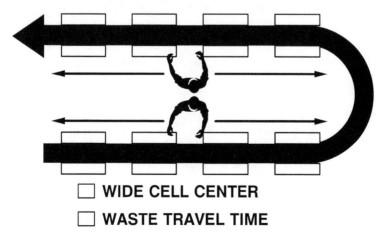

WORK ASSIGNMENT - POOR

□ WIDE CELL CENTER
□ WASTE TRAVEL TIME

EXHIBIT 5–17

WORK ASSIGNMENT - BETTER

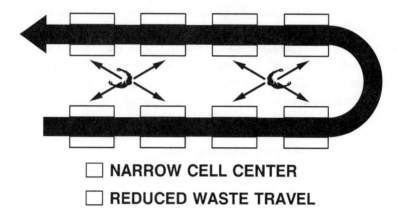

☐ **NARROW CELL CENTER**

☐ **REDUCED WASTE TRAVEL**

EXHIBIT 5–18

distance is significantly greater than that between any two machines on both sides of the center of the U.

Conventional line-balancing theory and practice would require the use of detailed motion information to develop operator assignments, even if cooperative recovery were utilized. Nevertheless, in the best possible example of cooperative recovery, there would be no requirement for detailed, job-specific data. The operators would automatically determine, by the actual time required to do a job, how to apportion the work performed. Thus, cooperative recovery would be based on a combination of each worker's natural speed and actual work performed rather than on a theoretical, detailed standard. With the phasing out of detailed standards for determining assignments, the question arises, "What new standards will be used for cost and inventory accounting?" It might be followed by a second question, "Are there simpler accounting alternatives for labor costs than developing labor standards?"

Assuming the continuation of some form of labor standards, one could answer the first question by using either historical cost as the basis of the standards, or standards based on approximate labor times for the entire cell. Direct labor today rarely accounts for more than 5 percent of customer price and usually represents no more than 10 percent of manufacturing costs. Yet an inordinate amount of management system time and expense is devoted to preparing detailed reports that monitor labor costs. By contrast, overhead costs, which are typically two to five times greater than labor costs, are pooled and charged to product cost, according to the amount of labor in the product. In answer to the second question, it might be just as logical, and perhaps much simpler, to apply overhead to products based on the cost of material used. For that matter, direct labor could be included in the overhead pool, and be applied to product cost based on the price of material used.

The superior manufacturing operation will aim to eliminate detailed standards in its plan for becoming the factory of the future. It will develop new interim procedures for creating estimated and historical standards. In the short term, it will recognize the important benefits of matching work assignments to individual natural speeds and will launch training and implementation programs to teach employees how and why to work together cooperatively. Finally, some of the most progressive superior manufacturers will develop new incentive programs that are simple, require little administration, and truly motivate individuals by enabling them to understand that their efforts will increase their earnings.

EQUIPMENT MAINTENANCE: CONTINUOUS UPTIME

In many factories, machine downtime represents a substantial percentage of the total time a machine is in production, being changed over, or down. Ten percent downtime for a machine not directly linked to others is usually not a significant problem. The operator, and perhaps the job being worked on, can frequently be moved to another machine. When 10 machines, with an average downtime of 10 percent each, are moved into one cell, there is potential for a sizable problem. The theoretical downtime for the entire cell would be 55 percent, with the probability that two machines would be down simultaneously 90 percent of the time.

Because 55 percent downtime might cause serious shortfalls of available machine capacity in the cell and/or could create large amounts of operator idle time, a special maintenance productivity improvement program is often required to bring downtime to an acceptable level. In many companies, this project is not a high priority for one or more of the following reasons:

1. Downtime in the cell is usually much less than in the functional department organization, without any special maintenance improvement project. This is the case because cell operators develop a heightened awareness of the need for rapid repair since cell disruption is much costlier than the disruption of an individual machine.

As a result, they are accustomed to think in terms of improving maintenance.

2. Numerous machines used have relatively insignificant downtime.

3. The number of machines in typical cells are few—two, three, or four. Thus, the multiplier effect of the number of machines times average downtime, factored for the probability of being down simultaneously, may produce an acceptable range of cell downtime.

4. There may be backup cells and/or machines to which operators and/or jobs can be moved when downtime occurs.

Throughout the world, presentations and publications on increased productivity stress total preventive maintenance as an important key to the successful operations of a world-class manufacturer. Preventive maintenance, however, is only part of the story. It would be a disservice to the manufacturing world if we were to encourage the belief that a preventive maintenance program alone is the only way to avoid or reduce machine or equipment downtime.

Machines and equipment do need preventive maintenance, and where it makes sense, it would be a major mistake to fail to perform it. Nevertheless, the only sure remedy for old, unreliable, worn pieces of equipment is either to rebuild them to a state of good operating condition, or to replace them altogether. Thus, preventive maintenance is important to productivity improvement, but it is not a cure for all equipment downtime.

Two major objectives of a maintenance productivity project are: first, to minimize the amount of time that machines and equipment used in manufacturing processes are down due to breakage or machine failure; second, to minimize the cost of maintaining equipment in sound operating condition (which includes reducing the time required for repairs and the cost). Goals for maintenance productivity improvement should be as aggressive as those in other areas. To begin, machine downtime should be reduced by as much as 90 percent, as achieved by the Brunswick Corporation's Pin Plant in Muskegon, Michigan, with its improvement of 80 to 85 percent. Then a second goal should be reducing the time lost by direct labor, as a result of machine downtime, by 75 percent. If the time required to repair a machine in a manufacturing cell can be reduced from one hour to five minutes, the potential cost savings of direct labor time would be as much as 55 minutes per person in the cell.

The cost and time needed for planned and unplanned repair can be cut by 40 percent through the use of improved maintenance productivity methods and techniques. The techniques, several of which are described in this chapter, decrease the amount of labor required and thereby bring about significant savings. For instance, a machine presumed to be repaired is frequently returned to service and subsequently produces bad parts or experiences further problems. Maintenance people must then correct their errors. In factories where this is a serious problem, improved methodology can significantly reduce flaws in machine maintenance by as much as 90 percent, thus contributing to the decline of total maintenance costs.

By providing better planned maintenance and improving maintenance errors, it is possible to reduce the consumption of spare parts. Through the use of improved focused inventory control, the level of equipment and spare parts for machine maintenance and repair should be lowered by as much as 50 percent. As a result of maintenance improvements that provide machines that hold closer tolerances, the quality of products produced should be enhanced. Work-in-process inventory reductions of as much as 90 percent can be achieved by reducing the need for safety stock required to protect against machine downtime since downtime can be correspondingly reduced.

As discussed in Chapter 2, maintenance should be decentralized so that each subplant has one or more maintenance workers assigned to it, and each maintenance worker should have his own area with a workbench in his subplant. Although most of the maintenance organization can be decentralized, the central shop would still house machines used for repairing components of shop machines and some storage. Maintenance supplies and component parts used by more than one subplant would continue to be stored in a central storage location.

In the future, the operators and entrepreneurs of factories will have jobs with considerably more interest and satisfaction. As it was, many machine operators and assemblers spent all day, every day, repeating the same basic tasks. In new machining cells and on assembly lines, employees will have the opportunity to learn a variety of production operations and to switch back and forth among different workstations as frequently as team members feel it desirable. This freedom will enable workers to minimize boredom and give each the opportunity to master various operations. Also machine operators and assemblers will be responsible for maintaining the machines and equipment, carrying out both preventive and corrective maintenance. Other responsibilities of each team of operators and entrepreneurs will include:

- Meeting schedules on time, neither early nor late
- Participating in controlling and limiting the inventory investment of work in process and the materials used

- Managing the team's capacity to control work assignments that are consistent with producing the products required at the highest level of productivity
- Meeting and exceeding quality requirements, with sole responsibility and authority for achieving quality objectives (separate inspection and test specialists will not be required)

There is great opportunity for reducing the amount of time lost by machine operators idly waiting for repairs. However, supervision in many manufacturing operations is lax when it comes to quick reassignment of workers when their machines are down. Immediate improvement can be made by implementing procedures that move operators to other machines the minute specialized repair work is needed. When this happens, the entire team of operators can be shifted to another cell. In most cases, moving operators from one to another cell should be practical since the number of cells designed for manufacturing plants is usually greater than are required for full operation on a daily basis. Therefore, additional cells should always be available for operator moves. Another alternative is to temporarily blend operators into other work teams. This will increase the output of those teams. After repairs are completed, workers from other cells can be assigned to help regain the schedule position of the affected cell.

A longer-term objective is training machine operators in the cell or assembly area to assist or to do the actual repair work. A majority of repair and maintenance operations involve the partial disassembly of equipment, replacement of component parts, and equipment reassembly. Because disassembly and reassembly are fairly routine, most factory personnel should be capable of performing these tasks. Thus, rather than standing idly by, waiting for maintenance to repair the equipment, the operator or cell team could do the disassembly and reassembly work. Sometimes, however, specialized personnel are needed to perform repair or maintenance work because of its complexity or special requirements, or because machine operators have not been trained to do it. In these situations, there is still potential for major savings. Since each subplant will have maintenance personnel assigned to it, the response time will be much faster than when these workers were dispersed throughout the manufacturing plant.

A primary reason for the wasted time and motion of the maintenance worker is the centralized storage of repair parts. If the parts are available, they can be carried back to the equipment. Very frequently, however, the parts are not in stock. Maintenance personnel must then leave pieces of equipment disassembled or partially disassembled while they place requests for the needed parts. Machinery will then stand idle, in a disassembled condition, until the parts are obtained. In addition, there is the difficulty of controlling a large number of parts. The responsibility for central inventory can become very bureaucratic. The person deciding how much to stock, when to reorder, and how much to reorder is often located too far away from factory areas where spare parts are actually needed to be able to make reasonable choices concerning inventory. Instead, each subplant should have its own focused inventory of machine repair parts, just as it has its own focused material storage. It is not unreasonable for productivity project teams to recommend the allocation of space for this purpose. The spare parts stored can either be unique to the subplant or commonly used on machines in subplant areas. It may also be advisable to continue stocking repair parts *common* to many subplants in a central storage location. The options are to stock these parts only in a central location or to maintain additional stock in one or more subplants that are replenished from central storage.

The focused maintenance organization eliminates the wasted time maintenance personnel typically spend in travel to the repair site, then back to the central maintenance department to get special tools. After they return to the repair site, they may need to go back to the central maintenance area several times to retrieve parts required. Travel is reduced by portable tool kits designed for tools routinely carried from machine to machine. The tools stored in these kits should be easily portable and have frequent use. Certain tools will need specialized tool storage. Such tools are used within an area or for a group of machines, but they are too expensive or large to duplicate and store at each site. Thus, housing them in a focused storage location is an appropriate solution. Another alternative for storing tools specific to certain machines would be to design a special portable tool kit that could be stored close to where the tools would be used.

Opportunities to employ quick-change modules should also be identified. For example, if electric motors on equipment fail and need annual or semiannual repair, a practical decision may be to make quick-change modules with fast connect/disconnect hardware that make it faster and easier to replace motors.

In a centralized maintenance organization, one of the most difficult management jobs is scheduling and controlling maintenance operations. To provide some basis for these processes, many companies enter maintenance requests into a computer system. These are then prioritized and kept on file, until a report is issued on the task completion, the time required, cost of the component parts used, etc. Simplifying computer system monitoring activities and eliminating excess reporting will provide substantial additional savings. In the new subplant organization, scheduling and controlling maintenance operations become quite simple. The supervisor determines where the maintenance employee should work, and the maintenance materials required are stored in the same area.

In summary, the total time required to repair a down machine can be reduced by decreasing the time spent waiting for repair people to respond. Necessary spare parts and tools can be located close by to minimize retrieval time, and the time needed to do the repair work can be lowered by using machine operators. Reductions of downtime will ensue from designing improved methods for performing maintenance repairs and by improving preventive maintenance procedures. Realistically, shortening downtime as a result of routine/preventive maintenance will not be significant compared to the improvement opportunities previously mentioned.

TIME AND MOTION: IMPROVEMENT OPPORTUNITIES

Although other areas of machining improvement may yield greater savings, personnel cost reductions of at least 30 to 50 percent are achievable. They require reorganizing not only the flow of machining but also the design of each machine operation. In Exhibit 4–1 (see Chapter 4, p. 74), the effect of poor work arrangement and methodology is apparent. The operator shown spends the majority of his time removing completed parts from the machine, bending to put them into the large container on the floor, straightening up and turning, picking up the next part and positioning that part. In this example, the machine cycle time is short compared to the time the operator spends handling the product. While the machine is cycling, the operator is idle. The amount of machine capacity utilized is low, and the operator is subjected to fatiguing physical demands that are likely to reduce his productivity. As each large container is emptied or filled, productive time is lost waiting for a lift truck to move the containers.

The productivity of both the operator and the machine is increased substantially by using short, low-cost conveyors or wheeled containers to bring smaller containers or individual items to the machining position and to move completed parts. As Exhibit 5–19 depicts, minimal time is spent by the operator removing and putting down a completed part and

ONE MACHINE -- LONG CYCLE

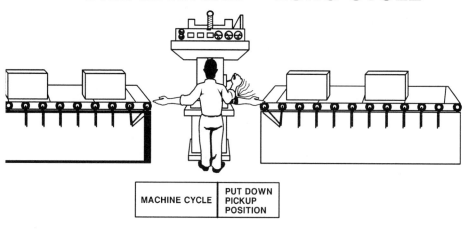

MACHINE CYCLE	PUT DOWN PICKUP POSITION

EXHIBIT 5-19

picking up and positioning the next part to be machined. In fact, it is short compared to the machine cycle time. This process reorganization can sharply reduce operator fatigue and eliminate time lost while lift trucks move containers. However, the operator is still nonproductive when the machine is cycling. Some factories have recognized nonproductive operator time and decided to purposely use it for measuring and gauging parts previously machined and maintaining statistical quality records. These companies tend to forget the difference between operations that add value to the product (machining) and those that add costs without value (inspection, measuring, and gauging). As we have repeatedly stated, inspection as a manual operation should be eliminated. Processes must be designed with built-in quality control or automatic detection and selection of defective items. Thus, any time spent by the machine operator in unnecessary motion, or performing non-value-added tasks must be viewed as time that can be saved.

An ideal way to further increase worker productivity is to combine two or more sequential machine operations, requiring numerous operators, into an operation with one operator. In Exhibit 5–20, one operator runs two machines. He removes and puts the completed part at the first machine and picks up and positions the next part. Then, while the first machine is cycling, he removes and puts the completed part in the second machine and picks up and positions the next part. Machine cycle time is almost entirely overlapped with takeout, pickup, and position operations, as well as with the cycle time of the other machine. Using this procedure,

TWO MACHINES - - LONG CYCLE

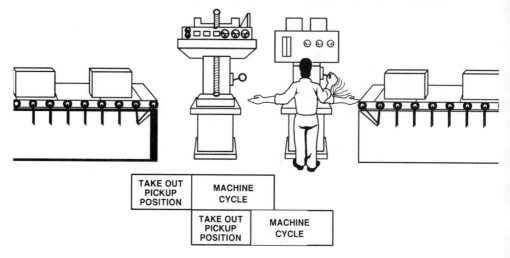

TAKE OUT PICKUP POSITION	MACHINE CYCLE		
	TAKE OUT PICKUP POSITION	MACHINE CYCLE	

EXHIBIT 5–20

the increase from the poorest productivity example (Exhibit 4–1) to this improved operation ranges from 125 to 150 percent.

It is also logical to combine two or more sequential machining operations with machine cycle times that are too short to overlap. In Exhibit 5–21, the operator picks up and positions a part at the first machine.

TWO MACHINES - - SHORT CYCLE

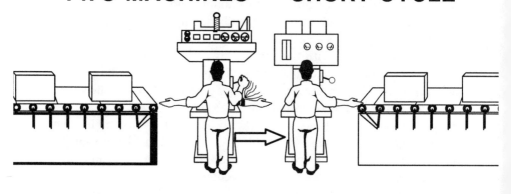

PICKUP POSITION	MACHINE CYCLE	TAKEOUT POSITION	MACHINE CYCLE	TAKEOUT PUT DOWN

EXHIBIT 5–21

After the machine cycle, he removes the completed part and positions it in the second machine. This eliminates putting the part down between the two machines, then picking it up at the second machine. After the short second machine cycle, the operator takes the completed part and puts it down. Operator productivity increase, compared to the poorest productivity case (Exhibit 4–1), ranges from 50 to 100 percent. However, following these steps usually reduces machine utilization. Thus, it may be necessary to operate the machines for additional hours.

Productivity improvement projects involve the study of time and motion in existing operations and the design of new operations to reduce waste. This often involves breaking down large, complex individual tasks into many small ones, performed by a larger group of people. In such cases, time savings in producing the product are expected to range from 50 to 80 percent.

Lately, it has been popular to speak with disdain of the accomplishments of the fathers of the modern industrial revolution, Frederick W. Taylor and Frank Gilbreth. Some go so far as to completely reject time and motion studies, blaming them alone for monotonous, dehumanizing assembly procedures. They also criticize the reliance on time standards for the measurement of performance of manufacturing tasks, comparing this practice to flogging galley slaves so that they will work faster.

It is unrealistic to argue against the successful application of time and motion study and task simplification to manufacturing production. The industrial revolution of the 1900s brought unparalleled benefits to mankind:

1. Reduced costs and prices of every mass-produced item to a level that everyone employed in the industrial world is now able to afford— products produced by methods of time and motion analysis and task simplification.

2. Higher working and living standards of employees of industries applying these techniques. In a 10- to 20-year period, the earning level of workers increased manyfold, while working hours and conditions constantly improved.

These benefits are even enjoyed by the very factory employees who are thought to suffer from mindlessly repetitive manufacturing tasks and the relentless speed and pace of power-driven, continuous-motion production lines. Unfortunately, critics of high-speed, repetitive manufacturing seldom recognize its benefits and the realities or potential for solutions to drudgery. Those who find fault with high-speed, simple task production, based on minimizing time and motion, are both right and wrong. Some people prefer simple, repetitive, high-speed tasks to more complex jobs; most enjoy the challenge of high-production goals. Many would have greater job satisfaction if their positions provided a broader range of experience and a greater depth of responsibility by allowing them to rotate among several simple tasks.

While it is practical and desirable to give production people more satisfying jobs, the advantages of simple, high-speed tasks are so great that it will remain necessary to design work assignments around them as much as possible. Greater job satisfaction has its price in higher costs and lower volumes that consumers will not tolerate.

Critics of time and motion analysis have one very sound argument against standards used to measure performance and, sometimes, to determine incentive pay. Every manufacturing professional readily recognizes, from his own experience, that factories using standards for performance measurement have higher rates of production. They also know that factories that use standards as a basis for extra incentive pay have the highest rates of production. The question remains, however, is more output per hour the best measurement of productivity? Those critical of standards do not recognize two of the best possible arguments for thinking about them in new ways. These are:

1. People are not uniform. When jobs on a factory line are based on a theoretical standard, the line will never be able to operate any faster than the slowest worker. A line that permits work to be assigned based on the natural speed of each worker will be the most productive line.

2. It may be better to produce exactly what is required, not more or less. Incentive standards usually encourage people to produce whatever they can. Thus, the amount produced is not what is necessary, but what the person assigned was able to accomplish.

Major export-oriented Japanese companies do not maintain or use labor standards. For them, labor is treated much like a fixed overhead expense. The reasons for this are:

1. The substantial costs for the personnel responsible for developing and maintaining standards are eliminated. In addition, since there are no standards, there are no incentive systems for pay based on the amount produced. This avoids the major costs of administering an incentive pay system.

2. Maintenance of standards tends to inhibit improvement of methods. When methods are improved, revised standards are needed, and the

standard section is usually too busy to develop them. Thus, ideas for improvement do not get processed.

3. In an environment of dynamic improvement (i.e., 19 percent per year), meaningful measurement against either the year-old standard or latest one is complex and costly.

4. With the design of new flowing machining and assembly processes, process costing is more applicable than standard costing.

5. People are not standard, as previously mentioned.

Moving away from standards systems may be a long-term improvement for most companies. Typically, overall productivity measurements by focused factory, cell, or line are preferable to direct labor measurement by individual. A majority of the most successful companies in the world operate without direct labor standards. Other companies should also start identifying how to manage in a new environment with no direct labor standards.

CONTAINERS

Containers used in machining, assembly, and storage are a major factor in determining the productivity of operations. They also affect the amount of inventory in the system resulting from the container size used. (Containers are discussed further in Chapters 4 and 6.) Although machining, storage, and assembly operations should all use identical containers for the same item machined, stored, or used in assembly, they should be selected or designed based on use in the assembly process, for the following reasons:

1. Larger-than-necessary containers on the assembly line can lead to wasted time and extra motion by the assembler. The potential waste of motion is usually greater than corresponding waste in either machining or storage.

2. Items produced in manufacturing operations can often be automatically ejected or dropped onto a conveyor or transported via chute into the container. Thus, time and motion associated with container size can be virtually nil. By contrast, assembly operations usually require manual access of the item from the container, with large potential for wasted time and motion.

3. Storage quantities should be reduced until zero or near-zero levels are reached. Since the target is to eliminate or minimize stored in-

ventory, it is usually logical to assume that design for productive storage is less important than that for productive machining or assembly.

Exhibit 5–22 illustrates how containers, chutes, and conveyors can be used to minimize the time required to pick up parts from large containers and put completed ones into outbound containers. In this graphic, a specially designed container (at left) drops its contents into a chute. Below that, the chute tapers to a small outlet leading almost directly into the hand of the operator of the first machine. This eliminates the time and motion that would be required to reach into the container, if the chute were not used. When the first machine operation is complete, the operator places the finished part on a very short conveyor that spans the shortest feasible distance between the two machines. The distance from the machine to the conveyor can be less than the distance from the machine to a point in a container, if a container were used in place of a conveyor. Thus, by avoiding the use of containers between operations, the time required for the motion to put parts into a container at one operation and to take them out of the container at the next is reduced to the amount needed to put the part in the conveyor at the first operation and pick it up at the second. The second machine operator picks the item up from the conveyor, machines it, and puts it into the next chute. The part then slides into the outbound container. Again, the amount of motion from

CONTAINER CHUTES

EXHIBIT 5–22

machine to chute is less than that which would be required from machine into container.

If the machine process designer sees opportunity for this type of process, or if the process is already operating this way, it is logical to consider whether automation of the transfer of processed items is feasible. A transfer line is simply a series of machines with automated transfer from one to another and through the machining operation. Some transfer lines are manufactured like one large machine, consisting of several machining stations. In general, transfer lines are applicable when relatively few items of roughly the same size, shape, and machining operations are produced in high enough volumes to use the capacity of the line.

In addition to designing chutes that minimize the motion required to put items in or take them out of containers, if wasted time and motion is significant factorywide, containers can also be purchased (or designed) with a side that opens. This reduces the time required to bend over the side of a container and then reach into it. Exhibit 5–23 provides an illustration of a commonly available wire container with a drop front. In the exhibit, the worker on the left shows the motion that would be required to get a part from the container if it had no drop front. The worker on the right demonstrates how time and motion are reduced by the use of the drop front.

A factory does not need to wait until machines are relocated and chutes

DROP FRONT CONTAINER

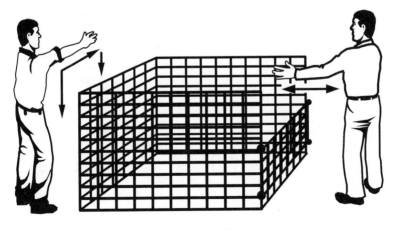

EXHIBIT 5–23

are fabricated to begin achieving some of the benefits of reduced time and motion. Exhibit 5–24 depicts an angled container stand on the left. Use of these relatively low-cost, simple stands can reduce some excess time and motion and may even be of longer term benefit. The exhibit also shows how shelves and racks, used on assembly lines, are angled to improve access to parts in containers, thus reducing required motion. Two essential points to remember are that the smallest size container is the best and that the ultimate in productivity will be reached when there is no container at all.

QUALITY: STATISTICS, PEOPLE, OR EQUIPMENT?

Although it is impossible to eliminate 100 percent of human error from the production process, instant feedback of errors heightens the awareness of the person responsible. It is especially effective in reducing errors caused by a lack of understanding of the quality requirements of the operation. Undetected defects attributable to human error can be sharply reduced when inspection is performed by one of the other operators in the machine cell, or when inspection closely follows an assembly operation. Unfortunately, defects will still occur, since not all are the fault of workers. After all, nothing has been done to eliminate the possibility of error or other types of defects. Moreover, the inspector is human, and thus also subject to making errors.

ANGLED STANDS / SHELVES

EXHIBIT 5–24

The quality level of parts going into complex products consisting of hundreds of components must be very high. For every million parts produced for such purposes there cannot be more than a few that are defective. Higher rates of defects may cause customers to switch to a competitor's products. For example, consider a product with 300 components, each of which has a defect rate of 1 out of 10,000. Although 99.99 percent component quality seems quite satisfactory, the chances of any product having a defective part are 3 percent since there are 300 part numbers, each one with a potential for defect of 1 in 10,000. If product sales are 1 million per year, defects may alienate 30,000 customers. The question is how to achieve quality in the parts-per-million range, or even better, in the zero-defects range. Statistical methods of inspection or quality control, however, are not the answer. Neither can detect defects to the extent of virtual elimination. The answer lies in designing the process to eliminate the possibility of producing defective parts. For the few defects that cannot be eliminated, the solution is to design automatic devices for identifying and taking these parts out of the process. The authors believe that assembly and machining process design must always consider quality problems and requirements. In cases of unacceptably low-quality performance, where quality should be an overriding concern, the major part of the design effort should be directed towards process quality improvements.

A quality audit of the frame machining and assembly plant at Harley Davidson's Utilimaster factory identified many simple methods for reducing quality problems. One such problem involved an occasional failure to drill one of the holes on the vehicle frame depicted in Exhibit 5–25. The fixture used to drill them had drill guide brushings at each hole location. Yet, since the frame was long, there were enough holes to make it easy to overlook the position requiring drilling. To rework the frame later in the process, without the large drill fixture, was quite expensive.

In factories where higher volumes of frames are drilled, the process should usually be mechanized. Computer control of the drilling would thus eliminate the possibility of missed holes. Utilimaster's lower volumes, however, precluded the possibility of automation. A simple operational improvement involved painting a bright-colored square around each drill brushing, making it difficult to overlook the drill site. Colors played a big role in reducing problems of fasteners which were either too loose or too tight. Bins for parts requiring the same torque were coded with the identical color. Each workstation was then equipped with color-coded tools for every torque setting needed.

HIGHLIGHTED DRILL FIXTURE

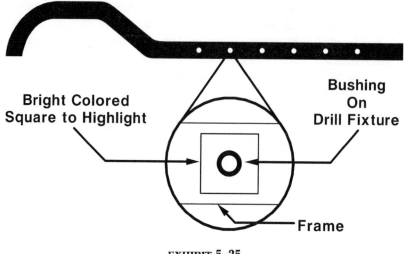

Bright Colored Square to Highlight

Bushing On Drill Fixture

Frame

EXHIBIT 5–25

MACHINING AUTOMATION

Robots and flexible manufacturing systems are widely regarded as the keys to the factory of the future. For many manufacturers, however, the fascination has waned. Large investments in automation have had disappointing results. All too often, automation has produced no significant improvements but has increased the cost of manufacturing. The promise of automation is real. Every company should continuously update processes by both selective automation of some operations and complete automation of an entire series of operations. Avoiding the pitfalls experienced by others can produce much better results than adding cost to the product.

We view *all* types of machines, tools, and storage and conveyance mechanisms—not just robots and flexible manufacturing systems—as potential components of the flexible system. In addition, we believe that the transfer line, designed especially for only one or two items, will continue to be an economically sound approach for machining some items. Chapter 4 described the use of robots and transfer lines in manufacturing. This section will focus on the utilization of flexible manufacturing systems.

The objectives of flexible machine systems are specifically related to the hardware used by them. For example, the goals and related hardware implications are to:

1. Reduce the number of machines required to decrease the people needed, machining lead time, and work-in-process inventory. By using automated tool exchangers, computer-controlled machine centers are designed to do this. Then one machine can do a variety of operations normally performed on several machines.

2. Reduce the amount of labor required to convey and store jobs between two machines performing operations on the job, by automating the transport and storage. Some forms of transport utilized include:
   • Wire-guided vehicles
   • Self-powered shuttle cars
   • Powered monorail conveyor
   • Towline conveyor
   • Powered roller conveyor
   • Car on track

3. Reduce the variety and complexity of fixtures required. Computer numerically controlled (CNC) machine centers can use simple pallets to hold the items to be machined, making most of the surfaces accessible to the machine tool. These machines do not require fixtures with tool guides; thus the new pallets without them are simpler. This procedure speeds up the process of getting new designs into production by reducing the time needed to manufacture numerous, complex fixtures.

4. Relieve the machine operator of the responsibility for setting machine feed and speeds, with the corresponding potential for error, by putting these values in the computer control program. Doing so reduces unusual tool wear and breakage that can result from improper settings.

Most of the automation objectives listed above are related to non-value-added activities, such as tool changing, transport, storage and machine adjustment and/or setting. The need for tracking statistics on these items can be virtually eliminated through setup reduction and development of new cells, using conventional, low-cost, general purpose machines. The message here is clear: first simplify the operation and then consider whether or not flexible machining systems provide additional benefits and fast payback.

The objectives of flexible systems are realistic but most have had disappointing outcomes. Some common reasons for unsatisfactory results of flexible machining systems include:

1. Flexible machining systems work best when used for low-volume, complex machining jobs. Many companies are misapplying these systems to higher volume production of a less complex nature.

2. Systems are overdesigned by the user's engineers. Companies in the United States have spent more than 400 percent[1] as much time on design and installation as their counterpart Japanese companies.

3. The number of engineers trained in the design and use of flexible manufacturing systems is too low. The time that companies devote to training is not enough.

4. System designers have not been given direct responsibility for operation of the system until it is performing the desired results.

The complex network, illustrated schematically in Exhibit 5–26, depicts a form of flexible system in which the sequence of operations performed may be different for various items machined and may include the need to return to one machine for additional operations after performing operations on another. Empty pallets, palletized raw castings, and completed items in the exhibit are kept in pallet storage. In some factories,

SEQUENTIAL / RANDOM SYSTEM

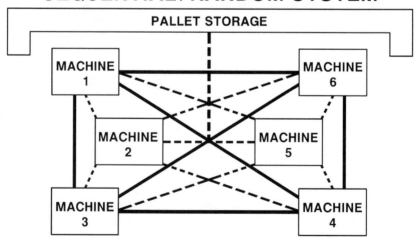

EXHIBIT 5–26

[1]In his study of flexible manufacturing systems in the United States and Japan, Jaikumar made an excellent summary of the reasons for disappointing FMS results. See Ramchandran Jaikumar, "Postindustrial Manufacturing," *Harvard Business Review,* November–December 1986, pp. 69–76.

pallet storage is an automated storage/retrieval system. The lines in the schematic, both solid and dotted, represent the automated conveyance devices used to transport jobs through the required sequence of operations. This system is probably the most complex, in terms of the computer systems necessary to maintain the status of all jobs in process, to control and monitor the operations of several machines, and to schedule and control the movement of all jobs in the network. More frequently encountered is the dedicated flexible system, which is merely an automated cell. In this case, all items follow the same sequence of operations; thus, complexities of scheduling and control are virtually eliminated.

Machine system flexibility is too often misunderstood. Its actual and practical limits can best be comprehended when examining the specifications of systems developed for different companies, or even for different systems in the same company. The fact is that every system is different. Each company must develop system specifications that match the machining requirements of a family of items to be machined. The reasons flexible machine systems lack alterability can be readily understood by asking if it would be feasible to produce shafts for miniature motors on the same system used to produce shafts for turbines used by power plants. Obviously, product size has a major impact on the size of the machining system. Although it might be technically possible to machine smaller items in a system designed for larger ones, it assuredly would be uneconomical. Using the very expensive machine for small items would reduce the time available for large ones, thus perhaps forcing a need for an additional system.

SUMMARY

Different types of machining techniques are applicable to different volumes of production and complexity of operations. Choices are available for selecting machining methods applicable to groups (or families) of parts of similar characteristics. For instance, conventional transfer lines are suitable when the size of the family of similar parts is very low. Transfer lines of machines are typically constructed for the specific part or parts to be produced. Thus, modification of the machines due to changes in part configuration are, at best, time consuming and costly. Moreover, changeover of tooling required for one part to that needed for another is usually a long and expensive process. At the other extreme is the family of parts that consists of a very high number of items. In this case, the most applicable choice is stand-alone, numerically controlled machines or other conventional machines. For families of items with the fewest family members, the system is likely to be dedicated. This means that one or more of the machines is inclined to be uniquely suited to the machine requirements of only few part numbers, all of which need the same sequence of operations. Sequential and random flexible machining systems, by contrast, are suitable for larger family sizes of differing sequences of operations, since the machines involved are of a more universal nature. The cell, which is just like the dedicated system, but with less automation, is usually applicable when the family of items machined is somewhat larger and automation is more expensive.

Tremendous benefits can be achieved by improving machining process design. The separate physical location of machinery and other manual operations, in relation to others used to manufacture the same items, causes unnecessarily high work-in-process inventories. It also wastes the time of human or automated operators and material handlers. New cell or semicell organizations will not only benefit these areas; they will also make improvements on late delivery and quality. It is not necessary to make massive investments in new equipment to start realizing major benefits.

6

■□■

Material/Product Storage

WHETHER FULLY AUTOMATED OR MANUALLY OPERATED, the ideal factory of the future will be organized as a production network. Assembly lines will be directly linked to subassembly lines, and machines and machine cells will be tied directly to the assembly and subassembly lines that use the components produced by them. Throughout this network of operations, the tempo of production will be consistent. Components, subassemblies, and assemblies will be produced one at a time, at the same scheduled rate. Then, manually or automatically, these items will be transferred from one machine or line to the next machine or line.

In this ideal factory, individual components and materials will be fed directly from delivery trucks into the line, or containers of parts will be taken straight from receiving docks to storage areas on the line.

There will be no need for storing purchased and manufactured materials, components, and subassemblies, except for a minimal time on the line itself. Thus, it may seem paradoxical to be concerned with designing new, highly productive storage facilities. But realistically, it will take most companies years to come even close to achieving the ideal factory and/or the supplier network that requires no storage. Most manufacturers, therefore, should plan to reduce the cost of storage as long as it continues to be a practical necessity.

The percentage (not dollars) of reductions of equipment and building investment as well as operating costs of storage are usually as impressive (or more impressive) than corresponding savings in machining and assembly processes. The most important targets for improvements are reduc-

161

tions in storage space (50 percent) and in personnel (50 percent). This 50 percent reduction of storage space, however, presumes storage of the current level of inventory. Long-term objectives could be to reduce inventory by as much as 90 percent. Thus, storage space requirements may be much less by the time the target inventory level is reached. For example, if the amount of inventory is reduced by 90 percent and the remainder is stored in 50 percent less space, the total space reduction is 95 percent.

In many companies, a great deal of space may be required for materials, components, work in process, and finished goods, especially if the product is large, has strong seasonal demand, and is produced to inventory in anticipation of sales peaks. Reductions in inventory and increases in space utilization will provide a short-term opportunity to discontinue leasing outside warehouse space and/or company-owned storage buildings. These temporary improvements can shift these investments in buildings, inventory, and operations to cash for financing other opportunities.

In recent years, many companies have invested in automated storage and retrieval systems to further increase centralized storage productivity. Their investments could have been avoided by focusing (decentralizing) components and materials inventories, virtually doing away with work-in-process inventory, and eliminating finished goods by making to stock rather than producing to order. Thus, millions and even tens of millions of dollars tied up in storage facilities and equipment can be saved when a company decides to improve production rather than improve storage. Increased cash flow is not the only reason for improving utilization of storage space. A great amount of the labor involved in storage operations can be attributed to travel time required for putting parts away and retrieving them when needed. Thus, reduction of the size of the storage area will result in decreased time spent traveling to and from it.

Some additional opportunities to reduce storage cost are:

1. *Decentralization of storage to the subplants that use the item stored.* This not only decreases the time required to put away and retrieve parts in each of the small focused stock locations, it also eliminates central bureaucracy and reduces long travel distances between central stores and using locations.

2. *Use of activity-frequency zones.* More frequently used items are stored closest to the points of receipt and issue, and those used least often are kept in the most remote areas of the storage facility.

3. *Picking components required for several different production orders simultaneously.* This order-filling method, often called "wave picking," requires the worker to make only one trip to each component's

stock location. While at the location, the worker retrieves enough of the item to fill all of the production orders which require the item. By traveling efficiently by the shortest route to all stock locations in a single trip, the total travel time is usually much less than that required when making several separate trips through the stockroom to gather all the components for each production order. However, the time saved in travel by the wave method is at least partially offset by the additional time required to sort the component parts retrieved into the kits of parts for each order.

4. *Eliminating the counting of receipts and issues* through standardizing the quantity per container, and receiving and issuing only full containers.

FOCUSED STORAGE

Decentralization of the receipts and storage of materials and components (focused storage) is one of the radically different concepts of new, superior manufacturing methods. The basic objectives of focused storage (introduced in Chapter 2) are to receive and store materials as close to the point of use as possible. The primary reasons for this are to: (1) provide better management authority and responsibility for stored inventory, with the twin objectives of avoiding surprise shortages and minimizing inventory investment; and (2) reduce all costs of storage and transport associated with material receipt and storage. Since these costs do not add value to the product, they should be eliminated, or at least minimized.

Exhibit 6-1 depicts the five long and costly movements of materials into and through the centralized receiving and storage facilities. Reduction of the number and distance of these moves can sharply reduce these costs of operation. Trucks are usually unloaded at the receiving dock in their sequence of arrival by forklift truck. Unless there are enough forklifts and docks for peak arrival periods, there are delays between the truck's arrival and its completed unloading. Further, the most urgently needed materials and components might be contained on the last truck in line. In most receiving departments, the incoming items are counted and a receiving report is prepared to update the inventory of items held in the receiving area. Exhibit 6-1 shows a very progressive factory that has eliminated receiving inspection. As previous chapters pointed out, it is practical to design manufacturing processes and tests that either produce only perfect products, or else select defective ones automatically from the process. If suppliers have these types of processes, or if they

FIVE MOVE STORAGE

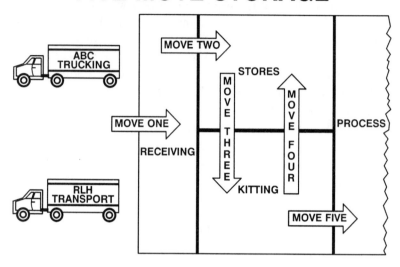

EXHIBIT 6–1

are qualified to perform any remaining tests and inspections, receiving inspection can be eliminated.

After counting and paperwork processing, the receipt is taken by forklift truck to the central storeroom. In factories with central storage, this move is usually hundreds of feet. In stores, the receipt is often counted again to catch instances of loss between receiving and stores. Then the receipt is placed in stock. Frequently, the stockkeeper must record the location in which the item is stocked on the stock receipt transaction, thus deducting it from the receiving inventory and adding it to the storeroom inventory balance. If the location number is erroneously recorded, it may be impossible to locate the receipt later. Periodically taking complete physical inventories or cycle counts may be necessary to locate misplaced items.

In many factories, stored items are issued according to authorizing production orders in a specified quantity. In these cases, kits of materials or components are prepared by retrieving the required items (move three in Exhibit 6–1) and counting the precise quantity needed. However, there are many opportunities for errors in the count and in processing the issue transaction. This transaction typically reduces the storeroom inventory for the item and increases its work-in-process inventory. After counting the required quantity, the unused portion of a container is returned for storage (move four). The items issued are transported, as seen in move five, to the process needing them. This move, by lift truck, again is usually hundreds of feet. Issues are usually delivered to a setdown area in the processing location, then picked up by the material handler responsible for the process, using hand lift or cart. He then delivers the items to the machine or assembly station.

Some of the best focused storage facilities now receive, store, and issue materials and components, using only two moves, as shown in Exhibit 6–2. In this illustration, as in most factories, the forklift may still be required to move skids of material off the truck directly into storage or to set them on wheeled dollies, which can be moved manually to a temporary stock location in the combination receiving/storage area. As each item is received, a bar-coded CONBON (kanban) card received with it is read with an electronic wand or other device to record the receipt into the subplant. Counting the quantity of received items is no longer necessary. All containers in which the item is stored hold the same amount, and the quantity in them is always accurate.

Because receipts arrive just in time, the item is moved a short time later by pushing the wheeled container or cart to the process area. This location is often only a few feet from where the item is temporarily stored. In Exhibit 6–2, the skid of part A holds several small containers rather than a single giant one. These are designed to minimize space, time, and motion in the operation at which they are used. In the case of components

TWO MOVE STORAGE

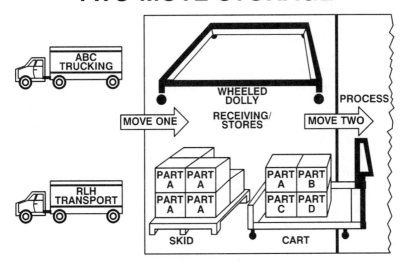

EXHIBIT 6–2

used in assembly, the wheeled cart makes continuous circular trips between the line and focused receiving/storage. While making deliveries to the line, the material handler picks up CONBON cards for items requiring delivery to the line, then returns to the focused storage area to load his cart with the necessary items.

Frequently, the subplant is considered to have only one inventory of materials and components, which is a total of the stock in both the focused receiving/storage and the process areas. Thus, the transactions needed to transfer an item from storage to work in process are eliminated. The transaction used to report completion of a manufactured item is used simultaneously to add it to the subplant inventory and automatically to deduct its materials and components from this inventory. For example, for each of 50 components used on an assembly, 200 transactions would be required in a factory tracking daily receipts and issues on the receiving dock, through inspections, and into and out of stores. Seventy-five percent fewer are needed if two-move receiving is combined with automatic, computer-generated issues of components when assembly is reported to be complete.

In the past, long lead times and floor loss have been reasons for individually issuing required components from central stores to the shop floor. For example, if assembly lead time were one week, and assembly production were used to reduce component inventory, the storeroom inventory balance would be inaccurate until completion of the entire lot is reported. Further, if floor loss occurs—i.e., defective parts are scrapped or good components are dropped, swept up, and carried off in the trash—and the using area does not report it, inventory records are even less accurate. Superior manufacturers must plan to reduce lead time and to virtually eliminate unreported scrap and loss. This will make it feasible to change from reporting the issue of individual components, to computer updating of all components based on a single report of the completion of production of the item on which the components are used.

As containers are emptied, users of CONBON cards may decide to read their bar codes with an electronic wand as an alternative to using completion reporting to reduce component on-hand inventory balances if lead time and floor loss problems have not been resolved. Thus, the on-hand inventory balance would be timelier. This solution, however, fails to address and correct the real problems.

Because today's process area is, on average, 50 percent smaller than in the past, the travel path of the material handler is usually less, or no more, than the distance from the former putdown point to the previous location of the machine or assembly station using the items. For example, at GM's Fisher Guide Monroe (Louisiana) Plant, a productivity team revised the headlight system assembly lines, shown in Exhibit 6–3. Doing so sharply reduced the space occupied and, accordingly, the travel path of the material handler. Exhibit 6–4 depicts one of three cells that replaced the single assembly line. The travel path of the material handler, from the focused stores directly adjacent to the new cell to every point of use in it, is a fraction of the distance traveled in the previous line. Reduction of material-handling time was only one of the benefits of compressing the space required for assembly by 69 percent. In total, the personnel needed by this subplant was reduced by 40 percent.

It has been especially difficult for many manufacturing managers to understand how frequent deliveries of small containers to the assembly line can cost less than infrequent deliveries of large ones. Exhibit 6–5 illustrates a method for reducing transport costs. The old system had trucks travel with an average of half a load or less, and some trips were made empty. For example, a delivery to shipping meant an empty trip back to the factory to pick up the next load. In addition, several containers were transported less than full despite the fact that, in most factories, the travel path to and from central storage is hundreds of yards. By contrast, the new wheeled cart depicted in Exhibit 6–5 transports the same cubic volume as the lift truck but carries it only tens of yards.

If a company has already achieved two-move storage for most materials and components, there is still no room for complacency. Many of the

MATERIAL DELIVERY - BEFORE

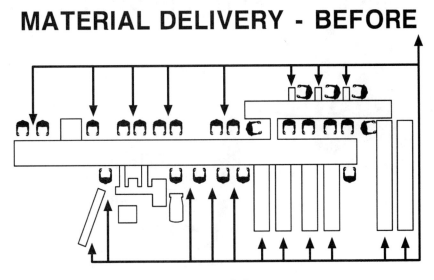

EXHIBIT 6-3

MATERIAL DELIVERY - AFTER

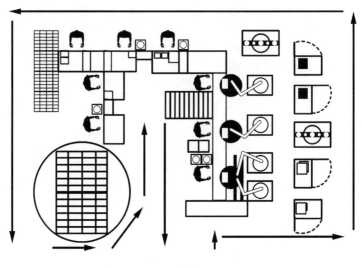

EXHIBIT 6-4

95% TRANSPORT REDUCTION

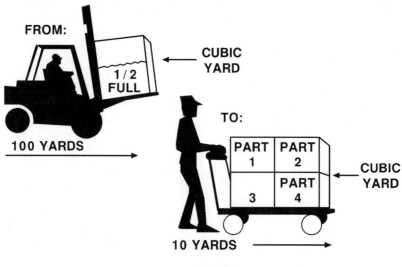

FROM:

CUBIC YARD

1/2 FULL

100 YARDS

TO:

PART 1 PART 2

PART 3 PART 4

CUBIC YARD

10 YARDS

EXHIBIT 6-5

best companies are achieving one-move storage, as shown in Exhibit 6–6, for at least some materials and components. In this type of storage, several items are unloaded from incoming trucks directly onto the main conveyor line or onto feeder conveyors. In other cases, receipts are moved directly to the point of use by any one of several transport devices, including lift trucks, carts, wheeled containers, and containers on wheeled dollies.

Changing from centralized receiving/storage to focused receiving/storage has the potential for reducing an army of employees. For example, most personnel on the left side of the arrow in Exhibit 6–7 perform operations that do not add value to the product and that can be eliminated by focused organization. These non-value-added operations are:

1. *Receiver:* the material handler who helps unload trucks and counts items received
2. *Receiving clerk:* the person responsible for paperwork and/or computer system updating
3. *Stockkeeper:* the worker who counts receipts and moves them into stock
4. *Storeroom clerk:* the individual responsible for paperwork processing and/or computer system updates

ONE MOVE STORAGE

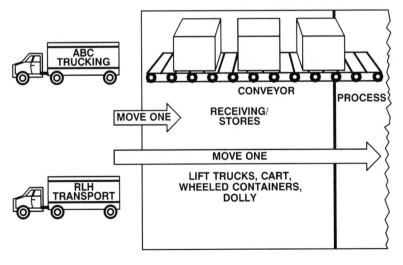

EXHIBIT 6-6

CLASSIFICATION REDUCTION

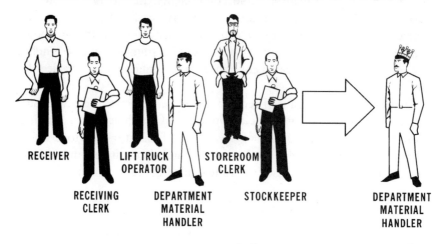

RECEIVER · LIFT TRUCK OPERATOR · STOREROOM CLERK → DEPARTMENT MATERIAL HANDLER

RECEIVING CLERK · DEPARTMENT MATERIAL HANDLER · STOCKKEEPER

EXHIBIT 6–7

5. *Lift-truck operator:* the driver who transports material to and among all of the above

6. *Department material handler:* the employee who receives inbound materials and components and delivers them to the specific operators who use them

In reality, all of these workers could be eliminated, except for the department material handler (shown in Exhibit 6–7 on the right side of the arrow). Since he replaces six people, the crown he wears signifies his new importance. He unloads trucks, records receipts by entering CONBON cards into the system, places receipts in stock, and maintains adequate supplies of materials and components at all machine and assembly stations. If these tasks are simplified and the layout of the work areas improved, even the number of material handlers can be reduced.

In the ideal factory, which consists of several subplants, each subplant should have its own focused receiving dock/storage area. In the practical world, however, existing factory construction may not permit separate docks. For example, several sides of the factory might be impossible or impractical for receiving due to barriers such as adjacent factories, inadequate space for vehicle traffic, or hills or rivers that border the walls. In most factories, it will be necessary to designate each dock as a receiving point for one or more subplants. In some cases, the focused storage and process areas for one or more of the subplants served by a dock may be adjacent to it. Other designations may require transporting receipts to subplants not directly adjacent to the dock. The objective of the plant-wide layout should be to minimize transport by locating subplants with the highest volumes of receipts and shipments closest to available docks.

Most executives accept the logic of point of use receipt and storage. The few who resist this idea are often those with recent involvement in centralizing inventory, who have found that decentralized inventories are improperly controlled (for instance, receipt and issue transactions are not always processed or, when processed, are incorrect). Thus, computer records of on-hand balances contain many inaccuracies that caused production shortages and surpluses, or obsolete inventory.

By centralizing all inventories, usually in locked storage areas, it is possible to introduce new controls that ensure all receipts and issues from stock are accurately documented. In the new subplant, the person responsible for focused storage is more directly a part of the manufacturing team. As a small entrepreneur, his job of receiving, stocking, and disbursing heightens his awareness of the importance of accuracy. Thus, a focused organization can result in increased record accuracy, lower obsolete and surplus stocks, and fewer shortages.

It is not logical to compare controlled, locked storage and its associated control procedures to decentralized stores, even assuming that decentralized storage will not feature locked doors and the control features of central stock. Locks and control procedures used in central stockrooms should be as (or more) effective in small or focused storerooms. Ideally, however, only a small quantity of valuable, dangerous, or difficult-to-control items should be kept in locked storage. It is also important to keep in mind that walls and fences increase the travel time and the complexity of getting parts from storage space to assembly lines. Therefore wherever it is practical, locked storage should be avoided.

TIME AND MOTION: OPPORTUNITY KNOCKING

As in every other aspect of factory operations, wasted time and unproductive motion in storeroom operations are major areas for productivity improvement. To analyze opportunities for improved efficiency, all the procedures and elements of storeroom time and motion should first be documented on videotape, the most efficient way to "document" the required procedures and time. Most storeroom activities include traveling to and returning from stock locations, counting receipts and issues, repackaging receipts and issues, and transporting issues to the process or to a shipping dock. The greatest productivity gains can be achieved when counting and repackaging are eliminated, and when travel and transport time and distances are reduced to a practical minimum.

Exhibit 6–1 (shown earlier) indicates the basic flow of material from receiving into the storeroom, including the counting of receipts. The process of kitting, illustrated in Exhibit 6–8, starts after the material is placed in stock. To begin, the stockkeeper travels to the locations where the required items (parts 1 and 2) are stocked, takes these parts to a mechanical or electronic counting scale, counts the quantity required of each part, and packages each separately. All parts of one assembly, assembly operation, or customer order are placed into a larger package (a kit), which is then delivered to the assembly line or, in the case of customer orders, to shipping.

A lower-cost alternative for receiving, stocking, and issuing parts to assembly is to do so in set lots. For example, the container size and a standard quantity of, say, 150 parts per container is specified to the supplier. The supplier then delivers containers of 150 each. Thus, on receipt, counting is unnecessary. The container received is simply placed in stock, and issues from stock are always in multiples of 150. As a result, issues can also be made without counting or repackaging. This process of issuing stock to assembly without kitting is usually referred to as *line stock replenishment,* and demonstrates the ideal situation. Unfortunately, though, the elimination of kitting in every type of manufacturing has not

CONVENTIONAL KITTING

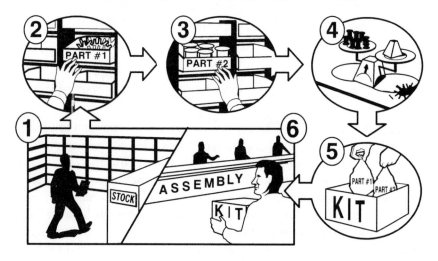

EXHIBIT 6–8

yet been achieved. It is not difficult, however, to do away with kitting for assembly processes that require a high degree of common components and/or processes that repetitively produce a limited range of different products. Examples of manufacturing processes that lend themselves to replenishing stocks on line are those for producing vehicles and small and large appliances.

On the other hand, make-to-order and assemble-to-order products (those with few common components), and processes with numerous different products, are most applicable to kitting for specific production lots. For example, processes for making products such as power plant generators and low-volume, printed circuit board assemblies can benefit from kitting. There are also innumerable processes and products that fall somewhere between kit or line replenishment. Where change to line stock replenishment is possible, time and motion will be reduced. Thus, every effort should be made to convert to this method.

Too often the location assignments of items in storerooms and warehouses are made randomly or are not organized to minimize the amount of travel to and from the storeroom entrance/exit points to stock locations. In medium and large storerooms and warehouses, organization by issue-frequency zone can sharply reduce travel time. Exhibit 6–9 illustrates how such zones are used. In the example, the relatively low number of stocked items that have the highest number of issues are located closest to the stockroom point of receipt and issue. Therefore, those items that move most frequently have the shortest travel path possible to be put in stock and to be retrieved for issue. The second most frequently issued

ISSUE FREQUENCY ZONES

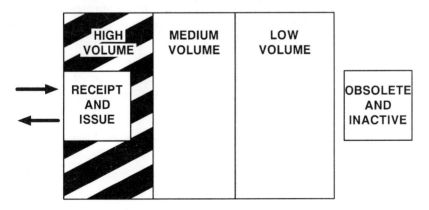

EXHIBIT 6–9

items are stored in the medium-volume area, requiring somewhat more travel per trip, but fewer total trips. The items that have the lowest volume of issue transactions, usually the highest percentage of items in all three categories, are stored in the most distant area of the stockroom. Also, there is a separate, remote storage area for obsolete items and those with little or no expected demand. By removing these items from the main stores, travel time for other items is decreased. More important, physical segregation will permit a worker to permanently dispose of the nonproductive inventory, giving him physical control over, and visibility of, this troublesome stockpile. Thus, the three main objectives of storeroom reorganization should be: elimination of counting and repackaging, use of issue-frequency zones, and compression of space.

MATERIAL FLOW

In reviewing factory operations, it is a good idea to routinely plot the flow of selected parts and assemblies through the plant, and in selected operations, to chart the travel of the operator. In both cases, these diagrams can help management and operating personnel see where wasteful time and motion exist and to highlight changes that can be made. (Original flows are often described as "spaghetti" charts, due to their irregular and lengthy paths.) For storeroom operations, these same types of diagrams are useful. Frequently, there are lengthy, and therefore costly, flows in storerooms for small products, such as electronic and electromechanical assemblies. In one case, Andersen Consulting filmed the kitting operation of a small subassembly requiring three components. First the storekeeper traveled to the stock location of each component to pick up containers and then to the counting/kitting area. After counting the required components, he followed the same path to return the remaining parts containers to their locations. Each trip was approximately 200 feet, taking 2 minutes.

In observing this process, it was clear that utilization of the stockkeeper's cart was very low, compared to that of the most productive operations. For example:

1. The order used up less than 50 percent of the stockkeeper's cart's capacity.
2. The cart was completely empty before the first component was picked up, and only 50 percent full after picking up the last part.
3. Since the cart was comparatively small, a taller, wider one could have been easily maneuvered in the aisles. In this situation, the pro-

ductivity of component picking could be increased in several ways, but primarily by filling more assembly orders on each trip to the storage locations. By tripling the size and capacity of the cart, it becomes possible to fill four orders in one circuit. Each circuit required visiting a few more aisles, however, reducing the walking time for one circuit by 60 percent. Second, the larger cart accommodated a low-cost counting scale, eliminating the need to take every part to a counting area and then to return unneeded parts to storage. This further reduced walking time to a total savings of 80 percent per component. The scale on the cart should be a temporary measure. Eventually, only complete standard containers of specified quantity should be received and issued, eliminating any need for counting.

In this factory, simultaneously picking four orders with a larger cart increased the utilization of cart capacity to close to 100 percent by the time the last component was retrieved; however, the cart was still only 50 percent utilized, on average. A new procedure required that each circuit begin with loading newly received containers on the cart. Thus, the cart traveling out on the circuit was full of containers to be added to stock while retrieving items to be issued. Prior to this, receipts and issues were each handled separately, thus one of the trips to or from a location was with an empty cart. In addition, issue-frequency zones concentrated the highest volume of transactions in a small area close to the point of receipt/issue, further reducing the time and cost of stocking and issuing.

LOW-COST KITTING

Kitting is not only inherently costly, but also increases manufacturing lead time and total inventory requirements. Because kitting is like the process of assembly, time must be scheduled for both performing the operation and for completed kits to sit in queue awaiting assembly. Kitting is also like setup. Its cost should dictate the quantity of kits prepared and the resulting investment in kitted inventory. It is entirely feasible and desirable to decouple assembly lot and kitting lot sizes. The assembly process itself is likely to have little or no tangible setup cost. Consequently, it can be expected to produce daily needs minimizing finished goods and poor customer service which result from producing large lot sizes.

Cutting the cost of kitting can justify reduction of kit sizes and, therefore, kit inventory investment, and can significantly decrease the number of shortages created by kitting requirements greater than minimum immediate needs. There are several ways in which kitting costs can be reduced. Some, like picking more than one kit at a time or eliminating the requirement to kit by replenishing individual items on the line when the supply is low, have been discussed previously.

The permanent kit technique, in conjunction with others, is useful for achieving the decoupling of assembly lot and kitting lot sizes, while minimizing kitting costs. This kit is illustrated in Exhibit 6–10. One or more permanent trays/boxes contain spaces for each part number listed in the bill of material. In this example, the target kit size for assembly A is 50 units. Since part 1 is used three times on assembly A, the target kit quantity for part 1 is three times 50, or 150. Parts 2 and 3 are used once per assembly, and thus have target kit quantities of 50 each. Also the compartments in the kit should be somewhat larger than the size of the component containers. This permits the stockkeeper to put a full container into the compartment when the quantity within it is low. It also may allow him to place the container directly into the kit compartment to avoid the time and cost of transferring parts. In the kit, the compartments are of different sizes to match the size and required quantities of each component.

PERMANENT KIT

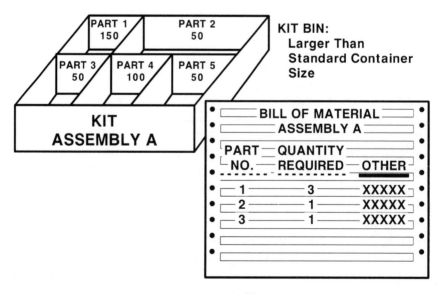

EXHIBIT 6–10

Permanent kits usually contain the equivalent of several assembly production lots. For example, 10 units would be produced daily on the assembly line; thus, the kit of 50 would last about five days. The flow of the kit is from kitting to kit stores, which is often directly adjacent to the line. Each day thereafter, the kit is taken from kit stores to assembly where 10 more products are assembled. If the entire kit contains enough components for the next lot, it is returned to kit stores. When many of the components are low, the kit is returned to be replenished. The kit container and the label on each component's compartment eliminate the need for CONBON cards for every component, thus simplifying the procedure and system.

The simplest kind of inventory information would be a single balance for the total quantity of each component in stock, in kits, and in the assembly process. This, however, complicates the reconciliation of physical inventory to record inventory, if such routine reconciliation is necessary. The alternative is to maintain two balances: one for component stock and the other for stock of kits and assemblies in process. Since the greatest percentage of inventory is usually in component stock, maintaining accuracy of component inventory may be enough to satisfy company and outside accountants and auditors and to avoid most problems associated with record inaccuracies. The CONBON card, seen in Exhibit 6–11, is used in one of 3M's factories. Subplant M475 indicates the stores

AMERICAN CON BON CARD

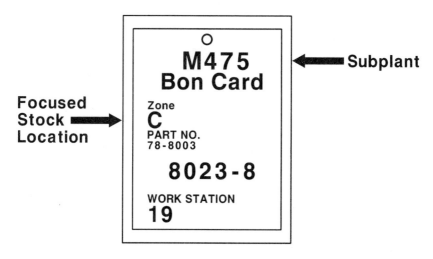

EXHIBIT 6–11

area within stores in which this part number is stocked. The specific stock racks, based on container size (one of eight standard sizes), is indicated on the BON card used to replenish parts on the assembly line. (BON stands for "bring out notice," which instructs stockkeepers to bring more parts from stores to the assembly line. The development of the acronym CONBON as a Western alternative to the Japanese kanban is described in Chapter 8.) In this case, the 3M part number contains 11 digits (78-8003 8023-8), too long to easily scan on the storage shelves. Thus, the latter 5 digits (8023-8) are enlarged on both the BON and on the storeroom CONBON cards on each container and/or container label.

To sum up, small, focused stores, at the point of use for purchased items and at the point of supply for manufactured ones, are the ultimate in storage technology for these types of items. There will always be a need, however, for larger storage facilities for certain types of items, such as finished products and service parts. The best in modern storage technology matches containers to demand, part size and weight, and racking systems. Efficient receiving, stocking, and issue procedures and facilities have the potential to bring about major reductions in needed cubic space and in the costs of storage labor and equipment.

7

□□□

One-Touch Changeover

WHEN COMPANIES WORKED on setup reduction, on the same machine, over a period of several years, they learned it is possible to reduce change-over time from double-digit to single-digit hours. Later, on the same machine, those single-digit hours can be reduced to double-digit minutes. Still later, the double-digit minutes can be reduced to single-digit ones. A few companies have even achieved the ultimate objective: one-touch changeover, where the time required for changeover is near zero. No company can afford to stop work on setup reduction until this goal is reached. The issue is not if it is feasible, but rather what is necessary and how long it will take.

Although there are an unlimited number of techniques that contribute to superior productivity, a few of these warrant special attention: (1) organizing small, focused subplants; (2) improving space utilization (both of which have been discussed); and (3) reducing the time, costs, and complexity of setup or changeover. Of the three, setup reduction is the easiest, lowest-cost, and fastest type of improvement that most manufacturers can make.

Reduction of setup costs is important for three reasons:

1. Production lot sizes are large when changeover cost is high; thus, inventory investment is high. When changeover cost is insignificant, it becomes possible to consider daily production of the amount required for one day, virtually eliminating inventory investment that results from large lot sizes.

2. Fast, simpler changeover techniques eliminate the potential for the mistakes in setting tools and fixtures. Thus, new changeover methods substantially reduce defects, while eliminating the need for inspection.

3. Fast changeover techniques can be used to make additional machine capacity available. If machines are operating at or close to seven days a week, 24 hours a day, reducing changeover time may make it possible to delay purchasing new ones to gain additional capacity.

A simplified production schedule for a plastic injection press requiring a 120-minute setup is illustrated in Exhibit 7-1. The machine is used to produce, each week, part numbers 1 through 5. The setup of each part requires two hours, the production of each, six hours. In the five-day week, the machine runs 30 hours and setup requires 10. Because of the lot size of one week, inventory investment is an average of half a week's supply of each of the five parts. Thus, there is no time available, in this one shift operation, to produce any other parts.

When setup in this machine is reduced to three minutes, as shown in Exhibit 7-2, it becomes practical to run every part each day. Although setups are increased from 5 to 25 per week, each is so small that the total setup time is reduced from 10 to a little over an hour, leaving more than 8 hours available to run other parts. (Incidentally, 3- to 10-minute changeovers on plastic injection molding presses are now fairly common. In

120 MINUTE SETUP

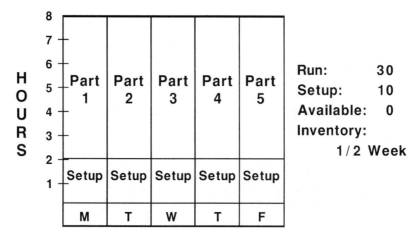

EXHIBIT 7-1

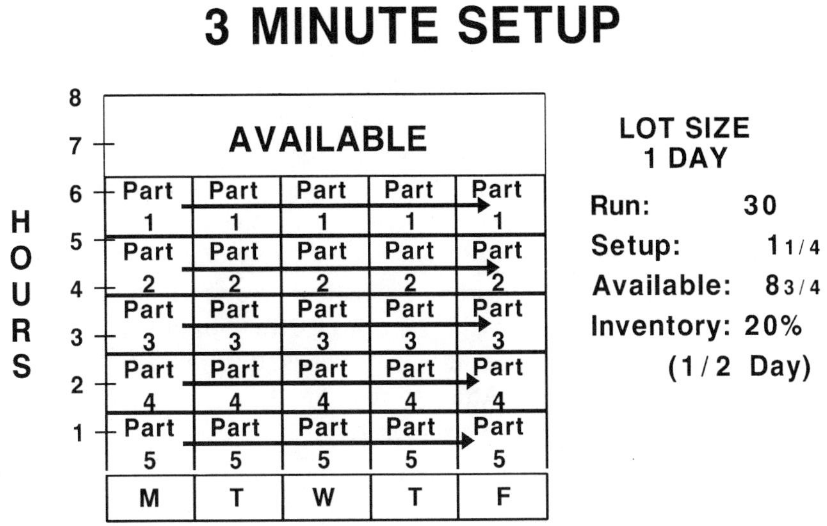

3 MINUTE SETUP

HOURS	AVAILABLE					LOT SIZE 1 DAY
8						
7	AVAILABLE					
6	Part 1	Part 1	Part 1	Part 1	Part 1	Run: 30
5	Part 2	Part 2	Part 2	Part 2	Part 2	Setup: 1 1/4
4						Available: 8 3/4
3	Part 3	Part 3	Part 3	Part 3	Part 3	Inventory: 20%
2	Part 4	Part 4	Part 4	Part 4	Part 4	(1/2 Day)
1	Part 5	Part 5	Part 5	Part 5	Part 5	
	M	T	W	T	F	

EXHIBIT 7-2

1984, a Kodak project team's first effort reduced changeover from approximately 2 hours to 30 minutes. A few months later, it was decreased to 6 minutes.) One of the most important benefits of reducing setup minutes to single-digit numbers is that a company can then focus on changing from manufacturing-to-stock to manufacturing-to-order. Since finished goods inventory investment is the greatest asset in some factories, converting it to cash can free capital for alternative investment or debt reduction.

Plantwide benefits of fast, low-cost changeover are clearly so great that it is puzzling that improvements have been started on less than 5 percent of the millions of machines in existence. (This estimate is based on visits to hundreds of factories around the world.) There are several reasons that progress has been shockingly slow:

1. Full-time teams are not assigned to make improvements. Using part timers, in periods when urgent production problems do not interfere, is not viable for most companies. Participative worker groups are also less than effective in all but the best plants.

2. Too many factory managers prefer to buy new machines, instead of improving existing ones. Therefore, they do not try to improve existing equipment. In most factories, machines can and should be used up to 20 years or more. Improvement of existing machines should be undertaken as rapidly as possible.

3. Most engineers are routinely accustomed to designing overly complex and/or automated setup reduction solutions. One company that Andersen Consulting subsequently helped implement low-cost reduction originally indicated that it could not justify setup reduction because its engineers, who had extensive training and experience in factory automation, could only conceive of high-cost, automated solutions. In reality, the majority of potential improvements can (and should) be designed to pay back their costs in six months.

4. Tool, machine, and fixture improvements require toolmaker time. In most factories, toolmakers are loaded to capacity with assignments to fix broken machines and tools and to make fixtures and tools for new products. Attempts to reduce changeover are thwarted when toolmakers are not available.

5. Conventional methods for cost justifying changes inhibit some companies from making them. Management needs to recognize the global benefits of reducing changeover time and to establish pools of funding to minimize bureaucratic roadblocks.

6. In some cases, new equipment has fast changeover features. However, it is often mistakenly believed that purchasing new equipment is the *only* way to achieve reduction.

Shigeo Shingo, one of Japan's pioneers in setup reduction, has written one of the most comprehensive and detailed books[1] on the subject of setup reduction. In it, however, he focuses primarily on punch and plastic molding presses. Further, several of the designs in his book, while quite good, do not offer the best solutions possible. Indeed, our experienced practitioners find the quality of solutions improves on each type of machine and on every individual machine on which work is performed. Although a comprehensive set of examples of setup improvements for each type of machine might be useful to those with little or no background in setup reduction, experienced practitioners are not likely to find value in such a product. They quickly learn that:

1. The basic types of setup reduction inventions are universally applicable to every machine. After working on two or three different types, the kinds of improvements designed are similar from one machine to another, 80 to 90 percent of the time.

2. Within various generic groupings of machines, there are wide variations in both design and tools and fixtures developed for them. Even when identical machines are used in different companies, the

[1]Shigeo Shingo, *A Revolution in Manufacturing: The SMED System* (Cambridge, Mass.: Productivity Press, 1987).

tools and fixtures employed on the machine are different. The result is that almost all improvements must be designed for the specific machines, tools, and fixtures used.

Since relatively few factories do not have changeover costs, most have opportunities to reduce these and their accompanying penalties in inventory investment. Setup costs are not limited to conventional metalworking machine shops but also affect process industries and assemblers—the pharmaceutical, paper, food, chemical, wood products, plastics and electronics industries, to name a few. In this chapter, our objective is to identify the major types of setup reduction. We will use case examples to illustrate how these concepts have been applied to a variety of machines in order to demonstrate the general applicability of these techniques.

MAINLINE/OFFLINE: SAVINGS OR ILLUSION?

In 1982, Andersen Consulting introduced the use of video cameras to record and analyze the process of changing tools, fixtures, and machine settings from the production of one item to another. In that same year, they applied the standard methodology of documenting major setup steps and classifying each one as either mainline, offline, or unnecessary, as illustrated in the worksheet found in Exhibit 7–3. The simplicity of this worksheet is in line with our dedication to simplifying factory operations.

SETUP ANALYSIS WORKSHEET						
WORK CENTER / MACHINE DESCRIPTION GEAR MACHINING				NUMBER 64		
PART NUMBER (IF UNIQUE) N/A	SETUP MINUTES			SETUPS PER MONTH 10		
	ELAPSED 75	TEAM 1				
STEP NO	MAJOR STEP DESCRIPTION	MINUTES	TYPE			IMPROVEMENT
			M	O	U	
1	GET TOOLS	15			X	TOOL KIT
2	REMOVE GEAR NUTS	10	X			SPRING CLIPS
3	GET GEARS	5		X		MACHINING SIDE STORAGE

M - MAINLINE   O - OFFLINE   U - UNNECESSARY

EXHIBIT 7–3

As the exhibit indicates, there are three types of setup operations—offline, mainline, and unnecessary. Offline setup operations are those which could be performed before the machine is stopped to change over to production of the next part, for example, bringing the required raw materials, tools, and fixtures to the machine. Mainline setup operations are performed while the machine is stopped, after the last item is produced, but before production on a new item is begun. However, there are plants that perform offline setup operations while the machine is still running. In these cases, these preparatory elements are classified as offline, and are also conducted as offline operations, as Exhibit 7–4 illustrates. Unfortunately, many of these projects stop there and claim a reduction of elapsed setup time of 50 percent since half the work is performed while the machine is in operation, and even though the offline work still costs as much as it would when the machine is stopped for mainline setup.

Simply by moving setup operations offline does not justify changing lot sizes since setup cost remains the same. Thus, there would not be savings in lot size or inventory reduction or significant benefits in reduced payroll and fringe benefit costs. There may be a benefit, however, associated with making more machine time available, which cuts overtime costs and/or delays the purchase of new machines. The savings in Exhibit 7–5 are real, not an illusion. Actual minutes of work in both offline and mainline have been reduced. In most factories, very few machines run 24

MOVE SETUP OFFLINE

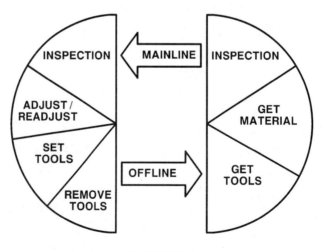

EXHIBIT 7–4

REAL SETUP SAVINGS

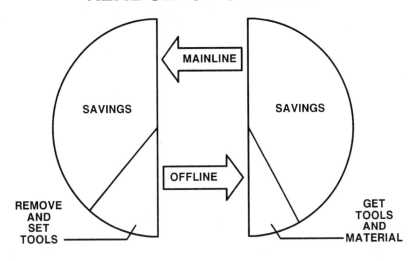

EXHIBIT 7-5

hours a day, 7 days per week. It is usually wisest to count setup reduction only in terms of decreasing the total minutes or hours of work required to change over, and to claim savings in machine utilization only where new machine purchases are actually avoided.

In his book on setup reduction, Shingo discussed the need to reduce *both* mainline and offline time. Many in the field claim that operations moved offline could produce savings, as these offline tasks could be performed by someone paid less than the person who has done the setup in the past. Although this argument has merit, the difference in cost between those who perform offline and mainline setup could be negligible in the long run. New, simpler machine setup and operating methods will eliminate the skilled machinist classification; thus, offline setup, if there is any remaining, would not be likely to be performed by a lower-cost person.

Machinists' real skills lie not in the fact they can operate a machine, as most operation can be simplified to the point where this entails putting parts into the machinery, pushing a button, and removing completed items. The real skills machine operators possess are related to machine setup. Because these kind of machinists are in short supply, worldwide, many factories have established a separate classification for them. These specialists do nothing but set up machines that can then be operated by personnel with virtually no special talents or training.

All this changes radically when setups are simplified. It is easy to understand that a setup that takes 24 hours of work requires special skills. When the same task is reduced to 15 or 30 minutes, the new job needs a lower skill level. In existing factories, it is hardly feasible to downgrade skilled machinists to lower pay classifications in the short term. It should, however, be possible to eliminate setup specialists and to give the new, easy setup job to cell operators. In the long term, all plants should work toward updating job classifications and pay scales to match new simplified tasks.

FIX THE BASE

In Japan in the 1970s, one of the basic principles of setup reduction was "Don't Move the Base." A slightly more accurate way to phrase this is "Fix the Base." Part-holding fixtures can usually be attached to a machine table at any location on the table. Thus, setup requires adjusting the starting position of tools to the location of the part in the fixture, based on where the fixture is placed. If, by contrast, the fixture is always positioned on the table in exactly the same spot, adjusting tools to the location of the fixture can be eliminated. The reasons that fixtures are placed randomly in different areas on the table are usually as follows:

1. Until the 1960s and 1970s, setup time was universally accepted as a necessary evil. All ingenuity used in the design of tools and fixtures focused on speed and efficiency of operation. Setup time, if long, could be minimized by doing so infrequently.

2. Over a long period of time, many different fixtures, of various sizes and shapes, were designed. Consequently, it is difficult to design a device for the machine table that will hold each fixture in the same position every time it is used.

3. The same fixture might be used on any one of several similar machines. The other machines, even when they are theoretically identical, vary in dimension between table and machine heads. Thus, a fixture requires somewhat different positioning on various machines or else it will be necessary to continue to adjust the machine head to the fixture location.

One of the most inefficient factory practices is routinely permitting parts to be produced on different machines each time they are required. Conversely, each part should be run on the same machine each time it is produced. One of the most important concepts of process quality control is to adjust each variable until perfect quality is achieved and then use that same setting every time the part is produced. When this is done, it should be virtually impossible to produce defective products. If, however, a different machine is used each time a part is produced, it eliminates the possibility of stabilizing the most important variable, the machine.

It is often difficult to convince the longtime factory foreman that parts can be assigned to specific machines or cells. Such a veteran knows that large quantities of items produced have very infrequent and erratic requirements. When these infrequently required parts are needed, the preferred machine is likely to be loaded to or above its capacity. To meet the schedule, the order must be produced on another machine or cell. Even higher volume parts have fluctuating requirements. If they are assigned to specific machines, some will always be overloaded, while others will be underloaded. The solution is to assign all parts to specific machines and cells and run the majority of them where designated. By exception, a few items can be transferred to other machines or cells to keep machine loads reasonably balanced.

The fact that fixtures are of different size and shape is not really a serious problem. For example, a grid of locator holes on the machine table could correspond to matching locating pins in each fixture. The largest fixture could have pins corresponding to all the holes. This arrangement, and numerous other small inventions, makes it easy to place every fixture at the same location on a machine each time a specific part is produced.

ELIMINATE TRIAL AND ERROR

Factory management often views the setup operation performer, setup man, or skilled machinist as a wizard. He is thought to be capable of adjusting machine settings and positioning tools without the benefit of predetermined calibration values and, indeed, without the aid of calibration scales or measurement devices. In thousands of videotaped setups, we have seen tremendous differences between this myth and the actual facts. In virtually every setup initial settings (usually brief) are followed by lengthy periods of trial-and-error runs of sample items, measurement of these parts, and additional adjustments of the settings. As Exhibit 7-6 shows, the trial-and-error process usually produces defective items, which may need to be scrapped or reworked. Finally, the machinist deter-

TRIAL AND ERROR

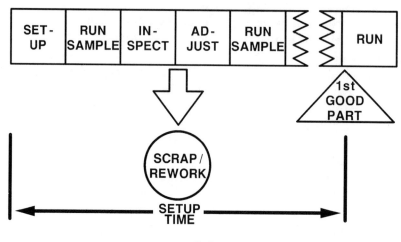

EXHIBIT 7-6

mines that the parts meet the required specifications and produces an entire production lot. When his original measurements are wrong, all or part of the lot must be scrapped or reworked.

In Exhibit 7-6, note that setup time includes initial setup and subsequent trial-and-error cycles until the first good part is produced. Many manufacturing personnel, when asked the length of setup time, routinely answer two hours, yet it actually takes eight to produce the first satisfactory item. Their definition of setup time includes only the initial operation, not the trial-and-error adjustment cycles. The objectives of every setup reduction project team should include eliminating trial and error. It is feasible to place machine setups and tool and fixture locations at the precise settings necessary to start production, confident that the first part produced will always be good, as illustrated by the lower bar in Exhibit 7-7.

There are an infinite variety of ways to place machine and tooling settings at precise required positions. In many cases, calibrated scales, gauges, and meters are on the machine but are illegible because they are encrusted with grease and oil. The reason these devices have fallen into disuse or never have been used is usually because of one of the following:

1. Setting specifications were never developed for each manufactured part, simply because no one took the time to document required settings.

ELIMINATE ADJUSTMENT

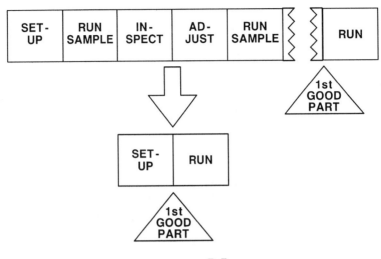

EXHIBIT 7-7

2. Because of machine variations, required settings are different for the same part produced on different machines. Thus, documentation of the settings for one machine would be helpful only when the part is produced on that particular machine. Due to the amount of work required, it would be impractical to develop and maintain data on separate settings for every machine.

3. Because of play caused by wear and machine vibration, the components of a machine move, over time. As a result, machine measurement devices are often inaccurate.

When the machine has setting measurement devices, it is usually not too difficult to put them to work, but it is often necessary to clean, repair, and reset them. Part numbers must be assigned to specific machines/cells and almost always produced in them. This makes it beneficial to document correct settings for use in setups. Daily, weekly, or even monthly measuring device readjustment can catch "wanderings" of machine components. Doing so allows operators to reset these devices before they deviate outside the dimensional range that must be maintained.

Johnson & Johnson, in Montreal, Canada, was successful in eliminating trial and error adjustments on one of several similar manufacturing and packaging lines. The carton magazine on its sanitary napkin packaging line was used for different sizes of packages (see Exhibit 7-8). When changing from one carton size to another, operators had to measure

CARTON MAGAZINE - BEFORE

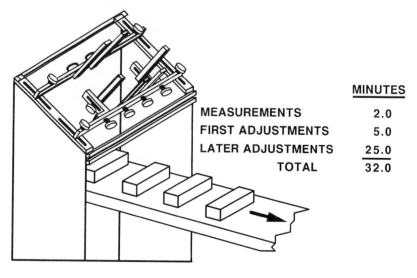

	MINUTES
MEASUREMENTS	2.0
FIRST ADJUSTMENTS	5.0
LATER ADJUSTMENTS	25.0
TOTAL	32.0

EXHIBIT 7–8

the new carton, set all 10 movable parts, and subsequently readjust some or all of these movable parts until the cartons were perfectly aligned with the mechanisms that unfold and form them. To remedy this wasteful changeover operation, a relatively inexpensive carton positioning fixture was designed for each of the four cartons. The slide-in feature shown in Exhibit 7–9 was developed to simply slide out the old fixture and slide in the new. This and other changes resulted in reducing line changeover cost by 90 percent.

Even computer-controlled machines continue to require changeover, with time needed to find and maintain the tapes containing the various programs. At the Slurry Pumps Division of Gould Pumps (Ashland, Pennsylvania), programs for parts machined on Giddings and Lewis vertical turret lathes were stored randomly on five different tapes, with an index to identify where each part's program was stored. For a new setup, an operator had to locate and reference the index and, 20 percent of the time, change the program tape currently in the machine. This procedure, on average, required four minutes. Each machine had different characteristics and needed its own unique programs, and every part number could be run on any machine. Thus, each part number was stored on five tapes, one program for *each* machine.

The first step towards reducing the time required to change the com-

CARTON MAGAZINE - AFTER

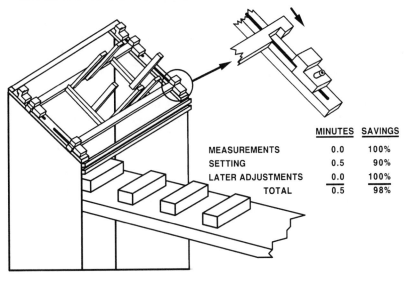

	MINUTES	SAVINGS
MEASUREMENTS	0.0	100%
SETTING	0.5	90%
LATER ADJUSTMENTS	0.0	100%
TOTAL	0.5	98%

EXHIBIT 7-9

puter tape was to designate a specific machine for every part number and store the programs for each machine on one of two tapes unique to it. One of the two tapes contained programs for the most frequently run parts, and this tape was on the machine more than 90 percent of the time. Items produced least often were stored on a separate tape. The majority of setups required programs on the tape of frequently produced parts. For those cases, the time needed to change a tape was eliminated. Further, the machine operator quickly became familiar with the new limited number of parts produced on each machine and was easily able to remember which of the two tapes held each part's program. Thus, the need for the index was eliminated. Tape changeover time, when necessary, is now well under one minute, a savings of more than 75 percent. The advantages of designating one machine to produce each part are of major importance. It not only reduces setup but also decreases the variability of the quality of parts that is attributable to variances in different machines.

FAST-FASTENING HARDWARE

Fastening hardware that require loosening, removal, subsequent replacement, and tightening can cause hours of unnecessary setup work. But improvements can be made and generally fall into four major categories: standardization, fast-fastener designs, fast tools, and elimination. In machines where the product being processed is guided through by fence-like devices, it is typical that tens or even hundreds of different types and sizes of fasteners must be loosened and retightened in changing from one size of product to another. Therefore, the operator responsible for the setup is equipped with dozens of different types and sizes of fastener tools, including screwdrivers and wrenches for hexagon, square, Phillips, Allen, and slot fastener head types. In these cases, setup procedures normally consist of:

1. Looking at the fastener to be loosened or removed and estimating the tool size required.
2. Searching through the tool box to find a tool of the estimated size.
3. Trying the tool on the fastener. If it does not fit, repeating steps 2 and 3 until the proper tool is found.

These procedures may be repeated hundreds of times during the changeover of one machine.

When a single fastener head size and type are used in every fastener application, only one tool will be needed. Once retrieved, this standard tool can remain in the changeover person's hand until all fasteners have been loosened or tightened. *Standardization* of fasteners, in the most complex machines, can reduce changeover time from hours to seconds. The time necessary to loosen and tighten the fasteners, however, will still be the same, unless other changes are made.

When machine clearances and required torque permit, conventional bolts and screws that need a separate tool for loosening and tightening can be replaced by T and L head fasteners like those shown in Exhibit 7–10. These eliminate the need for a separate tool since they are part of the fastener. This reduces tool retrieval time to its optimum—zero. In addition, no time is required to position the tool on (or in) the fastener head, cutting the time even more. The T and L fasteners are one type of fast-fastener design. The fastest, but not necessarily the lowest cost, fast-fastener design is power activated, with the power being hydraulic, electric, or spring. Since innumerable ingenious types of quick fasteners and fastening devices are available on the market, every setup reduction project team should become familiar with a broad range of these items.

In some cases, because the torque required to loosen or tighten is too high for T- and L-type fasteners, it may take too much time to position the tool, rotate the fastener, then reposition the tool. For example, when obstructions prevent a boxhead wrench from being rotated in a complete

T/L TYPE FASTENERS

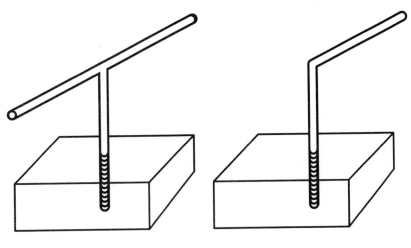

EXHIBIT 7-10

circle, the tool must be repositioned several times. Further, the length of the exposed thread, when excessive, adds wasted time and motion to the operation. If bolts are longer than necessary, this can easily be resolved by replacing them with shorter ones. When numerous high-torque rotations are still required, power tools can significantly reduce the time needed to loosen and tighten nuts.

Dies, fixtures, and other types of tooling are frequently attached by more fasteners than are structurally required; and these are often held in place by threaded fasteners when guidepins, without threads, are all that is needed. This is a result of overdesign. When there is no great pressure for minimizing the material used in a structure, engineers tend to overdesign products and tooling. In such cases, the designer need not make a detailed structural analysis to identify how many fasteners are required to attach a fixture to a machine table. Without any structural analysis, however, it is not clear that eight fasteners far exceed the requirement. But, clearly, the time for analysis is eliminated. Thus, a few hours of engineering time is saved, at a cost of three to five extra fasteners. However, two other important costs are overlooked—that for tightening the additional fasteners hundreds or even thousands of times over the life of the tooling and that for the inventory caused by added setup cost.

When too many fasteners are being used, the setup reduction project team should perform or request a structural analysis to determine how many should be used. Even better, when workers and equipment are not in danger, experiments with fewer or different fasteners may be the easiest way to find the answer.

At Triangle Industries' Rowe International plant in Whippany, New Jersey, operators found a way to eliminate the need for many of the fastener removals and replacements required to change a heavy brake press from one die to another. As Exhibit 7–11 indicates, a relatively small area of the brake press was needed for each of four components manufactured. Changeover required that both the upper punch and lower sections of the previous part die be removed and replaced by the next die set. Permanently attaching all four upper dies and replacing only the lower one when changing setup from one part to another eliminated the need to loosen and then retighten fasteners used to attach the upper die, as seen in Exhibit 7–12. The changeover design for the brake press was improved in many ways, including the installation of an indicator for readout of the ram setting and the addition of a ram adjustment control lever to the front of the machine. The correct ram setting for each die was printed on the press, directly above the die. These and other changes reduced changeover time from approximately 37 to 4 minutes, a decrease of 89 percent. Since the requirements for the four components made on the press and the press capacity were reasonably balanced, this design was highly practical. Not all brake presses, though, fall into the same category. Incidentally, the improved design also featured a second set of hand

BRAKE PRESS - BEFORE

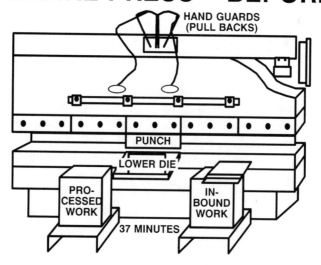

EXHIBIT 7–11

BRAKE PRESS - AFTER

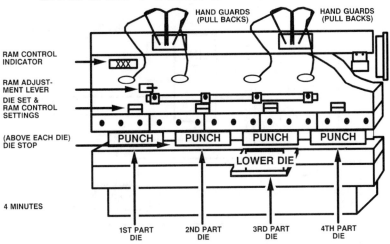

EXHIBIT 7-12

guards—a common safety device used to pull a worker's hands out of the press as it closes—which made it feasible to use any area of the press without adjusting the guards.

FOCUSED SETUP STORAGE

One of the easiest, fastest, and least expensive techniques for setup improvement is focused setup storage. Up to one-third of the total setup time (and, thus, of the cost) consists of the setup person leaving the machine to get the raw material, fixtures, dies, tools, and documentation required for changeover. With focused storage, all of these items are stored as close as possible to the machine on which the setup is performed. Every cell that consists of a single machine should be organized with its own raw materials, fixtures, dies, and tools. Whether in a single or multiple machine cell, focused storage has the same target. Even when storage is focused by department, the penalty in unnecessary wasted time and motion can be significant. For example, one of our earliest projects for Siemens, in West Germany, involved analysis of the changeover of machine lines used to stamp, form, and assemble electrical contacts. A punch press at the start of the line and another at the end of it required die changes. Exhibit 7–13 is a schematic of the movement of the setup man as he removed old dies from the machine lines, took them to the

OLD DIE TRANSPORT

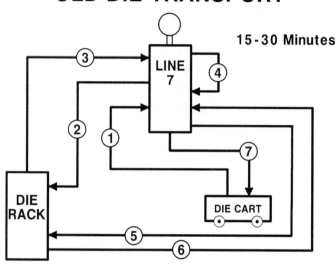

EXHIBIT 7-13

centralized department die racks, and returned to the machine lines with the next required die. Even before starting this process, he had to find the only die hoist available in the department and move it to the first machine in the line. This entailed walking back and forth between a dozen lines. Moreover, sometimes an additional delay occurred when the die hoist was in use on one of the other machine lines.

The die hoist was equipped with a hydraulic foot pedal for raising and lowering the die platform. To align the height of the hoist tables with the bolster of each of the two punch presses for both old dies when removed, and new dies when inserted, required as much as a half a minute. Additional time was needed to adjust the table height to the storage shelves to which the old dies were returned and from which the new ones were retrieved. This complete procedure took 7 trips and from 15 to 30 minutes per machine line, depending on the distance from the machine line to the die storage and how long it took to locate the die hoist.

The new die change procedure assigned two die carts and a combination die shelf/cabinet to each machine line. As illustrated in Exhibit 7-14, the cabinet and carts for machine line 7 were located between it and line 6. The new carts and cabinet were designed to be the same height as the punch press bolster, thus eliminating that adjustment. In the new process, the next two required dies were put on the carts, offline, while the first of two jobs was running. The carts were then moved to the two

NEW DIE TRANSPORT

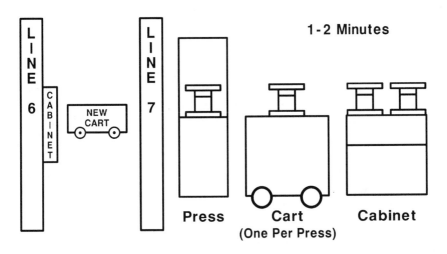

EXHIBIT 7-14

machines. When the first job was completed, the old die was moved off the press onto the cart. The cart was then reversed, and the new die moved from it to the punch press. Repeating the procedure at the second machine took only one to two minutes per changeover, a reduction of about 93 percent for just this one element of setup time and cost.

TOOL KITS

Imagine how inefficient it would be for a worker to stop between each unit assembled, return tools he used to the tool crib, and pick up those required for the next unit. Setup tools should be a permanent part of the assembly facility. Further, they should be located as close as possible to their points of use to minimize wasted time and motion. In the past when machines ran large lot sizes and were set up as infrequently as daily or weekly, having tools close at hand for the setup was not so crucial. Today, in the new factory, in which the minimum practical lot size is the production ideal, rapid access to setup tools is vital. Tools required for setup include hand and cutting tools that are usually kept in the centralized tool crib. When requested by the setup person, all tools must first be gathered from their storage drawers, bins, and shelves. Sometimes the setup person must wait his turn in line at the tool crib and be delayed even longer while tools are being gathered.

In the reinvented factory, tools are stored at or near the machine on which they are used. If hand tools are required for setup, they should be mounted on hangers on the machine. When this is impractical, portable tool kits or tool carts, as shown in Exhibit 7–15, can be positioned close to the machine and are the next best alternative.

The tool kit is advantageous not only because it can be located close to its point of use but because it can also highlight which setup tools are missing. Frequently, setup personnel return to the tool crib to get a tool that was overlooked. When a custom tool kit is used, a quick glance is enough to verify that all required tools are in it. However, even when the setup person has his own tool box, he frequently leaves it on a table somewhat distant from the machine on which he is working, increasing the time required to gather tools.

A productivity improvement project team designed the setup cart in Exhibit 7–15 for the Tipper Tie Division of Dover Industries at Apex, North Carolina. As illustrated, it is used for storing and transporting cutting tools and tool holders, computer numerical control program tapes, setup and job documentation, and all other setup parts, fixtures, hardware, and hand tools. The shop order document provision is transitory since it is replaced by CONBON cards as soon as feasible (further described in Chapter 8).

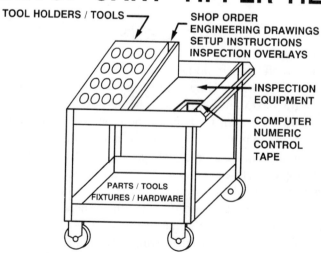

SETUP CART-TIPPER TIE

EXHIBIT 7–15

DIE/FIXTURE STANDARDIZATION

With rare exception, dies and fixtures that mount on machines are individually designed, with no attention being paid to standardization to eliminate setup time required to make adjustments from one size die or fixture to another. Frequently, the result is that if 800 dies are used, there are 800 different sizes. Few companies, if any, will find it economically practical to build new dies and fixtures of standard dimensions. Most can selectively, over time, make low-cost modifications to existing dies and fixtures to standardize their sizes. Shigeo Shingo described several techniques of die standardization, including attaching shims and plates to build up die size and using jigs to which existing dies can be attached. Even with low-cost modifications, standardization will require a prohibitively high expenditure and excessive amounts of toolmaker time to change all dies and fixtures. Fortunately, most companies can use selective analysis to identify the smallest number of dies and fixtures that can be modified to produce the best increase in profits.

As an example, a factory with 10 large and 10 small punch presses and 400 different dies wants to convert to standardization. To begin, it should dedicate only one or two presses (one large, one small) to running dies that have been standardized, specifically dies for part numbers of highest usage value. After enough dies have been modified to fill the capacity of the initial one or two presses, work should start on the group of dies that has the next highest usage value. Over time, more dies can be modified. It might never be necessary or desirable to alter the dies of lowest usage value. If so, one or more presses could be dedicated to making only parts for which die sizes have not been modified.

DIE/FIXTURE TRANSPORT

The equipment used to move dies and fixtures from storage to the machine may add time and cost to the setup. For instance, punch press dies are almost always moved by forklift truck. Few factories can afford to have enough trucks available to have one waiting at each machine for the next setup. Thus, the changeover man usually wastes time requesting and waiting for the lift truck.

Die carts, like the one illustrated in Exhibit 7–15, can limit or even eliminate the amount of lift-truck assistance required during changeover. Where the truck still needs to be used, scheduling procedures should be controlled so that neither the truck operator nor the setup man wastes his time waiting for the other. Beds of rollers into and out of many machines can be used to slide dies or fixtures in and out of them. When the roller system includes space for both previous and subsequent dies or fixtures, further movement to and from storage can be done completely offline. Overhead cranes that service large factory sections waste time and motion if they are not instantly available to the setup man. But smaller one-per-machine cranes can often improve this situation.

PRODUCTION TIME SAVINGS

Not all setup savings are confined to the time of changeover. At Quebec's Rolland, Inc., a manufacturer of fine business and printing papers, paper sheeting machines required unloading the last paper produced at the time of machine changeover. They also needed to be unloaded every time one set of pallets were filled. The time to unload one set of pallets was only 3.4 minutes, as shown in Exhibit 7–16. A forklift driver unloaded the completed skids of paper, and one of two machine operators moved between upper and lower elevations to place two new pallets on the elevator. In a year the time spent on unloading was equivalent to about forty 24-hour days. With the design of new flow-through roller systems, there was

PAPER SHEETING SETUP - BEFORE

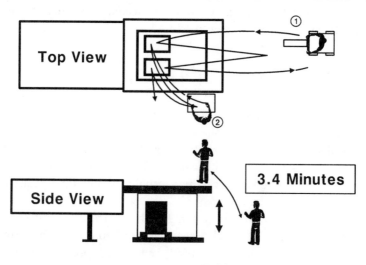

EXHIBIT 7–16

an excellent opportunity to use low-cost automation. As seen in the three side views in Exhibit 7–17, paper sheets are automatically loaded on the pallet. When the sheets on the pallet reach maximum height, the elevator descends automatically. An empty pallet is waiting to be loaded into the pallet elevator. The full pallet is advanced to the outbound roller, from which the hand-lift operator removes it at his convenience. At the same time, the empty pallet is advanced onto the pallet elevator. The center of the elevator bed is open. This opening is smaller than the pallet, but larger than the rollers. It permits the elevator to be lowered to a level below the rollers during the times that pallets are being moved. The hand-lift operator places a pallet on the outbound rollers, and it is moved into the inbound pallet position. The new procedure requires 36 seconds to execute, a decrease in elapsed time of more than 80 percent, but only of about 3 minutes each setup. Although a single unloading savings seems insignificant, the annual machine time gained is equal to thirty-two 24-hour days.

Even after major improvements in tools, equipment, layout and procedures reduce changeover time, continuous, near-optimal performance depends on motivated, conscientious employees and supervisors. Charting setup time before and after implementing improvements is one way to detect instances where backsliding occurs. Indeed, charting alone, without any other improvements, usually motivates the employees who per-

PAPER SHEETING SETUP - AFTER

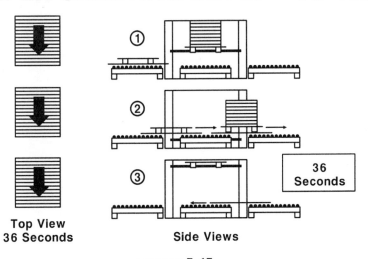

Top View
36 Seconds

Side Views

**36
Seconds**

EXHIBIT 7–17

form changeover to improve their performance. Charting is an activity, however, that does not add value to the product; thus, if charts are necessary because employees and their supervisors will otherwise fail to perform responsibly, this source problem must be solved, and the charting activity can then be discontinued. (Charting is discussed extensively in Chapter 8.)

Without a doubt, setup reduction is one of the most important foundations of superior manufacturing. Every company should have an aggressive program to achieve it, and should plan and accomplish rapid payback, thus financing additional improvements. Careful attention should be paid to developing simple, low-cost solutions and to training production management and technical personnel in the techniques of one-touch changeover.

8

□□□

Productivity Systems:
The Paperless Factory

SINCE THE 1950S, the unit cost of information processing has decreased dramatically, while its total cost has increased. In a recently published article, Robert J. Samuelson[1] pointed out that 14 million computers were sold in the United States from 1980 to 1987, some 20 times more than the total for all previous years. Yet there was no discernable corresponding surge in increased productivity. Most businesses face a deluge of information, new requirements to input data, and a need to analyze the resulting output. These have caused an increase in staff and clerical functions. If factories handled such matters in a similar way, automating production operations would lead to an increase in the number of factory employees per unit produced.

Manufacturing executives should insist that systems and procedures operate in a businesslike fashion, which includes drastic improvements in profit contribution. The goal of increased productivity should apply not only to computer system operations, but also to the people interfacing with the system. Additionally, attention should be paid to reducing computer system inputs and outputs, data records, and data record sizes. The

[1] Robert J. Samuelson, "Productivity Bounces Back." *Newsweek*, August 22, 1988, p. 50.

volume of printed reports, often a stack several feet high each day, should be a specific target for drastic reduction. It is the curse of nearly every manufacturer.

Examples of reasonable target ranges for productivity improvements are:

	Reduction
Personnel requirements	25–50%
Processing elapsed time	90–95%
Transaction volumes	75–90%
System development, maintenance, and operating costs	25–50%

Computer systems have often failed to reduce operating costs, and the reasons are complex and many. For one, in both the factory and the office, needlessly complex operating practices have not been eliminated prior to developing systems and procedures. Thus, as a result of being designed initially to function with poor operating practices, the systems have been unnecessarily complex. For another, information systems have often been installed where tangible benefits have not been identified or subsequently achieved. Too much credence has been given to the intangible benefits of information. Also, noting the results of human error in inputting and programming systems, responsible managers have been reluctant to eliminate routine manual reviews of computer output. Consequently, armies of personnel pore over pages of computer output to verify its accuracy and reasonableness.

In many cases, computer systems failed when systems and procedures were developed, at great expense, to routinely report on operating problems, such as scrap and rework. These types of problems are usually solvable, often at relatively modest cost. The proper focus of improvement should be to invest in solving problems, not in reporting them. Further, the cost and complexity of many systems is greater than necessary because many companies fail to use preprogrammed software to reduce system development time. The latest available software provides just-in-time features to support simplified factory operations.

In today's world, the computer is (and should be) a focal point for processing massive volumes of business transactions. It also serves as an extension of human intelligence in key areas, such as engineering analysis. Like many tools, however, the computer is often misused. The purpose of this chapter is to outline some ways in which systems and procedures can be improved to make a positive contribution to profitability.

FACTORY SIMPLIFICATION/SYSTEM SIMPLIFICATION

The superior manufacturing practices outlined in this book radically change both the amount of information involved in manufacturing and the number of required transactions. For example, at one time, every machine in the factory operated independently. Thus, it was necessary to track production through individual machines. In the superior factory, machine cells include several machines and operate like a single machine or assembly line. Parts started in the cell are completed in a few minutes; consequently, tracking production of individual machines within the cell is no longer necessary or desirable.

In the past, subassemblies were manufactured in separate facilities, well in advance of final assembly. Thus, it was necessary to plan and schedule subassemblies earlier than final assembly. This required additional levels in the bills of material, more production order paperwork, and higher-than-necessary inventory. By contrast, in the new assembly process, subassemblies are manufactured either in the main assembly line or on directly linked parallel subassembly lines. Now, both subassembly and final assembly use the same schedule. Inventory tracking of subassemblies is eliminated since there is no inventory between subassembly production and its use on final assembly. Thus, the physical changes in subassembly make it possible to reduce the size and complexity of bills of material and production order paperwork, while reducing the amount of subassembly work-in-process inventory.

In the traditional factory, central storage facilities stocked thousands of part numbers. Random assignments for storage locations were used to improve the use of cubic space. As a result, location control system features were required. Managers of small, focused stock locations, however, manage space utilization by eye. The need for detailed location control can be eliminated.

To better understand the potential for reduction in the number of transactions reported from the factory floor, consider these 31 routine transactions typically required to manufacture a single lot with eight routed operations.

1. One transaction to draw raw material from stock.
2. Eight transactions to record setup performance in the order tracking system and to pay the person who does it.
3. Eight transactions to pay each operator, maintain inventory accounts, calculate manufacturing variance, and track order progress.

4. Eight transactions to track movement between operations (relatively few manufacturers have this).

5. One transaction to add the completed order to stored inventory.

6. Five transactions to track order status, including firming, opening, releasing, issuing, and order closing.

In addition to these 31 normal transactions, others are often required to report scrap and rework. When these eight machines are organized into a cell, and raw materials and finished items are kept in inbound/outbound focused storage, the transactions mentioned above are replaced by a single CONBON for the quantity produced by the cell. This single transaction reduces the amount of raw material required for the quantity produced, and adds the completed item to inventory accounts and on-hand inventory status.

In the cell, transactions that would report the production of individual operators, machine production, and movement between machines do not make sense. The team of operators are responsible for running all of the machines cooperatively. Parts produced in the cell are completed a few minutes after they are begun at the first operation. Thus, tracking movement from machine to machine is not necessary.

Raychem's Wire & Cable Division was highly successful in designing ways to reduce the number of reported transactions in its Redwood, California, plant, as the following table shows:

| | Volume | | |
Item	FROM	TO	Reduction
Operation completion	51	0	100%
Order status	32	8	75%
Open shop orders	1,200	150	87%

Improvements in manufacturing operations not only reduce the number of records and transactions required but also simplify the remaining systems. For example: In the past, material requirements planning systems included both simple and complex order quantity calculations. However, with one-touch changeover, such calculations are unnecessary. The quantity needed is the same as the quantity produced. Also, the accuracy of keeping on-hand inventory was critical in the past because supplier schedules were based on the quantity required minus what was already on hand. When the quantity on hand was understated, shortages resulted.

In the new just-in-time world, the amount of inventory on hand is not material. The accuracy of scheduled deliveries is not critical since CON-BON cards or electronic CONBON messages draw inventory from suppliers as containers are physically emptied. Frequently, in the past, large amounts of scrap and rework necessitated calculations of allowances and/or safety stocks to avoid shortages. In the superior factory, quality levels measured in defects per million parts will make these calculations unnecessary.

Far from a complete list, these improvements in factory operations make it possible to simplify systems and procedures. When new systems are contemplated, it is important to minimize the effort and investment required. Thus, most companies should consider adapting software packages that contain as many simplifying features as possible.

When subplant problems and opportunities become the responsibility of the subplant manager, and the majority of problems have been eliminated, management information should be vastly simplified. Then continuously declining costs per unit of production should be the sole concern of executive management. If they do not decline, only the major elements of cost should be the focus of performance-oriented discussions between the subplant manager and his or her superior.

Other traditional forms of performance reporting that should no longer be necessary include:

1. *Efficiency reporting.* New cells and lines produce exactly the amount required rather than as much as possible. To encourage or accept production of either more or less than needed would mean failure to control production. Further, detailed operation standards and measurements against them should be eliminated to reduce the cost of administering standards and reporting efficiency.

2. *Quality performance.* Detailed, voluminous quality reporting is not necessary when defects are reduced to a few parts per million pieces of production.

3. *Inventory investment.* When new inventory levels are reduced to 90 to 95 percent of their previous levels, inventory investment will become less material. Accordingly, management should not require detailing inventory status by subplant.

4. *Schedule performance.* Measuring schedule to actual completion performance is not needed by the few companies in which production is currently virtually always on schedule. For many others, achieving just-in-time performance may require several years.

PAPERWORK SIMPLIFICATION/SYSTEM SIMPLIFICATION

Today, in most modern factories, the paperwork and procedures stem from, and are similar to, those dating back to the Industrial Revolution. The most noticeable difference is that now forms and procedures are automated and even more complex. Fortunately, new vistas can open for systems and procedures when outmoded methods are critically examined and new techniques are introduced. For example:

1. Orders for parts and materials can be replaced by an electronic transfer between customer and supplier. When achieved, this practice virtually eliminates the supplier's Customer Order Processing department and sharply reduces the staff needed in the customer's purchasing department.

2. Automatic generation of payment transactions from bar-coded CONBON cards, at the point of receipt, can eliminate invoices and the invoice matching process. Thus, accounts payable and accounts receivable department personnel can be sharply reduced.

3. Shop orders and shop-order packages of documentation (paper or computer display) can be eliminated by the use of CONBON cards, drastically reducing production control department and factory personnel involved in handling, tracking, and expediting shop orders.

4. Companies like Harley-Davidson have been able to eliminate annual physical inventories and simplify cycle-counting procedures by reducing inventory levels to a much lower percentage of company assets.

In all of these examples, CONBON methods are vital to superior manufacturing procedures and systems.

CONBON: THE WESTERN WORLD'S KANBAN

The card system, *kanban,* was one of the first unique aspects of Japanese manufacturing to receive wide publicity. Initial reaction from the West to this highly successful technique was that it is not a system but a joke, that it will work only in highly repetitive production; and that the material requirement planning system, MRP, is superior to kanban. Since then, however, numerous successful applications of customized versions of kanban in Western companies have proven that its users are laughing all the way to the proverbial bank and that the Westernized method of kanban, CONBON, has features suitable for both low-volume and high-volume items. As well, it's been discovered that it is nonsensical to discuss MRP and CONBON as two alternatives, since the best system is actually a combination of both.[2]

The Toyota Motor Co.'s kanban system is one aspect of superior manufacturing systems and procedures that has been studied to death and described to excess in innumerable publications. As an active practitioner in design and implementation of productivity improvements in Japan since the 1930s, Shigeo Shingo[3] is one of the leading authorities on the subject. Because the kanban system has been so widely publicized, this book will include only a brief explanation of the basic system, and some lesser known facets of kanban. In 1980, Western manufacturers needed to adapt the not-yet-famous kanban system for use in their own factories; however, both company and national pride deterred Westerners from adopting a system developed in Japan, regardless of the success of the system or its parent company. For this reason, Andersen Consulting coined and registered the acronym CONBON as a trademark. CONBON describes the two types of cards that are basic to kanban, which are:

1. The Card Order Notice (CON)
2. The Bring Out Notice (BON)

The acronym is also the correct Japanese pronunciation of kanban.

To visualize the CONBON method, one should imagine standing a few feet from the assembly line illustrated in Exhibit 8–1. On the line, two containers of part A are stocked and a BON card is kept with, in, or on each of the containers. When the assembler uses the last part A in one of the containers, he places the empty container and BON card on a special shelf to signal the material handler that another container of part A is required. At almost the same moment, just-in-time, the material handler picks up the empty container in a circular trip between the assembly line and the stockpoint. In each trip of a relatively short distance, the material handler delivers one load of full containers while picking up empty containers. At the stockpoint, the material handler (with the BON card for part A) locates a full container that is accompanied by a second type of card, a CON card. He removes the CON card, puts the container of part

---

[2] Even some of the leading manufacturing authorities now recognize this fact. In his 1983 "Education Curriculum," Walter Goddard was saying that the American companies need material requirement planning, not kanban. He now recognizes, however, that the two are complementary.

[3] Shigeo Shingo, *Study of Toyota Production System* (Tokyo, Japan: Japan Management Association, 1981).

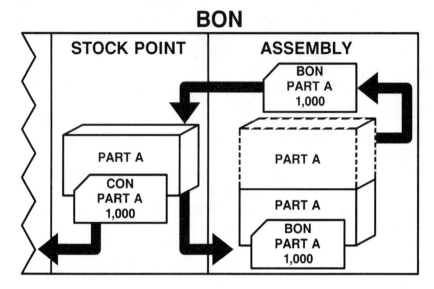

EXHIBIT 8-1

A and the part A BON card on his cart, and delivers the full container and its BON card to the line at about the same time that the next part A container is emptied. This will cause the cycle to be repeated. In this example, the material handler's system of scheduling delivery of components to the line is management "by eye." When he sees the empty container and BON card, he knows it is time to get another container, just-in-time.

In the meantime, the empty containers and the CON card that the assembly material handler removed from the container at the stockpoint are picked up by the supplier's material handler as he delivers more of part A. As illustrated in Exhibit 8-2, when the supplier's material handler returns to the supplying cell, he places the CON card for part A in the back of a short queue of cards waiting to be produced. The queue is produced on a first-in, first-out basis. When the cell is ready to produce part A, it makes exactly the quantity indicated on the CON card and sends the material handler with the card and full container of part A to the stockpoint. At about the same time that the supplier delivers part A, the assembly material handler arrives for another container.

Although there are several variations of the way in which CONBON cards are used, the prior example illustrates the most basic. When the supplier is located in a different plant, the concept is similar. For example, the card and empty container are returned, by trucks, to the supplier plant, and a full container and card are then delivered to the user. This

CON

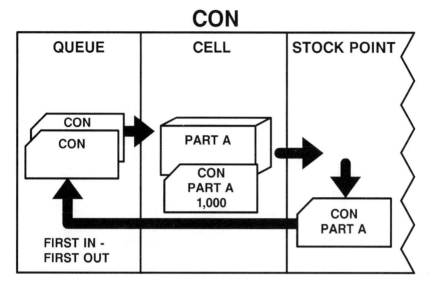

EXHIBIT 8–2

method is simple and easy to use with local sources of supply, especially when the user or supplier has dedicated delivery trucks that make frequent circuits between user and supplier. When these two are distant, electronic CONBON, as illustrated in Exhibit 8–3, is the practical alternative. When the container is empty, the card is transmitted electronically

ELECTRONIC CONBON
SUPPLIER / INTERPLANT

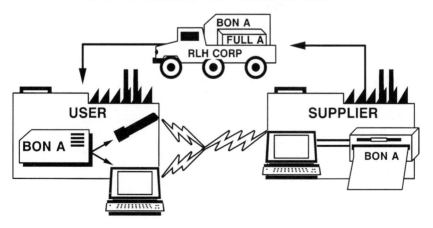

EXHIBIT 8–3

to the supplier, and the card is then scrapped. Electronic CONBON is not limited to use by remote suppliers but can be used in large factories to cut response time for replenishing parts. Chapter 10 includes a case example of General Motors using electronic CONBON.

Since nearly every factory has both higher-volume and lower-volume components and materials, they need normal CONBON for the highest, most repetitively used or produced items. A special one-time CONBON is used for items that have low volume and infrequent usage; this card is produced by using material requirements planning system information. Essentially a simplified manufacturing order, the one-time CONBON card is often a combination of order information, routing information, and schedule dates for each operation. When the item ordered is produced in a cell, the need for detailed routing information disappears. The use of one-time CONBON is simpler than the production order because its bar coding can be used to report completion and permits use of one system, CONBON, rather than separate systems and procedures for both CONBON and production orders.

In this case, the queue of CONBON cards waiting to be produced is different than previously illustrated in Exhibit 8–2. Instead of a single queue of cards, the queue now includes dividers for several days since material requirements planning systems, operated weekly, would generate one-time CONBON cards for the next five days. Normal CONBON cards are always filed in the front, in first-in, first-out sequence. It is precisely known when it is time to produce more of the item on the normal CONBON card because the card is processed when a container is emptied. By contrast, since the material requirements planning system rarely has such precision, the scheduled dates are normally earlier than required. One-time CONBON items, therefore, can have lower priority than normal CONBON items.

If normal CONBON items have highest priority, will one-time CONBON items ever be produced? This could be the case *only* if requirements of both were perpetually permitted to exceed the man/machine capacity. For example, if the target queue of CONBON cards is four hours, and eight hours of work arrives (as CONBON cards) every eight hours, eventually the only cards available to work on will be one-time cards, since less than 100 percent of the cards received daily will be normal CONBON cards. In fact, if the number of cards in the queue becomes more than an acceptable minimum, extra hours, shifts, or machines will be needed to reduce the queue to the target level.

Walter Goddard[4] points out that Toyota took four vital steps to estab-

---

[4] Walter E. Goddard, *Just-in-Time: Surviving by Breaking Tradition* (Essex Junction, Vt.: Oliver Wight Limited Publications, Inc., 1986).

lish the best possible CONBON system, including leveling the master schedule, using small order quantities (daily requirements or less) at all levels of production, reducing lead times to a minimum, and ensuring flexible capacity. He does not mention, however, that CONBON has had major successes even when some (or even all) of these conditions were not satisfied. Every CONBON system (including Toyota's) uses safety stock to protect against shortage due to unexpected variations in both requirements and supply. Companies that have wide variations in demand and supply have larger safety stocks (extra CONBON cards in circulation), while companies with a narrow range in variations have smaller safety stocks.

Still, the relatively level master schedule and just-in-time material requirements planning features that support stable and achievable schedules for all manufacturing processes are necessary for success. To meet schedules, it is necessary that capacity be flexible enough to meet almost all peak demands, or that production schedules not exceed critical capacities. Material requirements planning systems will always be needed, even when all items used and produced have relatively repetitive demand. There will always be a need to see future demand trends for the purpose of planning future capacity. This applies equally to items produced in a factory and by outside suppliers.

When items are produced infrequently, it may be better to use CONBON cards that do not specify the quantity of each specific part to be produced but only that more work is required at a specified machine, process, or line. Sometimes a physical space can be used to replace the CONBON cards. For instance, Muebles Danona, Soc. Coop., a manufacturer of wood furniture in Azpeitia (Guipuzcoa), Spain, machines panels for cabinets on three combination mills. Like most furniture manufacturers, it stored work in process on flow conveyors between the mills and the next operation—varnishing. Exhibit 8–4 shows 20 long conveyors, with a capacity of 8,000 units of production. Since various items are best varnished on different lines, sometimes the conveyor storage would be full, although it would contain no work for one of the three varnish lines in operation. Large amounts of inventory made it difficult to locate a specific job, or jobs for a specific line. Further, all mills could have been working to produce items for use on the lines for which the storage area already contained large amounts of inventory, while another varnish line was out of work.

Muebles Danona replaced its one large storage facility that held products from all three mills with small, focused outbound storage areas adjacent to each mill, as shown in Exhibit 8–5. The work-in-process inventory of milled components is now physically controlled by conveyors. When all conveyors are full, the mill must stop. When those for one

TWENTY LONG CONVEYORS

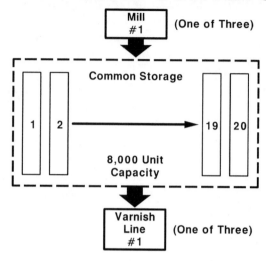

EXHIBIT 8-4

varnish line are full, production must be switched to items for another varnish line. The physical control of inventories at Muebles Danona goes a step beyond use of CONBON cards to cardless CONBON. In our long-term vision of superior manufacturing, all using and supplying operations will be directly linked and synchronized, thus not only eliminating the

TWELVE SHORT CONVEYORS

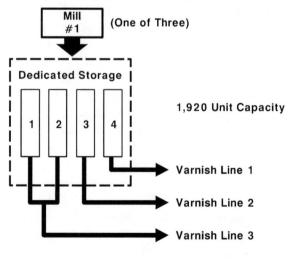

EXHIBIT 8-5

use of CONBON cards, but also of buffer inventories between user and supplier.

FROZEN MASTER SCHEDULE: ICE OR SLUSH?

Throughout the network of each manufacturer and his supplier factories, schedule changes are perhaps the most disruptive factor. For decades, the frozen master schedule had lured manufacturers to attempt the impractical: not to permit changes to the final assembly schedule on which all components and material schedules are based or, in other words, to freeze the schedule. The desire to freeze schedules was based on knowledge that materials and parts, once scheduled, start to proceed through the manufacturing process. Like a glacier, the scheduled production, once in motion, tends to proceed through the network. Schedule changes requiring later production of one item in process and earlier production of another may delay the item in process, but the clogged network usually also delays production of the item now required earlier.

Most attempts at freezing a schedule are relatively unsuccessful, and encounter the following problems:

1. Lead time of both the factory and its suppliers is far too long to freeze production schedules for all, or even a major portion, of the network. If the lead time is 6 months, 12 months, or even longer, customers expect to be able to change their scheduled receipt dates and to place new orders with much shorter response time.

2. All demands are ultimately driven by the marketplace. Market demand is subject to large swings, and the successful manufacturer must be prepared to supply surprise surges in demand while avoiding build-ups of surplus inventory when demand slumps. Thus, success demands rapid response to the market, not following an unrealistic schedule with head in the sand.

3. Many schedules, whether frozen or not, are unrealistic. Scheduled production is impossible to achieve with available capacity, materials, and components. When schedules are frozen unrealistically, they become meaningless.

Accordingly, one of the most basic requirements for any master schedule is that its early portion must be an almost perfect forecast of actual production.

Factory and supplier productivity projects will eventually eliminate most of the problems of excessively long production lead times. Supplier schedule systems will drastically reduce the time required to communicate schedules to suppliers. When lead times in a network are reduced from one year to one month, it becomes practical to freeze either all or a major portion of remaining production lead time. Master scheduling systems, however, must not freeze the schedule. Exceptional swings of market demand will always occur, and the superior manufacturer must be prepared to take exceptional action in response. Thus, the master schedule should be neither liquid nor frozen, but slushy.

LOAD LEVELING: PRODUCE TO ORDER VERSUS STOCK

For two sound reasons, almost every repetitive manufacturer tries to produce to stock rather than to order. First, production lead times are too long to provide required levels of customer service. Second, there are major peaks and valleys in demand that do not always equal the capacity for production. To meet variations in anticipated demand, competing manufacturers could pursue the following alternative strategies: (1) produce to inventory in anticipation of peak demands, or (2) produce at peak levels when demand occurs. In most cases, the company with the plant, equipment, and management techniques necessary to produce at peak levels when the peaks occur will be the superior manufacturer, in terms of minimizing product cost and meeting customer demands.

Unfortunately, the concept of production load leveling has dominated most of the literature describing the ideal type of scheduling. Attempts at leveling production schedules have kept thousands of production planners busy worldwide. The primary reason behind a uniform level of production is clear and understandable: every change in capacity takes time and effort. To reduce capacity, employees must be transferred from one area to another, perhaps laid off, or assigned reduced workweeks. Equally disruptive is increasing capacity, which results in employee transfers, overtime, and hiring and training new employees. In general, even when changes in capacity are finally made, production cannot keep pace with need because of the time required to execute change. Additionally, managers are often reluctant to make changes simply because they require so much effort.

Companies that level schedules should vigorously reexamine their policy and its real costs. In the past, load leveling had a tradeoff cost in inventory investment. This was due to producing to inventory in anticipation of future demand peaks versus incurring the costs of hiring and laying off personnel. There is no way to eliminate the costs of storing and financing load-leveling inventory, but the costs related to hiring and layoffs can be reduced and eliminated by improving systems to support planning capacity and implement changes in work assignments, and minimizing changes in the number of employees required. This includes:

1. Permitting production volume to vary, within a practical limited range, without changing manpower. This means employees agree to work less on some days and faster on others.

2. Shifting employees from one cell to another and from one subplant to another based on increases or decreases in demand. In order to minimize training and start-up production loss, manufacturers should design simpler jobs and encourage cross-training.

3. Promoting sales in traditionally low-demand periods.

4. Increasing the use of overtime to meet peak periods of demand.

Superior manufacturers are those most likely to produce to the level of highest demand during the peak periods. In Exhibit 8–6, the demand pattern (solid line) is for sales of a product with strong seasonal demand, with peaks in April and November. The trend pattern (dotted line) shows the increased sales that can be expected in the long term, except during cyclical economic downturns. However, there are some important points to keep in mind. Although the pattern of *past* demand is strong, the future forecast, for one discrete product, will be inaccurate. The further into the future, the greater the probable inaccuracy. Thus, leveling production to meet forecasted demand is likely to result in producing more of some items than required and less of others. Further, given a trend in demand, a completely level production schedule does not make sense. In Exhibit 8–6, high demand in the second year would require producing a substantial amount of inventory in the first year. The inventory investment required would usually be prohibitive. Companies must limit leveling to some short, practical planning period since all item-level forecasts are inaccurate and almost all item demands are trending either up or down.

An example of a short, practical load-leveling period would be a month or less. Leveling over a longer period, such as six months, usually carries penalties in terms of the inventory investment required. It is also likely the leveled schedule cannot be maintained after two or three months due to the high probability that actual demand will be substantially different

TREND / SEASONAL DEMAND

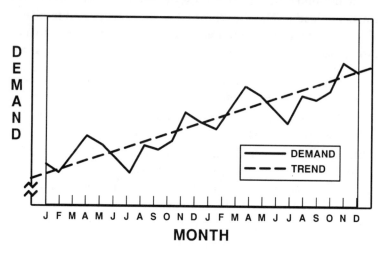

EXHIBIT 8-6

than initial forecasts. In Exhibit 8–7, an example of leveling production over six months, it is not readily apparent that simply planning to produce at the average rate of demand (as indicated by the dotted lines) fails to meet peak needs in time to avoid shortages. The reason is that extra amounts produced in the first three months are less than peak demand

PRODUCTION LEVELING
SIX MONTHS

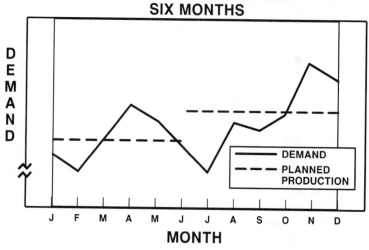

EXHIBIT 8-7

in the last three. As a result, leveling cannot simply average production over the six-month schedule, but may require producing more than the average both to level production and meet peak demands without experiencing shortages.

LOAD LEVELING: SMALL LOT PRODUCTION

The frequency of peaks and valleys in production requirements is one of manufacturing management's worst problems. Most manufacturers compound their problems by producing unnecessarily large lot sizes. (Until it became clear that setup/changeover costs could be drastically reduced, there were not too many alternatives to these production runs.) For most companies, running large lot sizes has meant an unreasonably high level of finished goods, work-in-process, and purchased material inventories. In addition, shortages have continued to seriously hinder meeting production schedules because some of the requirement peaks exceed normal production capacity. When production shortages are avoided, it is usually the result of either overtime work or excessively high inventory levels.

The effects of producing large lot sizes are illustrated in Exhibit 8-8. The end product X assembly schedule has been leveled at 10 units per day for the first 15 days of the month and 20 per day in the last. Presumably, this schedule would correspond with demand. It would be practical to meet this schedule by operating one shift through June 15, and two shifts thereafter. Although the final assembly schedule has been leveled,

ECONOMIC LOT SIZING

PART NO.	DESCRIPTION	JUNE				
		13	14	15	16	17
X	END PRODUCT	10	10	10	20	20
Y	SUB-ASSEMBLY		30		40	
Z	COMPONENT	70				80

EXHIBIT 8-8

converting subassembly Y to economic lot sizes results in requirements for only one of two days. The component Z of subassembly Y has even more erratic requirements because it is lot-sized for production only one day out of four. The efforts of peak and valley lot-sizing extend beyond producers to suppliers. Thus, factory production schedules that are really level will have far-reaching benefits.

Leveling production over long periods is not practical. It should be done over a shorter period. Uniform load, by half-month periods, is illustrated in Exhibit 8–9. Leveling becomes possible when setup/changeover costs are reduced to the level that enables production of each item every day. The ultimate goal of most manufacturers should be to supply customer requirements from production, not from stock. This becomes feasible when total lead times are reduced, setup costs become minimal, and the range of available, flexible capacity is sufficient to meet all but the most unusual peak demands. Ideally, every manufacturer should strive to achieve a make-to-order environment.

MATERIAL REQUIREMENTS PLANNING FOR SUPERIOR MANUFACTURING

If an entire network of a factory and its suppliers convert to superior manufacturing, their material requirements planning systems can be substantially simpler than those now needed in most factory/supplier net-

UNIFORM LOAD

PART NO.	DESCRIPTION	JUNE				
		13	14	15	16	17
X	END PRODUCT	10	10	10	20	20
Y	SUB-ASSEMBLY	10	10	20	20	20
Z	COMPONENT	10	20	20	20	20

EXHIBIT 8–9

works. The key differences between current and superior systems are that:

1. Flow orders (schedules) are used in place of purchase and shop orders.
2. Automatic flow-order rescheduling eliminates manual review of suggested orders and order changes.
3. Supplier schedules rather than orders are used to communicate requirements to factory subplants, to other company factories that supply components, and to vendors.
4. CONBON support features are provided, including the ability to control an item by order (not by CONBON), by CONBON, or by one-time CONBON.

The concept of flow order is relatively simple. The conventional production order requires a separate authorization for each date on which an item is scheduled to be produced. If the item is scheduled for production once or many times per day, the number of orders required could be staggering. Instead of authorizing production orders for each day separately, master scheduled items should be authorized for a daily rate of production for a specified period of time, such as a month or week. This single schedule authorization, thus, establishes a schedule for the next specified number of days, and eliminates daily paperwork. The uniform load, depicted in Exhibit 8–9, illustrates a master scheduled item with two different scheduled rates. It also depicts how master scheduled item requirements become the basis for lower level needs, without distorting those requirements by planning different order quantities. This example best demonstrates how demands for the product should be converted to component requirements. In the conventional planning system, it is necessary to manually review and approve every computer suggested order. Additionally, suggested changes to previously released orders must also be reviewed to determine whether or not to modify the date and quantity manually if they do not coincide with requirements. The reasons for manual review of computer calculations include:

1. *Difficulty in locating paperwork.* Released orders have accompanying paperwork packets on the shop floor, and it would, therefore, be necessary to find the shop packet to make a change. Usually, the number of orders released makes this impractical.
2. *Impracticality of changing orders.* Even if orders in process could be located, it would not be practical to change their quantities, since they are produced in lots, one operation at a time. Thus, increasing

an order from 100 pieces to 150 could require performing several operations on the 50 additional pieces until they catch up with the original 100, which had previously had 5 of 10 operations performed. Conversely, cutting the quantity of an order already completed through several operations results in inventory-completed items all over the factory.

3. *Skepticism.* Some planners fear that the computer-calculated action may be inaccurate or not as current as the knowledge of the person performing the review.

In the superior factory, flow-order items are produced continuously, one part at a time, and not in lots. Further, the shop packet is eliminated. As a result, schedules of these items can be changed at any time without modifying anything more than the scheduled rate of production. If errors occur in the new focused factory, shop personnel are much better equipped to detect and correct them than the inventory analyst. The person on the floor sees actual components and materials. By contrast, the computer inventory analyst peers at an abstraction of numbers on a display screen.

A diagram of both conventional and superior material requirements planning systems will highlight the differences. The typical order flow of the current system is shown in Exhibit 8–10. When the production

TYPICAL ORDER FLOW

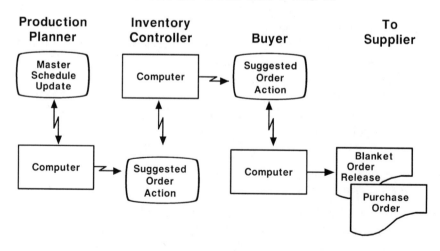

EXHIBIT 8–10

planner updates master schedules at a computer terminal, the material requirements planning system then displays suggested actions to the inventory controller. The inventory controller, in turn, updates the indicated orders by changing, adding, or deleting them. Next, the system displays the updated actions to the buyer, who selects a vendor and/or changes, adds, or deletes orders. Finally, the computer system issues purchase orders, usually one per item requested, to be mailed to the supplier. This process often takes a minimum of several days or it could even take weeks.

In more modern schedule communication, depicted in Exhibit 8–11, the production planner also updates the master schedule. Using rate-oriented scheduling in which both start and finish dates of the scheduling period and the rate of production are factored, he needs substantially less work to maintain the schedule. Manual overrides of the computer system are eliminated. Schedules of manufactured and purchased components and materials required to support the master schedule are delivered directly to each supplier. In some cases, requirements are transferred from computer to computer; in others, by magnetic media; and in still others by printed document. In the diagram, the time elapsed between master schedule updates and availability of new schedules is only a few hours or, perhaps, a day. The supplier schedule, for one or more items, is detailed by day for short-term requirements, and by week and month for longer term needs.

MODERN SCHEDULE COMMUNICATION

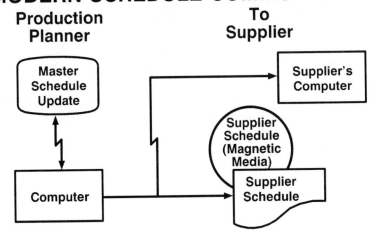

EXHIBIT 8–11

MULTIPLANT SYSTEMS

Most assembled-product manufacturers rely on a network of supply sources. A basic converter of ore, chemicals, or other raw materials, for example, supplies cast, rolled, extruded, or ingot products to other manufacturers. Thus, first-level (or uncut) products are converted by second-level suppliers into components. In turn, these components may be supplied to third-, fourth-, and fifth-level subassemblers and assemblers until, finally, one producer performs the final assembly operation. Some levels in the chain may be outside suppliers; others may be company-owned.

In the West, transmission of the latest requirements—from the end product, through all levels of the supply network, to the first-level converter—usually takes several weeks or months. Consequently, it is that long before any action is taken to produce new or increased component requirements at any level in the chain of suppliers. The results of long delays in communication are:

1. The suppliers in the chain, working hard to meet the most recent schedule, often produce items no longer required or needed later than originally planned. This means they are not manufacturing other, more urgent, components.

2. When the latest requirements become available, the pipeline is clogged with items in process that are no longer needed but usually continue to flow, delaying production of more urgent parts.

3. Little-used items, perhaps made from exotic materials, necessitate that weeks or months be added to paperwork processing lead time. Because of unreliable sales forecasts, suppliers and end-product users are unable to gamble on stocking inventories for these parts at each level.

4. For relatively common-use items, suppliers at each level are willing to stock inventories in anticipation of forecast demand. The maintenance of inventories, at all levels of the network, imposes the burden of inventory costs on each level and, ultimately, on the end-product supplier. In practice, forecasts for these inventories are also imprecise. Thus, when the supply network is clogged with the wrong item, the result can be that lead time will become as long as that for items not stocked at various levels in the network.

The ultimate solution to these problems is to turn the supply chain into a pipeline. This can best be accomplished either by the design of a single system that simultaneously updates requirements at all levels of the chain or by linking all supplier systems in the chain, level by level, with rapid response systems capable of receiving, processing, and passing current requirements to the next level in the chain. Such systems can reduce the time needed to pass requirements through the chain from weeks to a few days.

When broadcast of requirements to the chain is close to instantaneous, the chain can be transformed into a pipeline. Every supplier in the chain can simultaneously open its valves wider for some items and reduce the flow for others. Once this is achieved, lead time changes drastically. When all valves in the pipeline are adjusted simultaneously, response to the latest requirements can be almost immediate.

Decades ago, Andersen Consulting worked with several leading American companies, such as Outboard Marine Corporation and Hallmark Cards, to design and install multiplant requirements planning and operation scheduling systems. Although these systems are familiar to the West, they are not yet employed extensively to schedule and control the network of vendor factories and their suppliers. In Japan, leading manufacturers, such as Yamaha, Toyota, and their major suppliers, have been using multiplant computer systems for years to simultaneously schedule all levels of the network. They have learned to cut lead time through the network from months to days by taking all excess inventory out of the pipeline and using multiplant requirements systems. For example, the maximum lead time at Yamaha Motors has been reduced to 20 workdays. This is the total production time, from stocks of iron ore to shipping of motorcycles.

It will be years—even decades—before supplier-customer cooperation and new computer systems are operational in more than a few Western companies. Electronic data interchange between companies and their suppliers is a first step in this direction. Some North American automobile manufacturers—General Motors for example—have experienced major reductions in the time required to transmit requirements. As top executives insist on it, networks for multiplant requirements planning will become operational within the next decade. For those combining supplier programs with multiplant planning, target reductions of lead times and inventories in the supplier network should be 90 percent.

TRANSITION SYSTEMS:
LIVING WITH THE REAL WORLD

In most factories, modifying operations, including the coordination of changes in supplier plants, can take several years. In fact, the need to make improvements to maintain a position as the superior manufacturer never ends. For this reason, a new, superior system must include features of a less-than-ideal factory and office operations, which will continue to exist during a transition period. The modern systems and procedures should also be designed to support new cells, focused subplants, and vendors who have also implemented superior manufacturing techniques. This section addresses the issue of transaction reporting, particularly as it relates to operating problems. The eventual goal of superior manufacturing should be, however, to eliminate problems, and thus problem reporting.

Even in pilot cells and subplants, results are often so good that certain problems are immediately eliminated. The types of project performance charts illustrated in Exhibit 8–12 can be used to analyze performance. For example, a chart might track the time required for machine setup/ changeover. In this case, a full-time project team to improve setup tooling can be expected to initially produce a big one-time improvement. Thereafter, when the team moves on to other machines, additional improvement will not be experienced nor will performance worsen. This is because permanent improvements have been achieved by modifying tooling, fixtures, and layout rather than by expecting people to work harder and faster.

There is no advantage to reporting and tracking the performance pattern (see Exhibit 8–12, the upper left) when the remaining activity is no longer material, i.e., when machine changeover has been reduced from

PERFORMANCE CHART PATTERNS

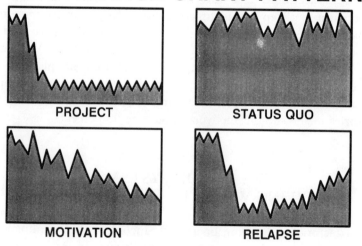

PROJECT   STATUS QUO

MOTIVATION   RELAPSE

EXHIBIT 8–12

hours to seconds and when there is no reasonable expectation of further improvement (for instance, no one is available to work on enhancing the design). Charting systems have been effective in highlighting problems and opportunities for improvement, especially when conditions are favorable for motivating responsible personnel. Such conditions arise, for example, when:

1. Executive and middle management is involved in reviewing charted activities and demand that improvements be made.
2. Personnel responsible for improvements are trained in the methods and techniques of improvement design and have the time and budgets available to implement changes.

In Exhibit 8–12, the pattern of the motivation chart reflects a steady, but relatively gradual, improvement (for example, a reduction of the amount of time required for setup). It is a typical realistic depiction of the slow pace of the part-time improvement assignments. Operating personnel rarely have the time and resources available to make the rapid progress expected of a full-time team.

In many factories, a majority of performance charts show that no improvement has occurred in a particular activity (see Exhibit 8–12, "status quo"). Reporting and charting of these types of activities, year in and year out, is clearly wasteful. Obviously, one or more ingredients of success is missing—management may not aggressively demand improvement, people may not have enough time or training to design improvements, or the activities may be too immaterial to warrant attention.

The objective of superior manufacturing is to eliminate the need for most reporting and tracking systems. This means temporarily discontinuing reporting by cell, subplant, or vendor as soon as improvements reduce an activity or problem to the point of its being immaterial. Eventually, data base provisions for recording unnecessary performance should be dropped entirely, thus simplifying computer system operations. A potential problem of eliminating reporting and tracking systems is that activities considered no longer crucial might suddenly become important again, as illustrated by the "relapse" pattern in Exhibit 8–12. Reporting and tracking systems applicable to relapse are temporary and focused.

TEMPORARY FOCUSED SYSTEMS

"If it's not broke, don't fix it!" These words of wisdom can be altered slightly to apply to manufacturing: "If there's no problem or opportunity, don't report it." Conversely, new problems and new opportunities will arise, making tracking and reporting necessary until these too are no longer important. In the past, the main thrust of reporting systems was massive review of all business transactions and reporting them to levels appropriate to each tier of management, and reporting performance outside these ranges to the responsible area, upper management, and staff analysts. The latter's role has been to understand what is happening in the factory, report his findings to upper management, and require action by factory management.

The problems that these systems and procedures tried to solve were that:

1. The size of the factory had become too large. Managers and executives could no longer be knowledgeable about all aspects of operations and, thus, were no longer able to make informed decisions concerning them.

2. Operating personnel did not have the training, authority, responsibility, and qualifications to manage their operations successfully.

3. Many operating problems were recurrent. These included excessive inventories, defects, late production, material and component shortages, machine downtime, and rising costs of manufacturing.

In the new, superior factory, these problems are solved by the formation of several smaller subplants within the factory; by upgrading the training qualifications of manufacturing managers, foremen, supervisors, and all direct and indirect personnel; and by structuring the subplant organization to place every resource necessary to its successful operation under the authority and responsibility of subplant management.

Since the new, superior subplant virtually eliminates all material problems and opportunities, the need for supporting systems and procedures shifts. It moves from permanent, massive reporting to temporary small-scale reporting of transient conditions as they occur. For example, a subplant has reduced setup in all machines to a few seconds each. Thus, reporting on setup would add cost to the operation; however, a new machine requires an hour's setup. Until this setup is reduced to seconds, reporting and tracking of this setup cost lets executive management know how well the supervisor is doing his job.

Clearly, this type of reporting is appropriate only when subplant managers and their personnel find it helpful to the process of designing improvements; the information should have no value for executives. Some transient problems and opportunities are unique to the process area of the factory. For instance, when the painting subplant manager and his staff employ methods that reduce pounds of paint required per product, it may be helpful to track their achievements temporarily. This detailed level of reporting is not appropriate for executive management; executives should only expect to review the continuous reduction of *total* costs of operation per unit of production. Thus, only when costs increase or stabilize would top management need further explanation.

PRODUCT COST: FACT OR FICTION?

Through simplification and automation, manufacturers, worldwide, are making quantum leaps in improving factory operations. Some companies are even pioneering the first computer integrated manufacturing systems. Virtually every company, however, continues to use traditional cost and performance reporting concepts applicable when direct labor was a major component of product cost, and when purchasing practice centered on frequent changes from one supplier to another in order to buy at the lowest possible price.

Companies involved in implementing superior manufacturing techniques have long recognized that traditional methods of accounting have not provided the type of information necessary to operate their factories and to make strategic decisions. In retrospect, most now see that many shortcomings of the methods used were due to poor manufacturing methods. Now that new factory methods are being implemented, the need for corresponding cost management systems is becoming more urgent, but the required system is simpler and, thus, more practical.

Today's best cost systems calculate the elements of cost to the ultimate degree of detail and summarize them by product. The results rarely represent useful information for making business decisions. Some of the problems are that:

1. Large expenditures for business operations are not considered to be product costs. For example, general and administrative, sales, and engineering costs are often several times more than theoretical product cost.

2. Large amounts of manufacturing overhead are charged to operations that might, only in one fleeting instant, represent some reasonable allocation basis. However, in day-to-day operations, the basis often does not accurately reflect the actual area benefiting from the cost incurred.

3. Direct labor standards are usually the base of labor costs to which manufacturing overhead is applied. Standards rarely come close to

actual labor cost incurred. Further, since direct labor is only 5 to 10 percent of the cost of manufacturing, it is questionable whether overhead should be apportioned to this small and often inaccurate base.

4. Costs of depreciation rarely match a realistic reduction of the asset value, considering its actual useful life. Most machines are usable for 20 years or more, especially when a maintenance program includes periodic rebuilding and low-cost modifications to update their basic capacities.

5. Direct labor efficiency reporting is designed to encourage management to keep workers and machines occupied rather than to eliminate unnecessary costs and unneeded inventory. In U.S. plants, labor efficiency reporting is one of the major contributors to the decline of this country's industrial base. Approximately 75 percent of accounting and data processing expenditures are aimed at controlling direct labor, which, as previously noted, is now only 5 to 10 percent of our manufacturing cost of goods sold, and 2 to 5 percent of retail price. As well, labor efficiency reporting causes factory supervision and employees to think of ways to "beat the system," for example, by overstating quantities produced and understating the time spent in production, and by allowing defective items to pass off as satisfactory.

6. Management attention to inventory is centered on, and usually limited to, the balance sheet. The direct, variable costs of carrying inventory are usually not included in the income statement as a component of the cost of manufacturing. Product cost calculations, therefore, usually ignore the inventory costs of various products.

7. The most frequently stated purposes of product cost calculations are to value inventory, to determine prices, and to make decisions to change product lines. It is, however, rare to find a company whose product prices closely approximate some costing formula—where the sales price of every product is a standard percentage over product cost. The market and competition are much more important factors in setting price than are product costs.

Leading companies are currently implementing the first of the new generation of cost management systems that will replace the relics that have served us since the early 1900s.

Superior manufacturers take an aggressive approach to solving the product cost dilemma. First and foremost, they undertake cost reduction, with special emphasis on the greatest elements of it, including those not considered to be direct manufacturing costs. Second, they move services provided by staff and indirect personnel into product-oriented subplant organizations, whenever practical. Thus, actual service costs need no longer be allocated. Services are the direct responsibility of, and are charged to, the subplant manager. Other costs, traditionally allocated to the area, are also better controlled to make it possible to charge actual costs to the subplant. Utilities, plant maintenance, and depreciation are examples.

After overhead costs are focused and reduced to a minimum, the remaining expense becomes a much smaller fiscal problem. Although allocation methods are numerous, depending upon the industry and product, it is important for accountants to think beyond allocation by direct labor only, which has unfortunately been a tradition in the West.

Given the new factory environment, the cost management system of the future should include:

1. New methods for allocating costs of business operations and expenses that cannot be focused
2. Elimination of primary reliance on cost reporting for business management in favor of an improved blend of quantitative data *and* cost information
3. Comparison of current costs to targets for improvement
4. Highlighting of those costs that do not add value to the product
5. New methods for considering how to treat equipment depreciation to better spread the useful life of a machine over the quantity of products actually produced
6. Simplification of the system, in contrast to previous systems, with corresponding reduction in the costs of accounting and data processing

There is, however, a distinct danger that the tradition of cost accounting may lead a company into more complex, rather than simpler, systems. For example, pursuing accounting's holy grail—actual product cost—always entails ever increasing levels of detail. External factors such as market demand can and do cause actual costs to fluctuate wildly from the standard cost. Thus, the marketplace can (and does) invalidate huge amounts of effort spent in developing decision criteria and operating plans based on standard costs and demand forecasts. If the calculated cost is merely a representative average value that presumes both a certain level of demand for the individual product and a certain level of equipment and factory utilization for a family of products, or even of all products, management should minimize the detail and, therefore, the effort and cost of developing the approximate cost.

Cost accountants often exaggerate the potential for making erroneous decisions based on misleading cost information. The classic example is the decision whether to buy an item, or to manufacture it on an expensive new machine burdened with an unrealistic amount of overhead. In reality, the managers of most factories are knowledgeable enough to recognize the real economics involved. That is, that reducing the work the machine must perform will not decrease overhead costs, thus direct comparison of purchase price versus manufacturing cost is nonsensical. In the new, small focused factory, it becomes even easier for the manager to understand the real economics of the operation.

For most companies, even a basic modern cost accounting system is several years down the road. The lack of factory automation is often considered the reason for poor productivity; however, complexity in our plants is the real problem. But as demonstrated by successful systems that exist today in simplified factory environments, the systems and technological issues can be solved.

COMPUTER INTEGRATED MANUFACTURING

One of the new areas in which some companies are aggressively competing is the ability to respond quickly to customer demands in both delivery and design. A company that can design new products faster than its competitors has a tremendous competitive advantage. Or if a company can respond to a rush order in days or weeks while his competitors require months, it will quickly capture market share and high-margin business. Many leading-edge companies are now adopting a competitive strategy to attack lengthy lead times in their efforts to keep pace with Eastern competitors. In most large organizations, all aspects of computer integrated manufacturing must be addressed if the companies are going to survive, grow, and prosper as reduced lead times for product design and delivery are an inevitable way of life.

Computer integrated manufacturing (CIM) is a relatively new concept, having been introduced in the early 1970s. Although no generally accepted definition exists today, the basic premise is to apply computers and information technology to the engineering and manufacturing activities to maximize the performance of people and equipment. This does *not* mean the total elimination of labor, but rather the redeployment of labor to work effectively with automation.

From a technical perspective, computer integrated manufacturing consists of several elements:

- *Product engineering systems,* including computer-aided design (CAD), computer-aided engineering (CAE), and group technology (GT). These systems assist the design engineer in creating accurate product design data in less time and at less cost than traditional methods.

- *Process engineering systems,* including computer-aided process planning (CAPP) and computer-aided manufacturing (CAM). These systems permit the manufacturing engineer to generate process plans and instructions for computer-controlled equipment more quickly, consistently, and accurately than typical manual methods.

- *Manufacturing planning and control systems,* frequently referred to as MRPII. These systems assist in planning and prioritizing delivery of raw materials, components, and subassemblies in support of master schedule and customer demand. Many companies are finding that MRPII and just-in-time (JIT) are complementary when MRPII is used for *planning* and JIT is used to manage *execution* in the factory.

- *Factory support systems,* such as scheduling, tool management, maintenance management, and direct/distributed numerical control (DNC). These systems concentrate on having supporting resources available when they are needed.

- *Factory execution systems,* including area and cell control systems. These systems relieve the foreman or factory supervisor of the many non-value-added activities for coordinating the sequence of events in the factory, so he can concentrate on helping operators produce a quality product.

- *Factory automation,* or the automated, computer-controlled equipment that processes, moves, and stores material in the factory.

- *Information networks* that store and transmit commands and data among the systems, people, and equipment.

The good, the bad, and the ugly sides of computer integrated manufacturing have been widely debated. Unfortunately, most manufacturers have reacted to this phenomenon by trying to determine *if* computer integrated manufacturing is right for them. Rather, they should be trying to determine *which* aspects are right for them. The secret to success involves a three-phase approach: (1) simplification, (2) automation, and (3) integration. Most companies that have tried computer integrated manufacturing and failed did not simplify the manufacturing process before applying automation. The "quick technical fix" approach, that is, trying to solve the problems of manufacturing competition by applying high technology to an inefficient production system, does not work. Automating an inefficient system is much more difficult than automating one that has been simplified.

Simplification streamlines the organization, product designs, and production processes, eliminating waste and unnecessary complexity. Organizational boundaries are realigned to improve communication within the company, and products are redesigned to make them suitable for automated production. Results include better use of factory and warehouse space and significant reductions in inventory, machine setup time, direct and indirect labor costs, and manufacturing lead time. By simplification alone, organizations have reduced their inventory and production lead time by 90 percent, their setup time 75 percent, their manufacturing space 50 percent, and their labor by 10 to 30 percent. Some have also improved quality by 75 to 90 percent. These benefits help pay for subsequent stages of computer integrated manufacturing.

Automation addresses the manufacturing process itself as well as the business functions that support it. Appropriately applied, automated engineering and production technology can improve a simplified and efficient environment. In some instances, selected use of automation can help in the simplification process and lay the foundation for integration. Automation provides greater design productivity, improves product quality, eliminates tedious and hazardous tasks, reduces lead time for product development and manufacturing, and reduces direct and indirect labor costs. Automated business applications provide timely and accurate information to manage operations efficiently.

Integration links all processes using computers, communication networks, and, on the shop floor, material-handling devices and robots. Successful integration allows companies to control and manage manufacturing and engineering information efficiently by eliminating barriers across departments and functions. As well, it increases a company's capacity for productivity, responsiveness, control, and innovation.

Since significant benefits are achieved through simplification alone, why should a manufacturing company consider the next two stages—automation and integration? The answer requires analyzing the following key factors:

1. *Product line flexibility*—the degree of product customization required to meet the demands of the marketplace

2. *Process precision*—the acceptable degree of variation from product and process specifications

3. *Safety and security*—the level of risk posed by the process to the human operator, the environment, and the product itself

4. *Information requirements*—process quality and schedule performance, process instructions, regulatory tracking requirements, and status information

5. *Process flexibility*—the frequency and degree of change in the design and mix of items produced

In general, the higher the degree of required excellence of these five factors, the higher the applicability of automation and integration. Noticeably missing from the list of factors is the reduction of labor. The authors believe that the labor reduction factor is often less significant than the other five factors. Consider the following examples:

1. A large lawn-care equipment manufacturing company needed to dramatically reduce costs, as well as product inventory levels, to remain competitive against foreign manufacturers. The product line (and hence, the process) was relatively stable; quality was important, but precision was not particularly challenging. The process posed no abnormally high safety or security risks, and the information flow, though fast, was not complex. In this case, a concerted effort to simplify the process had a significant impact on improving the company's costs, while automation and integration were required only in relatively few situations.

2. A major producer of complex, large machined parts and assemblies for military use needed to control costs, broaden its product base, and reduce delivery lead time. To accomplish this, the product and process engineering time, which accounted for at least half of the delivery lead time, had to be reduced. Due to increasingly tighter tolerance requirements, the capabilities of the manufacturing processes had to improve. Furthermore, the equipment had to perform a wider range of tasks to produce the newer products that were being introduced. Finally, the tracking requirements mandated by the customer increased the volume and velocity of the information flow. Simplification helped this manufacturer, but improved engineering, production, and tracking mechanisms were also needed. As a result, many computer integrated manufacturing tools such as computer-aided design, computer-aided manufacturing, computer-aided process planning, scheduling, direct numerical control, computer-controlled equipment, and realtime information networks are being installed today. Results thus far show that lead times and overhead

costs should be reduced by 20 percent or more, making this manufacturer a leader in its market.

Each of these companies is succeeding in meeting its strategic goals, but their solutions are quite different. In both cases, however, the companies first considered *which* elements of computer integrated manufacturing were appropriate for them. They then proceeded to follow the simplify-automate-integrate approach to making computer integrated manufacturing work for them. It is important for each manufacturing company to focus its attention on the simplify-automate-integrate process for improving cost, productivity, quality and flexibility. The individual tools themselves are not the answer but rather the mechanism employed. To sum up, the vast majority of today's computer systems and manual procedures do not support operating with small inventories, lot sizes, and clerical staff. Manufacturing software systems with just-in-time features are the low-cost way to provide new systems applicable to the superior manufacturer's factory operations. As computer costs continue to decline in relationship to processing capability, computer integrated manufacturing systems are the inevitable tide of the future. Simplified factory *and* office operations are a vital prerequisite to achieving superior computer integrated manufacturing.

9

■□□

The Step-by-Step Approach

DESCRIBING THE CONCEPTS of superior manufacturing is not very difficult, nor is reporting case studies of the specific changes to achieve it. But explaining how to design and implement superior factory and systems improvements step by step, however, appears to be virtually impossible, based on available methodology. Most how-to books and articles focus on what is easy: gimmicks and training. These may be important, but by itself, each represents only a small part of what is necessary. The objectives of this chapter are to contribute to the body of knowledge of step-by-step methodology to superior manufacturing and to explore dissenting viewpoints on gimmicks and training issues. The methodology that is overviewed fills a separate series of proprietary Andersen Consulting books. Clearly, it is not practical to discuss it in full detail. It *is* possible however, to outline the criteria for success and identify the framework of the methodology.

MANAGEMENT INVOLVEMENT

The factories in which Andersen Consulting has done productivity improvement projects have had varying degrees of success. But in every case, the degree of success has been easily attributable to the intensity of involvement at all levels of management, especially that of top executives. In many cases, executives want to see proof of the success of our concepts of superior manufacturing in a single pilot cell in their factory. Then, they say, they would broaden the scope of the project to include the entire factory. The validity of most simple, basic concepts, however, should not be questioned, as hundreds of companies have proven that they work. Experienced manufacturing executives almost instantly understand why these concepts are successful. On the other hand, executives unable to wholeheartedly support such improvement projects are probably not the leaders who will move their companies to the forefront of superior manufacturing. The executive and his management team must have the commitment to say "*when* it works," not "*if* it works." They, not the consultant, must be responsible for the degree of improvement achieved. It's far more productive when an executive says his company will learn these new concepts in one or more pilot cells or assembly subplants, build and train a design team, and then expand the program and the team to encompass the rest of the business.

Management involvement cannot be limited to one-time pronouncements of support. Radical changes in operations and systems demand active management participation at all stages of the project if the knowledge and skills of managers are to keep pace with that of their subordinates and competitors. Only if executive management lets it be known that superior manufacturing is necessary for survival and prosperity will an entire organization aggressively support the development of new operational methods. This does not mean that some individuals in the organization will passively accept change or actively resist it. Although it is human to fear and resist the new, it is not good business to tolerate managers who do not energetically contribute to achieving the goals and targets established by top executives. Only management itself can weed out the passive and active resisters of progress.

In one company, a high-level executive made a wager that a particular new technology would not work in his plant. Despite involvement of the company's top executive, he actively worked to minimize the benefits of the productivity project by resisting change at every opportunity. As a result, the accomplishments were much less than those of other companies in which some of the same changes were implemented. Early identification and removal of such individuals will accelerate the rate of progress and increase the benefits achieved. Unfortunately, this type of executive is more common than would be suspected, and behaves recalcitrantly for one of several reasons:

1. He feels threatened by the possibility that the project team may "show him up" by producing results better than those he has achieved in his years at the factory.

2. His ego is too large. No one—except him—has ever made substantive changes in the factory, and he is incapable of accepting ideas from others.

3. He is intellectually incapable of discarding outdated manufacturing concepts and accepting new, radically different ideas.

If every conceivable step is taken to convert this executive to the new manufacturing technology, and he continues to resist change, he should be moved to a different position. Then he could be replaced by a person more attuned to adopting new, improved manufacturing practices. The removal of active and passive resisters is management's first and most vital area of concern. Its second most critical task is to provide a budget to finance improvements. Before any work is done to define the potential costs of any improvement projects, executive management should budget annual amounts for personnel, relocation, tooling, and equipment costs. None of these expenditures can be precisely detailed until the improvements are designed, which may take several months. Initially, funds for designing and implementing improvements could come from the postponement of warehouse and factory additions. The investment in more facilities for storage and processing does not compare favorably to reducing inventory by 50 to 75 percent, and space by 50 percent.

Budgeted funds must ultimately be allocated to improvement projects in specific factory areas. Except in rare cases when a company can afford to fund reorganization of a complete factory, priorities must be assigned to various areas of the plant. In a large factory, with twenty areas, it may only be practical to work on four or five per year. At this rate, the project would take several years to complete. By then, the next generation of improvements should be started. The question that executive management must answer each year is which improvement projects to fund.

WHERE TO START? THE PROFIT MOTIVE

Although there are several alternative strategies for determining an implementation sequence, the overriding concern should be profit. The areas of the factory with the best potential for reducing operating costs and investment with the least effort and expenditures will obviously have the greatest beneficial impact on profitability. Superior executives understand this concept. They and experienced consultants also find it reasonably easy to know where to start an improvement program. They do not delay beginning the actual design work in favor of planning or strategy projects that could last for several weeks or months.

On our first visit to a factory, we often spend an hour or two with executive management. Then we take a fast, walk-through plant tour. Based on this brief overview of operations, we are usually prepared to suggest where in the factory to start and what kind of project organization is necessary to complete design and implementation of improvements in a relatively short period of time. The key questions consultants initially ask are:

1. Which final (assembled or packaged) products or product lines have the highest value of production?
2. Which types of machined and fabricated components have the highest value of production?
3. Which types of purchased items have the highest usage value?

Most of the time, similar production processes, such as three final assembly lines, have different degrees of automation and varied levels of personnel productivity. Nevertheless, the percentage of improvement in these areas usually differs by only plus or minus 5 to 10 percent. Thus, it is usually a safe assumption that the area that processes the highest value of production will have the greatest payback. Even if the choice of one of the top two candidates is wrong, there is likely to be only a relatively small difference in the resulting profit improvement potential. The issue is not whether or not a large increase in profitability will result, but whether the greatest improvement will be initially achieved.

When we tour a factory, we pay special attention to high-value production areas to assess whether or not the usual ranges of improvement would be achievable here. We rarely conclude that the high costs of improvement or limited potential benefits should dictate starting projects in other areas instead. In most factories, multiple initial projects achieve a vertical integration (a "pipeline") of improvements in areas ranging from the vendor of raw materials to completion of final products. For example, the areas for possible change include:

1. Final assembly (or packaging) process for a product or product family
2. A selected subassembly process for one of the types of major subassemblies used on the product or product family selected
3. Selected types of manufactured components used on the final product/product family and/or major subassembly

4. Selected suppliers of purchased components and materials used on one or more of the final product/product family and/or major subassembly

5. Purchased, manufactured, and finished goods storage

6. Selected machines on which to perform setup and maintenance improvement projects, usually corresponding to the areas selected for a type of manufactured component

In many companies, the personnel and budgets required for a project encompassing all of these areas are not available. But most projects should include at least three or four of them to ensure the best possible degree of successful integration. The selection of areas in which to start is not based only on potential for profit improvement or a vertical slice of operations starting with outside suppliers and ending with finished goods, but includes other considerations such as:

1. Manager and supervisor enthusiasm for participating in the project. Ultimately, the degree of success and the difficulty of achieving goals will depend on the support (or resistance) of these key individuals.

2. Management priorities, which may be based on quality and delivery problems or new product plans.

3. The amount of effort required to design and implement improvements.

4. Existing plans for automation/reorganization of areas.

5. The size of machines and equipment that would have to be moved and, therefore, the cost to move them.

FULL-TIME TEAM

The "quality circle" approach to productivity improvement is one example of an often ineffectual gimmick. Groups of employees who meet a few minutes per month cannot produce the same magnitude of benefits that highly trained, experienced, full-time teams can. Nevertheless, there is no reason to exclude employee groups in an improvement program, nor should a full-time project team serve as a substitute for management and employee participation. Every aspect of the project must be reviewed with all those involved, and their ideas and reservations must be part of the process of designing and implementing changes. When this involvement is productive, it does not take an inordinate amount of time. For example, one project team member prepares sketches of proposed changes and presents a design to all other individuals involved. This team member then records their ideas and concerns and incorporates any necessary variations in the design. Once this is done, the plan is again reviewed until a final design has been successfully implemented.

The organization of the project team, illustrated in Exhibit 9–1, is fairly conventional. The project manager reports to an executive, typically the vice president of manufacturing. For projects spanning several organizations, such as design engineering, materials management, and manufacturing, the executive responsible might be the president, or there may be separate, coordinated teams reporting to the vice presidents of each area. Too often, direct responsibility for productivity improvement is placed too low in the organization. This reduces the vital, ongoing involvement of management and the effectiveness of the project team.

The steering committee includes representatives of executive management from areas of the company from which participation and cooperation are desired. It should not expect to be a decision-making body, although, at times, it may be used to see that decisions are made. All important issues on which decisions might be required should be discussed with involved executives, individually, before any committee meetings. Thus, the purpose of committee meetings is typically to inform members of areas in which they may or may not have direct responsibility or involvement. They also provide an opportunity to learn the concerns

PROJECT ORGANIZATION

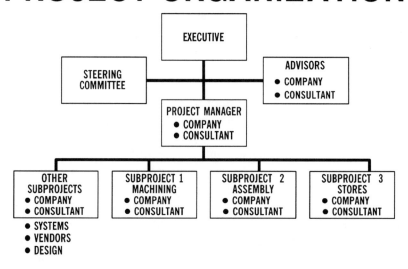

EXHIBIT 9–1

and suggestions of members not directly involved and furnish a report on progress.

By uncovering committee concerns and suggestions, the project team continuously develops ways to eliminate or minimize issues and modify proposals or incorporate them into the improved design. When this is successfully accomplished, specific decisions are rarely necessary since every area is worked on, clarified, and improved until it is no longer an issue.

On many productivity projects, union representatives are steering committee members. Managements that worry about union resistance to improvement are wrong in most cases. The union rank and file, and their representatives, usually understand the need for improvement in order to survive. They naturally want to preserve their benefits, resist demands for performance that would unreasonably fatigue or endanger workers, and earn a fair share of the gains derived from increased productivity.

It is rare for the union to have unrealistic expectations about productivity improvement. It usually understands that this process means reducing employee hours per unit of finished product. The best executives work hard to preserve as many jobs as practical and even add new ones. Whenever practical, productivity improvement projects should consider reducing product sale prices by some or all of the savings of greater productivity. The objective should be to either increase worldwide market share or else to invest in new products and product lines, thus making new jobs available. Those executives who favor keeping secrets from the union are usually misguided. Secrets are almost always discovered or revealed more quickly than could be imagined. Full disclosure of planned changes speeds up the process of identifying which issues must be formally negotiated. It certainly helps both management and the union to eliminate misunderstandings that could cause unwarranted confrontation.

Exhibit 9–1 depicts the use of consultants as advisers to the executive, in the role of co-manager of the project team, and as workers on each of several subprojects. It is important to consider the help of a qualified consultant to:

1. Avoid reinventing the wheel, in terms of dealing with problems that have already been solved or devising solutions inferior to those previously invented in other companies.
2. Obtain experience and methodology for conducting improvement projects.
3. Provide the necessary manpower to accomplish as much as possible, as soon as possible. Often, a company does not have enough personnel to completely staff a project and prefers to use a consultant as

temporary manpower, not on the permanent payroll after improvements have been implemented.

4. Bring fresh perspective to the project team.

5. Gain easier access to executive management than internal project teams. While this should not be true, there is a logical reason for it. Executive management understands that the most cost-effective way to benefit from the use of a consultant is to maintain frequent and substantive contact. The consultant often helps company personnel win approval for improvements that management has not previously taken the time to properly understand and evaluate.

Although we are certainly biased by our experience over the past 10 years, we believe that the best consultant is a worker, not an educator or adviser. While these latter two make valuable contributions to any project, they have considerably less effect than full-time consultants in the hands-on roles of co-project managers, designers, and implementors. Note that we distinguish between the educator and trainer. Most training programs with which we are familiar are educational. Education is concerned with teaching general applicability. Training, by contrast, teaches the industrial participant, step by step, how to do his job. A competent consultant brings hands-on manpower to a project, as well as a general education in superior manufacturing, standard training programs in improvement project methodology, and proficiency in developing training programs for the new factory, office, and systems operations developed by the project team.

To be most successful, every project team needs the periodic participation of an adviser. This person should have years of experience in manufacturing and have taken part in numerous productivity improvement projects in different types of companies. In a few hours, he can suggest approaches for improvement that may otherwise take months or years to recognize. The best advisers are members of a team that includes the workers capable of implementing the suggestions.

As previously mentioned, there are various types of potential subprojects in different areas of the factory and office. The typical manufacturing company should try to accomplish improvements in the mainstream of manufacturing, assembly, machining, and storage. Some of the other potential areas that could be included in the scope of the project are systems, office operations, engineering design improvement, and vendor programs.

The individual targeted to be the manager of the new, focused subplant should be someone who is actively involved in the project. This would be best accomplished by assigning him to the full-time project team. For a project whose scope is a single subplant, this individual might be the project manager. In one spanning multiple subplants, those targeted to be managers could be project leaders of the subprojects for their respective subplants. At a bare minimum, they must be involved in every step of the design process and must be given full responsibility for successful implementation.

Several functional areas are expected to make substantial contributions to the project on an as-required basis. For example, financial and cost accounting personnel should become intimately familiar with the figures behind projected costs and benefits. Their involvement assures support of the logic of the figures, as well as helps the project team present the "numbers" in accounting and financial reporting structures most familiar to executive management, through their day-to-day use of similar financial formats.

The plant maintenance manager is another person who makes a major contribution to the project. His familiarity with moving and construction initiatives should make it easy for him to provide quick, initial projected costs and to follow up with more precise internal and external contractor estimates. Marketing personnel should also be involved in reviewing reduced levels of finished goods inventories and in responding rapidly to customer needs resulting from planned cutbacks in manufacturing lead times. Tangible benefits of reduced inventory investment or projected increased sales due to improved customer service should be developed and/or supported by the marketing organization.

The people in the project organization who produce the design and support the implementation are the analysts who work in the subprojects. Poor project manning decisions must be avoided to ensure that superior operations will be designed and implemented in a reasonable amount of time. Common mistakes and problems are:

1. Assignment of marginal, rather than the best, personnel to the project.
2. Part-time assignment to the project. This rarely works because the time devoted is never the amount anticipated. Usually, demands of the regular job take priority.
3. Assignment of personnel to the project as analysts who consider themselves "above working." They expect only to supervise.
4. Assignment to subprojects in the area for which the person is usually responsible. This often makes it difficult for an individual to

see the possibility of improving something he designed. Someone with a fresh perspective usually produces better results.

The qualifications for productivity improvement project teams are so important that a formal, but simple, procedure for evaluating candidates should be considered.

PROJECT PHASES

Typically, the three main types of projects most often undertaken in factories are for: improved operations, design, and implementation; short-term improvements (e.g., setup reduction); and plantwide master plans (described in Chapter 3). Projects to improve operations are usually performed in three phases: (1) planning and initial design, (2) design, and (3) implementation. Usually, the areas selected for improvement are determined before phase 1 begins. The objective of the fast-moving six- to eight-week initial phase is to perform minimal design work in the areas selected to be able to:

1. Prove that improvements can be made and determine the specific changes that would be required. This would encompass designing new processes for a small, but representative, part of each area.
2. Quantify approximately the potential costs and financial benefits of the project.
3. Finalize a project scope and work plan for designing improvements for the total area.

At the end of phase 1, there is a checkpoint which allows management the opportunity to change project plans, and also enables it to better understand the specific types of change applicable to the area. For most factories, only the first project should need a phase 1 to satisfy executive management of its economic viability, and of the technical feasibility of the types of improvements that will be designed. Thereafter, it should be possible to complete all other areas of a factory, by performing only the tasks in the design and implementation phases.

In a phase 1 project, a limited sample of workstations are designed that may represent three to six stations on a 30-station assembly line. Their designs may be to approximate scale, and all design problems may not be answered. In phase 2, the final design is completed for all 30 workstations and every design issue is answered. For most projects, this phase takes about four months. When the project scope is limited to one small area of a small factory, however, less time may be required. Implementation of the new design usually takes two to three months. In factories that need a lot of new capital equipment, it is not unusual to encounter lead times of more than a year. Most plants, however, require relatively little new equipment; thus, cells can be implemented at once, with temporary inefficiencies, while awaiting one or two new pieces of equipment with long lead times.

On short-term improvement projects (for example, setup and inventory reduction), design and implementation phases of one improvement may overlap with another. Incidentally, some companies have only performed short-term improvement projects and then have failed to pursue longer term master plans. The results have been disappointing as compared to those of companies determined to continuously work on improvement. The outcomes of one small cell or new assembly line can be far more impressive when the complete network of cells, lines, and vendors of all components have also adopted new, superior techniques.

Most companies need a vision and a road map (a plantwide master plan) for reorganizing the factory from its present layout to a new one requiring 50 percent less space. For the average plant, completing the initial road map requires about two months; however, as mentioned in Chapter 2, it is outdated almost as fast as it can be produced. Thus, the new layout would be of relatively little value, unless the organization and procedures for maintaining it are put into place.

In most instances, work on a plantwide plan should start sometime after completion of the first phase of the pilot project. The reasons for not beginning earlier are that:

1. All levels of management will gain confidence in the potential for space improvements and other economic benefits when they see the partial designs created in earlier phases or projects.

2. The project team will gain knowledge and experience in phase 1 that will be helpful in the development of the plantwide plan.

3. Nothing should be permitted to delay the start of projects that will increase profitability. Often, however, companies spend months in strategic planning without designing and implementing a single improvement.

We are sometimes asked to do a master plan as a company's initial productivity project. Although this is technically feasible to carry out, the result often fails to recognize the importance of layout changes and drastic space reductions. Management, supervisors, and workers cannot accept change of this magnitude without thoroughly understanding the concepts and seeing them defined in the detail that is first practical in phase 2 design projects or following actual implementation in phase 3. Where master plans have been produced as the first company project, even with well-read, informed, and progressive management, the result is usually a series of compromises between the project team and operating personnel. This leads to a plan that is far from optimal, and excessive amounts of space are provided as a contingency to protect against the unknown.

The master plan project should logically be developed no later than the end of the first phase 2 design project. This stage produces a layout for the first pilot areas. The master plan identifies where these will be placed in the ideal factory. If the timing of the master plan is right, the pilot areas could be set up directly in their ideal locations, without moving the same area two or more times. If only a few pieces of large equipment require relocation, and moving and disconnect/connect costs are nominal, master planning could be delayed with some cost penalty for resituating some operations more than once.

PLANNING CHART SEGMENTS, TASKS, AND STEPS

Planning charts, a simplified form of critical path network, should form the basis for scheduling and managing any project. The planning chart overview, as seen in Exhibit 9–2, is the highest level of illustration of the

PROCESS DESIGN PLANNING CHART

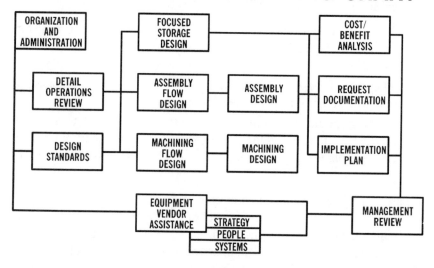

EXHIBIT 9–2

step-by-step process of a phase 2 factory design. Without detailing all the information presented, the most important types of segments are:

1. Organization and administration
2. Detailed review of all factory and related systems operations
3. Overall conceptual design of assembly and machining
4. Detailed design of assembly, machining, and storage
5. Wrap-up activities, including cost/benefit analysis, implementation plan, and management review

Each level of organization depicted on the overview has its own planning chart for tasks that make up that segment. Every task is then further documented with a series of steps and the associated procedures and products. Exhibit 9–3 is the task-level planning chart for organization and administration of the design phase. Space does not permit discussion of all such charts or their tasks. There are a few points related to organization and administration, however, that must be covered.

1. In this segment, project organization and administration tasks are performed in parallel with actual work in the factory. A mistake many project teams make is spending too much time in the office and too little at the site. The project analysts should be on the factory floor the first day on the job.

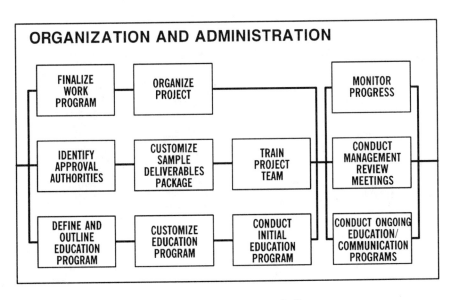

EXHIBIT 9–3

2. Project management's single most important product in this segment is a customized sample of the package of deliverables that must be produced by each analyst. It should eliminate any confusion about what work must be done and what format must be used when presenting results to all levels of management.

3. Also in this segment education programs are customized and conducted for all appropriate operating personnel. Standard training programs are used to train only project team members in the methodology of the improvement project. During implementation, phase 3, special programs are developed and conducted to train personnel in the new methods of factory operations.

Exhibits 9–4 and 9–5 are task-level planning charts for the machining detailed design segment. They are included, without extensive explanation, to make one simple, but very important point. Thorough methodology for conducting productivity improvement projects exists. One developed and used by hundreds of companies can be of major value to any project team.

FULL-SCALE MOCK-UP

Unfortunately, some implemented cells and assembly lines are sources of embarrassment, even though targeted improvements of 50 percent reduction of space and 95 percent reduction of work-in-process inventory have

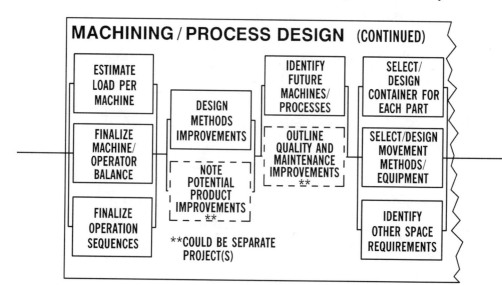

EXHIBIT 9–4

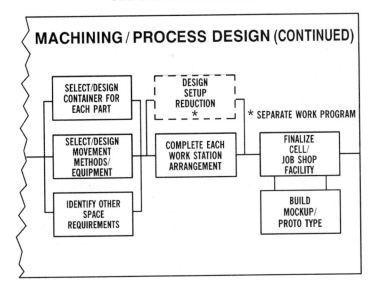

EXHIBIT 9-5

been achieved. Even though inventory has been removed from the process, the area occupied is still twice as large as necessary. The cause of this problem is simple. The layout of the revised area was a design on paper only. It is impractical to understand the realistic space requirements of an area drawn to scale. Very large factories are routinely built to the specifications of drawings or scale models only. As a result, areas may have too much or too little space.

It is simple and cost efficient to construct life-size models of lines, cells, and individual workstations. These should always be part of design and implementation projects, as depicted in Exhibit 9-5. But how does a project team responsible for the layout of an entirely new factory develop a low-cost, life-size model of a 100,000 square meter factory? First of all, the model can be as crude as chalk lines on the pavement of a parking lot. Second, it is not necessary to have one complete model. As each section of the large factory is completed, chalk lines can be drawn, the results reviewed, and decisions made. The parking lot can then be reused for the next section of the plant.

Often, chalk lines on the floor are not definitive enough to get a feel for the adequacy of space. Posts with connecting cords are a low-cost means of adding an element of vertical height to the model. The purpose of the mock-up is not only to satisfy the designer that the space is right, but also to provide an important tool for involving people in the design process. Workers, supervisors, managers, and executives should review and comment on the model with two objectives: (1) to answer whether or not the space is comfortable to work in and (2) to determine its efficiency from the standpoint of eliminating unnecessary, wasteful, and fatiguing motion. In the case of lengthy assembly lines, mock-up of at least one station should include three-dimensional models of the line, storage racks, and containers. This will permit the designer, workers, and managers to make sure that all elements of the workstation are sized correctly for comfort and efficency.

CONVERSION PREPARATION

Numerous preparatory steps can be taken to guarantee that a complex machining cell or lengthy assembly line can be converted to the new operation with a minimum of difficulty. One of the most important is developing and implementing the new, focused subplant organization in advance of actually converting it (as described in Chapter 2). Ready availability of responsible subplant maintenance personnel and process and product engineers during start-up will be a major factor in providing rapid solutions to unanticipated problems. The training and cross-training of personnel in their new tasks not only prepares them for the new operation, but also helps identify flaws in the process design that might otherwise be overlooked. It is usually feasible for assembly workers to be trained one at a time on the new assembly line. This line can almost always be constructed while the old one continues to operate, as the new line is typically much smaller than the old one, and uses new, lower cost equipment.

When dealing with both assembly lines and machine cells, employee assignments are rarely the same as on the old line or machine. The reason for this is that every individual job changes radically. In most cases, the number of people required is reduced, which is why employees should immediately start cross-training in every assembly operation or on every machine inclined to be part of, or adjacent to, their future workstations.

FIX IT: DO NOT ABANDON IT

Anyone routinely responsible for designing improvement should memorize the 101 reasons not to change that are the favorite responses of resisters. Close to the top of the list is, "We tried it once, and it did not work." Often, resisters will elaborate by saying that logically it should have worked, but for some reason did not, or even that it did not work because of such and such. Good ideas do not magically turn into bad ones. Usually, they do not work because of a failure to recognize and coordinate solutions to potential problems before implementation. Three keys to guarantee the success of good ideas are:

1. Spend enough time on the design to minimize oversights and design errors
2. Refuse to accept failure; make everyone involved responsible for success
3. Provide enough follow-up manpower to solve any oversights and design errors

Often the reasons for abandoning a new method are caused by difficult problems in other areas. For example, the quality of vendor-supplied materials or the engineering design might not be right. In the past, projects were discarded not because it was impractical to solve these subsidiary problems, but because no specific manager had the time, responsibility, and authority to tackle them. The productivity improvement team must unequivocably be involved in any and all follow-up activity until all serious problems are resolved.

In summary, people are the most important ingredient for successful productivity improvement projects. Those who can contribute the most, with respect to establishing motivation and direction, are executive management. They are also instrumental in staffing the full-time team with people who understand methodology and training and who have the experience and time to design changes. Last, but not least, operating personnel know existing operations, can offer ideas for improvement, and should have ultimate responsibility for the degree of the new operations' success.

10

□□□

Other Productivity Issues

WHEN WE STARTED THIS BOOK, our expectations were high. We rapidly saw that our outline would fill not one book, but three. We, therefore, found it necessary to focus on the issues of greatest importance to the largest number of manufacturers. Consequently, some topics have been treated in less depth than we would have preferred; others have not been included at all. Probably the greatest casualty of the cutting procedure was the process industry. Although we have made some reference to it, our coverage is much less than we would have preferred. For readers involved in process manufacturing, the important message is that the high goals and objectives of improvement described in the book are also applicable to them. This chapter touches briefly on some of the productivity issues that are most notably missing from this book.

PRODUCT DESIGN

The most vital opportunity for productivity improvement outside the realm of factory operations, which yields the highest return on investment and the lowest operating costs, lies in the area of improved product design. The best-designed product will capture the greatest market share, and give the greatest value to the customer, i.e., the product will have functions and features, including a long, trouble-free life, that the customer wants, in a price range he or she feels appropriate.

Most manufacturing companies have the potential for either designing replacement product lines or improving existing ones. The general objectives of any design improvement project should be:

1. Simplification of the design
2. Standardization of components within and across product lines
3. Rationalization of product lines to reduce the range of items produced
4. Design for producibility of the product

As a result of standardization and product simplification—including designs that use less exotic and, therefore, less costly material—cost reduction targets for material should be in the range of 30 to 50 percent. Decreasing material costs, in combination with reducing the number of items stocked, should result in lowering investment in materials inventories by at least half. Manufacturing costs, including both labor and overhead, should be slated for a 30 to 50 percent decrease. This results from systematically considering the producibility of the product design before finalizing it for release to production.

The reasons that product design offers a major opportunity for improvement are clear. In most companies, pressures brought to bear in the engineering organization to design and release new products in the shortest possible time always exceed its capacity to meet the demand. This means that too little time is spent on development. Second, the engineering design, manufacturing engineering, and quality engineering functions are poorly integrated. Usually, designs are released and later found to require manufacturing capabilities that do not exist. Consequently, manufacturing is forced to face higher costs than expected and unforeseen rework because design tolerances are tighter than existing process capabilities. Finally, design engineers, like other creative people, tend to operate in an insular manner. Management fails to set performance targets that demand new levels of excellence and yield better results. Design improvement projects, relatively few of which have been undertaken, need the discipline of full-time integrated teams of design, process, and quality engineering people. They also require management-specified targets for improvement.

PARTS PER MILLION QUALITY

The level of quality in some of the best Japanese companies is such that the only reasonable way to discuss defects is by their quantity per million units produced. In these organizations, the defects per million are rarely more than one or two digits. Consequently, in the Western world, a common theme for productivity improvement is quality before all else. However, quality improvement should be viewed primarily as an outcome of enhancing the design of the production process. Improved productivity, companywide, occurs as the result of dozens and even hundreds of improvements. In most instances, the greatest percentage of quality problems will be solved by setup design and machining and assembly facilities that eliminate the possibility of producing defective parts. Even achieving quality improvement for purchased materials and components requires going directly to the design of improved processes.

One example of a low-cost process improvement to control quality is illustrated by Fiat's Solex factory in Limay, France. Quality defects in aluminum carburetor bodies were reduced by 47 percent through several minor changes, one of which was to automatically monitor the rate of water flow to the mold as seen in Exhibit 10–1. The quality improvement project team found it possible for water flow to vary uncontrollably. Although flow meters were used, standards for an acceptable range of flow had never been established. Even if they had been, the meters still required manual monitoring. Since constant monitoring is not practical, several defective bodies could be produced before variance from the acceptable range would be discovered. By installing mechanical stops at the high and low limits of flow and attaching sensors to them, the machine could automatically be stopped the instant a fluctuation in flow caused a defective body.

WATER FLOW CONTROL

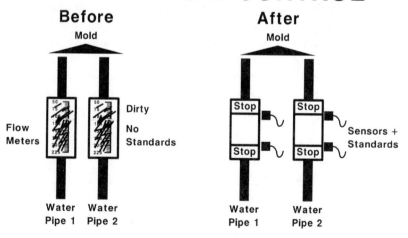

Before

Mold

Flow Meters

Dirty
No
Standards

Water Pipe 1 Water Pipe 2

After

Mold

Stop   Stop

Stop   Stop

Sensors + Standards

Water Pipe 1 Water Pipe 2

EXHIBIT 10–1

Unfortunately, the majority of quality improvement projects are designed to enhance quality by gradually identifying and solving problems through increased inspection or statistical sampling. A better approach is to have manufacturing professionals quickly identify opportunities for improvement in machine or assembly processes and design them, thus eliminating most of the delay associated with statistic gathering and analysis.

VENDORS: FUTURE PARTNERS IN PROFIT

Successful implementation of superior manufacturing techniques by every vendor will, in the long term, have greater total impact on product cost and quality than any other improvement, with the exception of product design. The reason for this is clear: purchased components and raw materials typically account for 50 to 70 percent of the cost of goods manufactured. Although supplier productivity improvement is of utmost importance, comparatively little progress is being made in convincing vendors that they must aggressively adopt superior manufacturing practices. Purchasing personnel have also been slower to accept the new principles, which carried to their ultimate, have the potential for sharply reducing their numbers. However, this is not the primary reason for resistance by purchasing personnel. There are important issues and practices that must be addressed if sweeping changes are to be accomplished. For example:

1. The typical company deals with far too many active suppliers. Thus, it is not practical to work with all vendors on improvement programs.
2. Customers frequently change from one vendor to another because of lower prices or improved quality and delivery.
3. Vendors frequently refuse to believe that customers will uphold their end of the relationship. All too often, vendors have made investments in improvements, only to see their customers switch to another supplier.
4. Small suppliers have less knowledge, education, and training in superior manufacturing techniques and usually are not staffed with enough personnel to design and implement changes.

To circumvent these roadblocks to vendor improvements, a superior manufacturer must engage in three fundamental practices: (1) reduction of the number of active suppliers; (2) establishment of longer-term (lifetime, it is hoped) relationships with the reduced number of suppliers; and (3) continuous quality improvement through upgrading the vendor's manufacturing process and the customer's design specifications. For many companies it will not be practical to immediately reduce the number of active suppliers of either a commodity or a specific part from several to one. It may, however, be practical to reduce the number from several to fewer. The most aggressive companies, however, will strive to achieve the goal of single sources of supply.

For a company to establish a long-term relationship with a single supplier flies directly in the face of tradition. Maintaining multiple sources has been a cornerstone of past purchasing practices and has been considered vital for protection against disruption due to natural disaster, labor problems, or business failure. Further, maintaining multiple sources has been a way to pressure suppliers to offer the lowest possible prices.

Often, a single vendor simply has not had the capacity to meet the customer's demand. Rather than encourage and even help a single vendor to acquire the required capacity, it has been easier for manufacturers to buy from multiple suppliers simultaneously. Conversely, many suppliers have been reluctant to supply 100 percent of a customer's requirements, even when they have sufficient capacity or could invest in more. They are all too aware of instances where they or other suppliers have had major customers withdraw their business, leaving the company with expensive excess capacity and sometimes forcing it into bankruptcy. In other cases, customers have threatened to go elsewhere to force the supplier to price his products far below a reasonable return on investment.

Superior manufacturers will realize that successful suppliers must earn a reasonable return on their investment in order to be, and to remain, superior suppliers. Two compelling reasons support this conclusion:

1. No reasonable management or board of directors would permit a business to continuously operate with marginal profits, or even losses. The supplier that is forced to sell at prices too low to bring a reasonable return on investment must move into other product lines or customers and/or abandon unprofitable business.

2. Process and product designs must be continuously improved. This requires investment in research and development, and in capital expenditures. Suppliers cannot invest in these areas, however, unless profits are adequate. Further, if the supplier perceives a high likelihood of losing a customer's business at some point, he would, naturally, favor investment in other areas of higher return and greater security.

The economies of scale, for a specific product or product family, still apply. Thus, the supplier with the largest volume can, and should, have the lowest manufacturing and overhead costs, especially when his factories, office, and indirect organizations are focused, as described in Chapter 2. Accordingly, fostering multiple sources of supply automatically pushes purchase prices higher than necessary. The collective capacities of multiple sources are much more likely to be higher than that of a single source. Customers frequently shift their business from one vendor to another, and suppliers have come to expect idle periods, simply because they may have been underbid in that time period.

Most component and material purchasers are gravely concerned about switching from multiple active sources of supply to a single source. They find it difficult to envision the day when, as a result of continuous elimination of inefficient suppliers, there remains only one source in a country, region, or even in the world. Typical concerns include the following:

1. Without competition, the single supplier can dictate prices, and will, therefore, ask much more for his products.

2. The single source of supply will have no incentive to invest in either improved process or product technology.

3. Numerous developing, and even some advanced, industrial countries have monopolistic manufacturers, most notably in production of basic raw materials, such as steel and chemicals. Most of the government, and even privately owned, monopolies are notoriously unconcerned with providing reasonable delivery service. Thus, the idea that a single source could be unreliable is of great concern. The supplier can dictate the production schedule of its customers by routinely delivering products later than necessary.

In most areas of the world, it is highly unlikely that the number of suppliers will fall to one for a given product or family of products. The logistics of product delivery, the need for backup to provide capacity flexibility, and the number of existing factories and machines almost guarantee that even if there is only a single source of supply, that vendor will have, and should have, multiple production facilities, which may even be in separate buildings in multiple locations. Only in the long term would one expect all but a single vendor to drop out of business in any individual country. If a country has a single source of supply, or even no source, there will continue to be multiple international sources for most products and product families. Although many find it difficult to accept the notion of long-term, single sources of supply, many companies have learned to work together in a fair, harmonious relationship with some select suppliers. Reducing the total number of active suppliers will not, therefore, be breaking new ground for them.

Superior manufacturing techniques apply equally to every manufacturer and to his suppliers. A supplier program, however, needs unique features. Two of the most important are long-term agreements and systems for rapid communication of customer requirements. The long-term agreement, pioneered at Harley-Davidson, is different than legally binding contracts, and is a supplement to the purchase contract. Its purpose is to define the intention of customer and supplier to work together in a relationship that will be perpetual. The agreement spells out the responsibilities of both "partners in profit" necessary for mutual success. Chief among these are the agreement by the supplier to continuously strive to improve his productivity and quality while helping to reduce inventories and delays in the pipeline of customers and suppliers.

Of primary importance to the supplier is the customer's agreement to rapidly communicate the latest requirement information. Almost every supplier experiences radical swings in his customer's purchase schedule as a result of delays between changes in the customer's market demands and changes in supplier purchase order schedules. Frequently, a supplier continues to supply at volumes of production far in excess of demands for several weeks after the market demand has dropped. When purchase order schedules are finally revised, production must often be stopped for weeks at a time while the customer uses up excess inventories that have accumulated. The use of stock purposely received earlier than required, or kept as safety stock, exacerbates the problem. (Chapter 8 outlines the tools with which the superior manufacturer can solve the problem of delayed transmission of requirements from customer to supplier. These include the use of CONBON, electronic CONBON, and supplier schedules to replace purchase orders.)

For many companies, reprogramming complex existing systems to eliminate lead-time cushions and safety stocks and to pass pure schedule information to suppliers is an expensive, long-term project. The interim solution for companies like Harley-Davidson has been handwritten schedules copied manually from internal reports and displays. Thus, supplier schedules for all of the most expensive parts could be used almost immediately, following arrangements with the supplier to adopt their use.

Nothing can eliminate swings of demand in the marketplace; however, rapid communication of requirements to suppliers permits the suppliers to rank production up or down in response to developing trends of demand. The alternative, caused by unreasonable delays in communication, is radical changes in demands, triggering massive temporary layoffs or major hiring and rehiring programs. Requirements passed through an entire network become greatly distorted, not only as a result of delays in processing schedule changes but also due to several other factors. The end result, illustrated by Exhibit 10–2, is that automobile assembly schedules, which are reasonably uniform, become uneven and unpredictable for suppliers in lower tiers of the supply pipeline. The major factors that contribute to this phenomenon are:

1. Safety stock provisions and changes
2. Lead-time allowances far in excess of actual process time
3. Inaccuracies in all types of inventory and requirement records and transactions
4. The effect of scrap and rework
5. Lot sizing
6. Systems with large schedule periods (weekly) operated infrequently (weekly)

The Inland Division of General Motors was able to virtually eliminate these scheduling distortions by changing from weekly schedules (sometimes called buckets) to daily schedules, and by adopting the use of electronic CONBON in some tiers of the pipeline network. Incidentally, elimination of safety stocks and lead-time cushions in the supply pipeline

NETWORK LOAD PROFILES

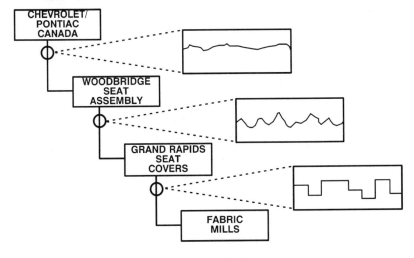

EXHIBIT 10–2

make it possible to react more rapidly. Fast reaction time is necessary to reduce reliance on surplus inventory to meet changed demands.

GM's Inland Division has been making giant strides in reducing supplier network lead times and inventories for its complex network illustrated in Exhibit 10–3. The pilot project included the vertical pipeline of supply from the producer of yarn, through the fabric mill, to the Inland Grand Rapids plant, which cuts and sews seat covers, through the Woodbridge seat assembly plant, culminating in the Chevrolet/Pontiac Canada automobile assembly plant in Ontario. The time required to pass the schedule for customer orders and forecast information down through the network was originally 14 workdays, while the time required to produce the schedule was 71 days. The production time of 71 days was reduced to 31 within 6 months. The longer term target is 22 days. Inland believes this pipeline lead time is superior to that of Japanese seat manufacturers and clearly unrivaled by that of other U.S. seat manufacturers.

GM's first-tier suppliers were scheduled just-in-time, even before this project was begun. Assembly line starts were, and are, broadcast every 57 seconds to the Woodbridge seat assembly factory to schedule seat production. Woodbridge, however, prepared schedules for the Grand Rapids seat cover facility only once a week, based largely on forecast rather than actual orders, and this schedule was in weekly increments. The seat cover plant typically produced the seats that were likely to be scheduled in the

CUSTOMER / SUPPLIER NETWORK

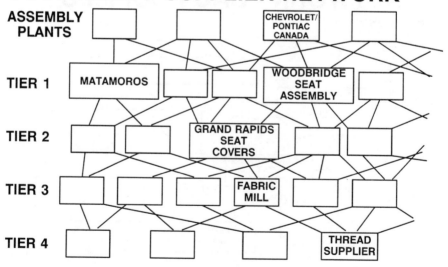

EXHIBIT 10–3

automobile assembly plant 3 weeks later. The fabric supplier's plants would typically be dyeing and knitting production 8 and 10 weeks in advance of forecast production, with thread manufacturing occurring even earlier. Now the seat cover systems have been revised to update schedules every day and to produce these schedules in daily increments. Further, the seat cover plant is connected to the fabric supplier by the electronic CONBON method.

As Exhibit 10-4 illustrates, the focused, seat cover plant starts the CONBON process by taking a roll of fabric from focused storage for cutting and sewing. At this point, the bar-coded CONBON label on the roll is read by a computer wand. This information is accumulated daily and transmitted to the fabric supplier, where the information is used to draw the required number of rolls from storage for shipment. The CONBON labels on the outbound roll are read by computer wand and are transmitted to Grand Rapids to update inventory status information.

If past transport systems had been used, the electronic CONBON system would not have worked successfully. Prior to the pipeline lead-time reduction project, fabric was scheduled to be delivered once a week from each fabric supplier, as illustrated in Exhibit 10-5. As shown in the exhibit, all of the fabric suppliers are located within a region which includes North and South Carolina, and is 30 hours by truck from the seat cover plant in Grand Rapids, Michigan. The weekly delivery schedules result in inventories no less than one-half of weekly usage. By scheduling

ELECTRONIC CONBON

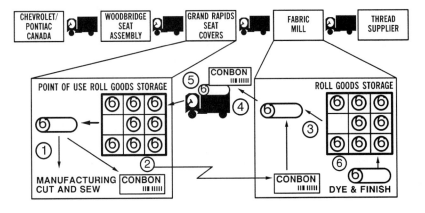

EXHIBIT 10-4

WEEKLY FABRIC DELIVERIES

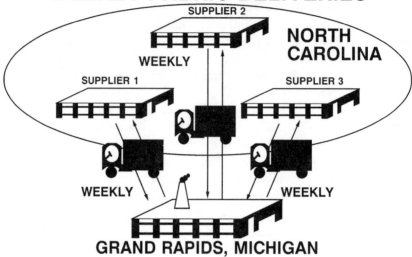

EXHIBIT 10-5

daily "milk runs" from all fabric suppliers, as shown in Exhibit 10-6, inventory was reduced to an average of one-half a day's usage—a reduction of 80 percent. In addition, total freight costs have been reduced by 67 percent. Trucks and drivers are better utilized on the continuous daily runs than on a weekly basis. Now that shipments are made daily, expedited shipment costs have been sharply reduced.

Decentralizing storage of roll goods and establishing focused factories for each customer were key ingredients in improving the Inland Division network's lead time. Each focused factory stores only a few fabrics. Thus, controlling the inventory of the few fabrics and communicating with their supplier are greatly simplified.

The number of quality problems in the pipeline has also been reduced substantially. Defects at the seat cover and seat assembly facilities have thus far dropped by 51 percent. The largest improvement came from simply reducing inventories. When stocks were large, slight color variations from two or more dye lots in stock sometimes resulted in a seat having different color shades. By sharply reducing the level of stock, the potential for mismatched dye lots dropped correspondingly. Subsequent to the pilot project described above, Inland's Grand Rapids plant has extended the pipeline improvement project to encompass all material from all suppliers, with similar benefits.

In sum, the supplier network will be the most important arena in which the struggle to achieve the position of superior manufacturer will be

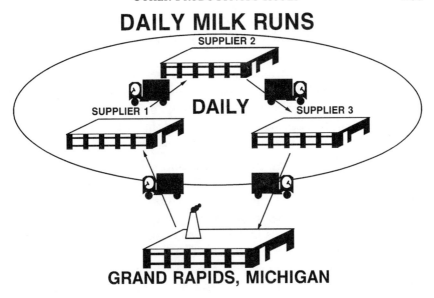

EXHIBIT 10-6

fought. The success of the supplier program will hinge on successful implementation of factory productivity improvements, transport improvements, and rapid requirement transmissions. It will also require a new era of fair, cooperative customer and supplier relationships, firmly based on the notion of single, long-term sources of supply.

OFFICE PRODUCTIVITY

Many North American and European companies that were once the finest in the world suffer a common malady: excessive bureaucracy. Simply stated, they have 10 times more employees in administrative areas than some of their Japanese counterparts, such as Yamaha and Toyota. The major reasons for this huge difference are:

1. Procedures and systems support old ways of doing business in the West. In the best companies in Japan, these have been streamlined to eliminate such wasteful procedures as reporting and administering direct labor efficiency, matching receipts and invoices to purchase orders, etc.

2. People work on tasks that are unnecessary. Corporate staff reviews and approves work previously evaluated and approved by group and division people, and originated by someone at the plant. In many

large companies, one or more employees decide which light bulb types are to be used worldwide. Worse yet, they monitor compliance.

3. Office and administrative employees are seldom subject to the objective types of performance measurement and control used for factory operations. As a result, work expands to fill the time. Time and again, industry has proven that deep cuts in staffing can be achieved with little or no negative impact on business operations.

Fortunately, the meat-cleaver approach can be applied to this problem. Corporate raiders use it all the time. They decree that, effective tomorrow, every administrative function will reduce its staff by 25 percent. Three months later, a second decrease of 25 percent could be required, followed by additional cuts of 10 percent each. As productivity consultants, we perform projects to increase office productivity by logical analysis and systematic improvement. As good businessmen, however, we have observed and participated in situations where the meat-cleaver approach, while more painful, has achieved major improvements at considerably less cost than study and analysis.

In the procedures and systems area, use of the meat-cleaver has been successful. By reducing the number of personnel, it forces the remaining staff to do more productive work. Real, permanent savings can only be achieved by designing and installing new productivity systems, with the goal of reducing the costs of operations and the number of people by up to 90 percent. For example, Harley-Davidson's engine plant was able to reduce the production control function from 22 to 2, while more than doubling the sales volume. Today, the area previously occupied by production control is used for training. Another important objective of office productivity improvement is decreasing the elapsed time required to complete transactions such as product design and order entry. Typical reductions and, therefore, target improvements, are 90 percent.

STRATEGIC ISSUES

Many of the productivity improvement projects included in this book have identified strategic issues of crucial importance to areas of the organization other than manufacturing. Initiatives have been undertaken to change the basic operations of a company, based on management's adoption of new policies and goals. The majority of strategic issues involve sales and marketing organizations. For example, the team responsible for designing new process layouts in a truck-trailer assembly plant learned that sales efforts were limited to a very small radius. Due to the high costs of delivery of trailers, manufacturers in areas beyond that radius had the market since delivery from the project team's plant would be costly enough to eliminate any profit.

The project team had discussed that, although the productivity project would ultimately produce major cost reductions, these savings were small in comparison to those that would be gained if production volume were doubled or tripled. The new layouts were capable of achieving such increased production levels. By having chosen to use cost reductions generated by the productivity project to pay freight costs, the new delivery radius could be doubled. The total market within the new radius was approximately four times that of the existing one. Based on these facts, groundwork was laid to establish a sales organization and effort within the new radius of delivery.

Although not every productivity project team uncovers strategic issues, the radical changes brought about by productivity improvements are more likely to permit strategic initiatives not before feasible. Management should expect the productivity improvement team to alertly recognize and report any such potential strategic issues.

SHORTAGE MANAGEMENT

The problem of part shortages is a persistent one for the majority of assembly plants around the world, but more so for smaller companies than for large ones. In many companies, part shortages are so severe and so persistent that management believes it impossible to solve the problem or to come even close to solving it. Executives worldwide frequently use the serious shortage problems as a reason to deny the possibility of adopting superior manufacturing practices. They believe that shortages necessitate high investment in inventory at all levels—purchased materials and components, work in process, and finished goods.

In our experience, shortage problems are unnecessary; they are permitted or caused. For example, on a recent trip to Venezuela, we visited two appliance manufacturers. One could not grasp the meaning of shortages. The management had simply never permitted practices in its own factories (or in the factories of its suppliers) that could cause shortages. In the second appliance factory, however, the management revolved around trying to keep employees busy regardless of constant component shortages. Very few units were assembled complete; semifinished appliances were constantly shuffled from assembly line to temporary storage areas, then back to the line when the missing part became available. In both of these cases, the same types of appliances were assembled, using the same types of components from the same types of suppliers. The key difference between the two, however, was management's attitude and operating practices. One company routinely accepted late delivery; the other company routinely expected and demanded on-time delivery.

At one of Harley-Davidson's assembly plants, Tom Gelb, vice-president of operations, said that the hardest decision he ever had to make was to close down assembly when a component was delivered too late or defective. It was, however, no great surprise that shutting the line down had an almost immediate impact on those responsible. Vendors learned very rapidly that they would be held liable for the costs of halting production. More important, they learned that it was practical to control schedule and quality carefully and that the improved control actually lowered their operating costs.

Late delivery problems were not only due to poor supplier performance but also to bad practices by Harley-Davidson management. For example, for years Harley-Davidson had rushed engineering changes into production. Routinely, the dates set for change were completely unrealistic. Insufficient time was allowed for developing workable tooling, for producing pilot samples, for testing pilot production to make sure the new design functioned properly, and to repeat the same cycle for changes necessary to correct problems uncovered during pilot production.

When a company perpetually sets unattainable goals and never learns from its experience, there is little hope for improvement. The philosophy of superior manufacturing is that goals should be set at highly ambitious levels, but that these must be attainable and even surpassable. Harley-Davidson learned, and most companies must still learn, that excessive haste in bringing new product designs to the market has a negative effect. Almost always the product is late, or otherwise enters the market with major design and/or production defects.

With a management team accustomed to routinely implementing radical changes, a company might expect its team to overcome most of the problems of late supplier deliveries in one or two years. Realistically, however, many manufacturers will require several years to significantly reduce shortage problems, especially if the company management is unwilling to go "cold turkey" by shutting down the plant as the primary method to force the development of permanent solutions.

VERTICAL AISLE SYSTEMS: MULTISTORY FACTORY

Many manufacturing managers are prejudiced against multistory buildings. Although we often talk as though it would be impossible to produce competitively in a multistory building, after analysis, we are normally able to construct the multistory factory at less cost per square foot of useful space than a single-level building. Further, it is a fact that multistory factories have been (and continue to be) among the most successful plants in the biggest cities of the world, where land costs are highest.

Some of the problems of the out-of-focused factory are magnified in the multistory factory. The biggest shortcoming in any large factory—single story or multistory—is the difficulty of direct communication of precise requirement schedules between user and supplier processes. But with the physical separation of process areas into multiple stories, there are even greater difficulties. If, in addition, the vertical aisle system (usually elevators) has inadequate capacity, the problem becomes even more serious. In most factories, the elevator capacity can be increased easily by improving the efficiency and utilization of the elevators and even by constructing additional one-level elevator equipment wherever transport between levels exceeds capacity.

SUPERVISORY PRODUCTIVITY

There are numerous reasons to expect improvement in the productivity of factory supervision and management, even before any other changes are made. For example, in many factories, there are large differences in the number of employees supervised/managed by each supervisor/manager. In reality, the number of employees supervised by any one person can usually be increased. Many factories also have more layers of management than necessary. Some of the largest Japanese companies, by contrast, have only five or six levels of management between the president and the factory employees.

In addition to increasing supervisor productivity, other changes made by the productivity project reduce the amount of supervision required. For example, worldwide results of many projects have achieved a decrease of 50 percent in the size of the factory. If the area of a supervisor's responsibility is reduced by 50 percent or more, the amount of time required to walk about while supervising should be correspondingly reduced. Similarly, the average productivity improvement team reduces the number of employees required by an average of 25 percent. Thus, a corresponding reduction of supervision should be feasible. Further, the main feature of productivity improvement is work simplification. For example, setup time reduction of 75 percent is achieved by cutting the amount of work required to change a machine from the settings and tools for one job to those for another. The reduction is achieved by simplifying and/or eliminating the work performed. When employees have simpler jobs, it follows that they should require less supervision. The new CONBON scheduling techniques and scheduling of flow operations further simplify the responsibilities of the supervisor. Finally, employee turnover and changing levels of demand result in a need for the supervisor to train new employees constantly. New, simplified work methods and systematic and routine employee cross-training can greatly reduce the amount of time required for training.

LOT SIZE DETERMINATION

The ultimate results of reducing setup time touches on numerous categories of expense and investments. With the exception of quality improvement, the largest benefits relate directly to the reduction of the lot sizes produced. In most companies, the benefits of setup reduction cannot be achieved unless lot sizes are reduced. The important issue then is the amount lot sizes should be reduced. Theoretically, based on setup reductions that average 75 percent the first time improvements are implemented, target reductions of lot size should be 50 percent.

Although the economic lot size formula and several sophisticated derivations have been the subject of numerous scholarly publications, relatively few manufacturers have adopted its use by rote. Real world needs and concerns have led most manufacturers to produce scheduled quantities, or multiples thereof, or to rely on the judgment of individuals charged with the responsibility of inventory management. In the case where production lots are specified in schedule periods (e.g., one week, four weeks, eight weeks), it is easy to see that the lot sizes should be reduced by half to achieve a balanced reduction in both setup and inventory carrying costs.

Justifiably, the purist may argue that production lot sizes expressed in schedule periods are probably not economic lot sizes, thus the reduction of half may also not be correct. Although this is true, it is, nevertheless, desirable to apply fast, practical logic to achieve reductions with minimal disruption in business. A change to strictly theoretical lot sizes, without setup reduction, almost always requires either substantially more setups or more inventory. More setups may result in exceeding the machine capacity. Further, few companies would purposely elect to increase inventory investment to accommodate lot sizes.

Even more important, every company should target inventory reductions of not just 75 percent, but eventually 95 percent or more. When virtually all setup cost is eliminated, new production lots become equal to daily demand. In other words, it becomes practical to produce a day's requirement every day. In this case, calculation of a lot size more precise than a day's production would usually be a waste of effort.

RELIEF PRODUCTIVITY

In factories reorganized for improved productivity, numerous manufacturing processes are changed from individual stand-alone operations to more productive flow processes, where all operations are directly linked and products are passed directly from one operation to another. Thus, in the new factory, if one operator leaves the process, it could potentially have the effect of stopping the entire process.

But in the best of the new highly productive operations, the assembly and machining lines have been so designed that one operator can step out of the line and the remaining crew will automatically adjust and compensate for the change. Production, therefore, continues at about the same rate. Theoretically, of course, this should not be the case. However, if one considers the almost undetectable effect on a hockey game when one player is sent to the penalty box, one can start to understand how a manufacturing line might operate, minus a player, for some period of time. At Yamaha, for example, most lines are still paced mechanically. The speed of the line during an eight-hour day never changes. Obviously, during each day, each operator leaves the line once or twice for personal reasons. When this happens, adjacent workers cooperatively perform each other's work and the work of the missing team member, and they work at a faster than normal pace. The techniques for this new mode of operation, called cooperative recovery, are described in Chapter 5.

In large factories of long flow processes, the most common method of providing relief is to maintain a pool of workers in excess of normal requirements. Since the most critical relief needs are for vacation, illness, and tardiness, and the amount of vacation, illness, and tardiness vary substantially from day to day, the relief pool is normally closer to peak need than to average need. A relief pool of workers available to the entire factory will usually have a lower difference of average to peak need than the sum of the averages and peaks of several departments; thus, the potentially nonproductive relief pool can usually be minimized by maintaining a plantwide pool. The plantwide pool, however, has the offsetting disadvantage of higher complexity and administration costs. For this reason, as many relief problems as possible should be handled within the subplant to minimize the need to draw on the plantwide relief pool.

Continuous reduction of costs, improved products and product features, quality, and reliability hold the promise of an incredible increase in the quality of life. The manufacturing industry can determine the pace of improvement by setting its goals high, by applying proven superior techniques, by inventing better methods, and by achieving even better results. Let us begin.

Appendix

◻◻◻

The Achievers

THIS LIST OF COMPANIES includes many of Andersen Consulting's more than 400 clients who have implemented the type of productivity improvements defined in this book. Most have made changes in *some* parts of the factory; few, however, have made changes in the *entire* factory.

For some of these companies, we have included case examples. All of the companies have had similar experience, but due to the limits of the book size, it was not practical to include them. In some cases, companies that made important achievements asked to be excluded entirely rather than allow competitors to learn of improvements, thus potentially alerting them to opportunities for copying any of their methods. The following compilation lists the company name, location, products, improvements achieved and, in parentheses, the Andersen Consulting contact person and the location of his office.

1. 3M, Medical Products Division, Brookings Plant, Brookings, South Dakota, U.S.A. Medical tape and surgical dressings. (Curtis G. Stangler, Stockholm, Sweden, and Peter R. Zirbel, Minneapolis, Minnesota, U.S.A.) Space reduction, 20%. Labor savings, 20%. Setup reduction, 80%.

2. Applied Magnetics Corporation, Seoul, Korea. Tape and disk heads. (M. Robert Leach, Los Angeles, California, U.S.A.) Manufacturing lead-time reduction, 20%. Space reduction, 50%. Total productivity improvement, 12%. Inventory investment: work in process, 97%; total, 50%. Quality defects, 60%. Payback period, 4 months.

3. Best Lock Corporation, Indianapolis, Indiana, U.S.A. Door locks and locking systems. (Robert L. Christianson, Indianapolis, Indiana, U.S.A.) Manufacturing lead-time reduction, 91%. Space reduction: assembly, 63%. Labor savings, 21%. Inventory investment: work in process, 96%. Payback period, 12 months.

4. Bostrom Europe, Northampton, England. Vehicle Seats. (Peter Sugden and Michael L. Ward, London, England.) Lead-time reduction, 85%. Space reduction, 20%. Labor savings, 30%. Inventory investment, 25%. Quality defects, 10%.

5. Brunswick Corporation, Bowling and Billiards Division, Muskegon Pin Plant, Muskegon, Michigan, U.S.A. Bowling pins. (Leroy D. Peterson, Chicago, Illinois, U.S.A.) Machine downtime, 75%. Quality defects, 65%. Production per labor hour, 20%. Capacity increase, 40%.

6. Brunswick Corporation, Mercury Marine Division, Fond-du-Lac, Wisconsin, U.S.A. Outboard marine engines. (Herbert W. Desch, Milwaukee, Wisconsin, U.S.A., and William A. Thurwachter, Phoenix, Arizona, U.S.A.) Assembly lead-time reduction, 85%. Space reduction: total, 30%; assembly, 68%. Direct labor savings, 14%. Inventory investment: work in process and material, 61%; finished goods, 71%. Total cost reduction, 20%. Increase in volume, mixed assembly for every model, every day, 53%. Reduction in number of vendors, 77%.

7. BSN, Inc., Sports and Recreation Division, Dallas, Texas, U.S.A. Weight benches, soccer goals. (Douglas Smith, Dallas, Texas, U.S.A.) Manufacturing lead-time reduction, 80%. Space reduction: total, 25%. Inventory investment: work in process, 80%; purchases, 50%; finished goods, 50%. Approximately 50% productivity improvement with major improvement in customer service.

8. Cambridge Instrument, Diecraft Division, Sparks, Maryland, U.S.A. Microscope, ophthalmic, and photogrammetric instrument components. (Steven A. Kruger, Boston, Massachusetts, U.S.A.) Manufacturing lead-time reduction, 60%. Space reduction: machining, 39%. Direct labor savings, 21%. Setup/changeover cost, 55%. Inventory investment: work in process, 70%; purchases, 18%. Quality defects, 54%.

9. Cambridge Instrument, Optical Systems Division, Rochester, New York, U.S.A. Microscopes, ophthalmic instruments. (Steve Kruger, Boston, Massachusetts, U.S.A.) Manufacturing lead-time reduction, 95%. Space reduction: assembly, 50%. Direct labor savings, 25%. Inventory investment: work in process, 95%; purchases, 80%. Quality defects, 80%.

10. The Cherry Corporation, Automotive Products, Waukegan, Illinois, U.S.A. Automotive switches. (Thomas A. Kaminski, London, England, and Ronald L. Luken, Chicago, U.S.A.) Space reduction: total, 40%; assembly, 40%; stores/warehouse, 40%. Direct labor savings, 35%. Indirect labor, 15%. Inventory investment: work in process, 80%; purchases, 50%; finished goods, 15%. Payback period, 6 months.

11. Machine tool manufacturer, U.S.A. Machine tool controls. (Roger E. Dunham, Cincinnati, Ohio, U.S.A.) Manufacturing lead-time reduction, 52%. Total space occupied, 27%. Labor savings: direct, 13%; indirect, 20%; stockroom, 30%. Inventory investment: work in process, 57%.

12. The Kendall Company, Hospital Division/Kenmex, Tijuana, Mexico. Urological and respiratory health-care products. (Douglas W. Cunningham, Orange County, California, U.S.A.) Manufacturing lead-time reduction; 80%. Space reduction: total, 50%; assembly, 20%; stores/warehouse, 60%. Labor savings: direct, 20%; indirect, 20%. Inventory investment: work in process, 77%; purchases, 68%; finished goods, 10%. Quality defects, 25%. Payback period, 18 months.

13. Cleaning products manufacturer, Alovera, Spain. Soap, cleaners, toilet goods. (Javier Tapia, Madrid, Spain.) Inventory investment: work in process, 75%; materials, 27%; finished goods, 38%.

14. Danaher, Partlow, Inc., New Hartford, New York, U.S.A. Temperature recorders and controllers. (William G. Stoddard, Hartford, Connecticut, U.S.A.) Manufacturing lead-time reduction, 80%. Space reduction: assembly, 50%. Direct labor savings, 34%. Inventory investment: work in process, 60%. Payback period, 2 months.

15. Datascope Corporation, Instrumentation Division, Paramus, New Jersey, U.S.A. Medical instrumentation. (Charles C. Searight, Roseland, New Jersey, U.S.A.) Pilot project results. Manufacturing lead-time reduction, 80%. Space reduction: total, 65%. Direct labor savings, 15%. Inventory investment: work in process, 85%. Payback period, 6 months.

16. Disston Company, Danville, Virginia, U.S.A. Hardware, tools, saws, rakes, tool boxes, power tool accessories. (Dow N. Bauknight, Charlotte, North Carolina, U.S.A.) Manufacturing lead-time reduction, 95%. Space reduction: total, 56%; machining, 69%; stores/warehouse, 20%. Labor savings: direct, 5%; indirect, 15%. Setup/changeover cost, 77%. Inventory investment: work in process, 65%; purchases, 42%; finished goods, 55%. Machine downtime, 35%. Quality defects, 60%. Vendor delivery lead time, 70%.

17. Dover Industries, Tipper Tie Division, Apex, North Carolina, U.S.A. Metal clipping equipment. (Dow N. Bauknight, Charlotte, North Carolina, U.S.A.) Space reduction: total, 33%. Direct labor savings, 35%. Setup/changeover cost, 80%. Inventory investment: total 50%. Quality defects, 96%. Payback period, 6 months.

18. Dumore Corporation, Mauston Plant, Mauston, Wisconsin, U.S.A. Electric motors. (David J. Storm and Christopher A. Coleman, Milwaukee, Wisconsin, U.S.A.) Manufacturing lead-time reduction, 85%. Space reduction: total, 50%. Direct labor savings, 25%. Inventory investment: work in process, 81%. Quality defects, 75%.

19. EG&G Torque Systems, Watertown, Massachusetts, U.S.A. Servo motors and encoders. (Steven A. Kruger, Boston, Massachusetts, U.S.A.) Manufacturing lead-time reduction, 99%. Space reduction: assembly, 25%. Direct labor savings, 50%. Inventory investment: work in process, 95%. Payback period, 7 months.

20. Eigen, Nevada City, California, U.S.A. Medical image-processing equipment. (Thomas D. Follet, San Jose, California, U.S.A.) Manufacturing lead-time reduction, 50%. Space reduction: assembly, 5%; storage, 40%; total, 20%. Labor savings: direct, 10%. Inventory investment: work in process, 60%. (Progress to date. See the projects in progress section for long-term goals.)

21. Elastor, Cumiana, Turin, Italy. Rubber automotive parts. (Federico Feyles, Turin, Italy.) Indirect labor, 20%. Setup/changeover cost, 85%. Inventory investment: finished goods, 50%. Machine downtime, 25%. Payback period, 3 months.

22. Electrotecnica Arteche Hermanos, S.A., Munguia, Spain. Transformers. (Raul E. Alvarado, Bilbao, Spain.) Manufacturing lead-time reduction, 65%. Space reduction: assembly, 30%. Setup/changeover cost, 70%. Inventory investment: work in process, 65%. Quality defects, 80%.

23. Ensign-Bickford Company, Simsbury, Connecticut, U.S.A. Blasting caps. (Henry S. Burgess, Hartford, Connecticut, U.S.A.) Manufacturing lead-time reduction, 65%. Space reduction: assembly, 40%; machining, 25%. Direct labor savings, 22%. Setup/changeover cost, 70%. Inventory investment: work in process, 65%; purchases, 50%; finished goods, 20%. Payback period, 12 months.

24. Fagor Industrial, Onate, Spain. Industrial cooking and washing appliances. (Raul E. Alvarado, Bilbao, Spain.) Manufacturing lead-time reduction, 40%. Space reduction: total, 30%. Direct labor savings, 29%. Setup/changeover cost, 55%. Inventory investment: work in process, 53%. Two factories merged into one. Payback period, 36 months.

25. Fiat, Solex, Limay, France. Carburetors. (Jean-Noel Deglaire, Paris, France.) Reduction of carburetor body defects, 47%. Payback period, 4 months.

26. General Motors Corporation, Fisher Guide, Anderson Plant 5, Anderson, Indiana, U.S.A. Automotive lights. (Robert L. Christianson, Indianapolis, Indiana, U.S.A.) Manufacturing lead-time reduction, 67%. Space reduction: total, 40%; machining, 90%; stores/warehouse, 90%. Labor savings: direct, 16%; indirect, 10%. Inventory investment: work in process, 86%; purchases, 70%; finished goods, 44%. Lift trucks, 40%. Payback period, 6 months.

27. General Motors Corporation, Fisher Guide, Monroe Plant, Monroe, Louisiana, U.S.A. Forward lighting systems (headlamps). (Bruce B. Piper, Houston, Texas, U.S.A.) Space reduction: assembly, 69%. Direct labor savings, 40%. Payback period, 12 months. Capital investment per unit of production reduced by 45%.

28. General Motors Corporation, Fisher Guide, RIMIR Plant, Matamoros, Tampas, Mexico. Fascia, plastic bumpers. (Bruce B. Piper, Houston, Texas, U.S.A., and Robert L. Wilson, Jr., Cincinnati, Ohio, U.S.A.) Space reduction: total, 35%. Labor savings, 25%. Inventory investment: work in process, 93%. Quality defects, 50%. On-time production, 99%.

29. General Motors Corporation, Harrison Radiator Division, Domchery Plant, Domchery, France. Automobile radiators and air conditioning. (Jean-Noel Deglaire, Paris, France.) Manufacturing lead-time reduction, 50%. Space reduction: assembly, 32%. Direct labor savings, 12%. Inventory investment: work in process, 40%. Payback period, 10 months.

30. General Motors Corporation, Inland Division, Componentes Mecanicos de Matamoros Plant, Matamoros, Tampas, Mexico. Instrument panel pads, steering wheels, brake hose. (Bruce B. Piper, Houston, Texas, U.S.A., and Robert L. Wilson Jr., Cincinnati, Ohio, U.S.A.) Manufacturing lead-time reduction, 94%. Space reduction: total, 35%. Labor savings, 25%. Setup/changeover cost, 90%. Inventory investment: work in process, 93%; total, 36%. Quality defects: rework, 47%; scrap, 50%.

31. General Motors Corporation, Inland Division, Grand Rapids Plant, Grand Rapids, Michigan, U.S.A. Automobile seat covers. (Robert L. Wilson Jr., Cincinnati, Ohio, U.S.A.) Manufacturing lead-time reduction, 93%. Space reduction: stores/warehouse, 40%. Labor savings: direct, 16%; indirect, 50%; office, 35%. Inventory investment: finished goods, 57%. Lift trucks, 16%. Quality defects, 51%. Inbound freight cost, 67%.

32. General Motors Corporation, Inland Division, Inlan, Ponte de

Sur, Portugal. Brakes, motors mounts, weather strips, steering wheels, and horn caps. (Robert L. Wilson, Jr., Cincinnati, Ohio, U.S.A.) Manufacturing lead-time reduction, 90%. Space reduction: total, 30%. Labor savings, 16%.

33. General Motors Corporation, Inland Division, Vandalia Plant, Vandalia, Ohio, U.S.A. Foam seats, instrument panel pads, brake hose, brake lining, steering wheels, ball joints. (Robert L. Wilson, Jr., Cincinnati, Ohio, U.S.A.) Labor savings, 20%. Setup/changeover cost, 70%. Inventory investment: work in process, 94%. Absenteeism, 60%; scrap, 75%; rework, 90%.

34. General Motors Corporation, Inland Division, Windsor Trim, Windsor, Ontario, Canada. Seat assemblies, interior trim, doors, seat covers. (Robert L. Wilson, Jr., Cincinnati, Ohio, U.S.A.) Manufacturing lead-time reduction, 84%. Space reduction: total, 34%. Inventory investment, 40%. Lift trucks, 16%.

35. Gruppo Industriale Ercole Marelli, EMC, Milan, Italy. Electric motors and pumps. (Alessandro Falchero, Milan, Italy.) Labor savings: direct, 60%; indirect, 30%; office, 30%. Purchases, 50%. Payback period, 8 months.

36. Gruppo Industriale Ercole Marelli, GIEM Condizionamento, Bari, Italy. Air conditioning equipment. (Alessandro Falchero, Milan, Italy.) Manufacturing lead-time reduction, 70%. Labor savings: direct, 30%; indirect, 30%. Setup/changeover cost, 80%. Inventory investment: work in process, 70%; purchases, 50%; finished goods, 20%. Increased volume 50% in available space, eliminated need for new finished goods storage. Payback period, 8 months.

37. Harley-Davidson Motor Company, Tomahawk Plant, Tomahawk, Wisconsin, U.S.A. Fiberglass and plastic motorcycle accessories. (Thomas E. Arenberg, Milwaukee, Wisconsin, U.S.A.) Manufacturing lead-time reduction, 80%. Labor savings, 18%. Setup/changeover cost, 88%. Inventory investment: work in process, 51%; finished goods, 55%. Quality defects, 75%.

38. Harley-Davidson Motor Company, Capitol Drive Engine Plant, Milwaukee, Wisconsin, U.S.A. Motorcycles. (Thomas E. Arenberg, Milwaukee, Wisconsin, U.S.A.) Manufacturing lead-time reduction, 80%. Inventory investment: increased turns per year from 7 to 20. Average reduction of setup costs, 75%. Total labor savings of 38%, in terms of employees per unit produced. Physical inventory-taking reduced from 5 days to 4 hours.

39. Harvard Industries, Snover Stamping Co. Plant, Snover, Michi-

gan, U.S.A. Stampings. (Jeffrey D. Bergeron, Detroit, Michigan, U.S.A.) Setup/changeover cost, 81%. Inventory investment: work in process, 50%. Payback period, 2 months.

40. Industrias Villares, S.A., Divisao Elevadores, Sao Paulo, Brazil. Elevators and escalators. (Ernesto J. Kuperman, Sao Paulo, Brazil.) Space reduction: total, 38%; assembly, 50%; machining, 34%. Inventory investment: work in process, 50%. Lift trucks, 50%.

41. Industrias Villares, S.A., Divisao Motores Eletricos, Sao Paulo, Brazil. Electric motors and generators. (Ernesto J. Kuperman, Sao Paulo, Brazil.) Inventory investment: work in process, 50%. Lift trucks, 70%. Payback period, 24 months.

42. International Rectifier Corporation Italiana (I.R.C.I.) S.P.A., Borgaro Torinese, Italy. Electronic devices. (Federico Feyles, Turin, Italy.) Manufacturing lead-time reduction, 80%. Space reduction: assembly, 20%; machining, 20%; stores/warehouse, 75%. Labor savings: direct, 20%; indirect, 35%. Setup/changeover cost, 80%. Inventory investment: work in process, 80%; purchases, 80%; finished goods, 75%. Payback period, 5 months.

43. Jaz-Zubiaurre, S.A., Eibar, Spain. Wire brushes. (Raul E. Alvarado, Bilbao, Spain.) Manufacturing lead-time reduction, 50%. Space reduction: total, 30%; assembly, 40%; machining, 10%; stores/warehouse, 50%. Labor savings: direct, 10%; indirect, 10%; office, 5%. Setup/changeover cost, 30%. Inventory investment: work in process, 50%; purchases, 20%; finished goods, 10%. Lift trucks, 40%. Machine downtime, 5%. Quality defects, 10%. Payback period, 16 months.

44. Johnson & Johnson, Inc., Montreal, Quebec, Canada. Personal health and patient health-care products (pilot project). (Stephen L. Brant, Montreal, Quebec, Canada.) Manufacturing lead-time reduction, 35%. Space reduction, 30%. Setup/changeover cost, 45%. Inventory investment: finished goods, 30%. Complete daily model mix.

45. Lennox Industries, Inc., R & D Laboratory, Carrollton, Texas, U.S.A. Air conditioning equipment (Gerald Gallagher, Dallas, Texas, U.S.A.) Labor savings, 30%. Setup/changeover cost, 94%. Payback period, 3 months.

46. Lockheed Aeronautical Systems Company, Burbank Operations, Burbank, California, U.S.A. Military aircraft and other military products. (M. Robert Leach, Los Angeles, California, and James M. Bernstein, Washington, District of Columbia, U.S.A.) Manufacturing lead-time reduction, 90 + %. Space reduction, 25%. Direct labor savings, 20%. Indirect labor, 75%. Setup/changeover cost, 40%. Inventory investment: work

in process, 90%; finished goods, 50%. Machine downtime, 50%. Quality defects, 80%. Payback period, 12 months.

47. Lufkin Industries, Inc., Lufkin, Texas, U.S.A. Oil field pumps, commercial gears, truck trailers. (Jerry C. Hassebroek, Houston, Texas, U.S.A.) Manufacturing lead-time reduction, 90%. Space reduction: total, 25%; assembly, 25%; machining, 10%; stores/warehouse, 50%. Direct labor savings, 15%. Indirect labor, 25%. Office labor savings, 25%. Inventory investment: work in process, 80%; purchases, 25%; finished goods, 50%. Lift trucks, 25%. Machine downtime, 25%. Quality defects, 30%.

48. Holophane Company, Inc., Newark, Ohio, U.S.A. Industrial lighting fixtures. (John Rife, Columbus, Ohio, U.S.A.) Office lead time, 88%. Space reduction: office, 65%. Office labor savings, 37%. Preprinted forms, 40%. Computer reports, 25%. Quality defects, 10%. Payback period, 5 months.

49. MHB (Messier-Hispano-Bugatti), Molsheim, France. Aircraft landing gear. (Francois Jaquenoud, Lyon, France.) Space reduction: assembly, 60%; machining, 50%; stores/warehouses, 70%. Labor savings, 18%. Inventory investment: work in process, 75%; purchases, 50%. Doubled output. Payback period, 12 months.

50. Muebles Danona, S. Coop., Azpeitia, Guipuzcoa, Spain. Furniture. (Raul E. Alvarado, Bilbao, Spain.) Manufacturing lead-time reduction, 75%. Space reduction: total, 45%; assembly, 35%; machining, 18%; stores/warehouse, 60%. Labor savings: direct, 21%; indirect, 13%. Setup/changeover cost, 75%. Inventory investment: work in process, 75%; purchases, 50%; finished goods, 60%. Payback period, 8 months.

51. Orscheln, Cabury Division, Salisbury, Missouri, U.S.A. Brake systems. (C. Robert Farwell, St. Louis, Missouri, U.S.A.) Space reduction, 29%. Labor productivity, 48%. Inventory investment: work in process, 58%. Scrap cost, 56%. Orders in backlog, 96%.

52. Pacific Scientific, Instrument Division, Silver Springs, Maryland, U.S.A. Electronic measurement instruments. (Steven A. Kruger, Boston, Massachusetts, U.S.A.) Manufacturing lead-time reduction, 80%. Space reduction: assembly, 10%. Inventory investment: work in process, 50%; finished goods, 40%.

53. Philips, Monza Video Factory, Monza, Italy. Television sets. (Luca Strambio, Milan, Italy.) Manufacturing lead-time reduction, 70%. Space reduction: total, 30%. Labor savings: direct, 10%; indirect, 32%. Setup/changeover cost, 88%. Inventory investment: work in process, 75%; purchases, 50%. Payback period, 10 months.

54. Polychrome Corporation, lithographic plates, Robbinsville, New Jersey, U.S.A. (A. William Kapler, New York, U.S.A.) Manufacturing lead-time reduction, 99%. Space reduction: assembly, 60%; machining, 60%. Setup/changeover cost, 84%. Inventory investment: work in process, 99%. Lift trucks, 50%. Machine downtime, 83%.

55. Quamco, Reed Rolled Thread Die Co., Holden, Massachusetts, U.S.A. Thread rolling machine dies. (William G. Stoddard, Hartford, Connecticut, U.S.A.) Manufacturing lead-time reduction, 70%. Space reduction: machining, 33%. Labor savings: direct, 10%; indirect, 50%. Setup/changeover cost, 68%. Inventory investment: work in process, 72%.

56. Raychem, Metals Division, Menlo Park, California, U.S.A. Fittings and couplings for aircraft and marine applications. (Thomas D. Follet, San Francisco, California, U.S.A.) Manufacturing lead-time reduction, 95%. Space occupied: total, 80%. Labor savings: direct, 26%; indirect, 40%. Setup/changeover cost, 95%. Inventory investment: work in process, 94%; materials, 75%; finished goods, 55%; total, 85%. Payback period, 9 months.

57. Rheem Manufacturing, Press Department, Fort Smith, Arkansas, U.S.A. Heating and air conditioning. (Neil F. Kidwell, Toronto, Canada, and John G. Schoen, Tulsa, Oklahoma, U.S.A.) Manufacturing lead-time reduction, 66%. Space reduction, 34%. Setup/changeover cost, 84%. Inventory investment: work in process, 83%.

58. Rolscreen Co. (Pella Windows), Pella, Iowa, U.S.A. Entrance doors. (Leroy D. Peterson, Chicago, Illinois, U.S.A.) Manufacturing lead-time reduction, 88%. Space reduction: total, 36%. Direct labor savings, 48%. Inventory investment: work in process, 49%.

59. Sargent, Exit Devices Division, New Haven, Connecticut, U.S.A. Architectural hardware. (William G. Stoddard, Hartford, Connecticut, U.S.A.) Manufacturing lead-time reduction, 80%. Space reduction: total, 50%. Direct labor savings, 10%. Inventory investment: work in process, 75%. Purchase price reduction, 10%. Payback period, 6 months.

60. Sargent, Hand Tool Division, New Haven, Connecticut, U.S.A. Electrical connector crimping tools. (William G. Stoddard, Hartford, Connecticut, U.S.A.) Manufacturing lead-time reduction, 60%. Space reduction: total, 75%. Labor savings: direct, 45%; indirect, 45%. Inventory investment: work in process, 60%. Quality defects, 25%. Payback period, 4 months. Sold vacated plant for $300,000, saving $75,000 per year in plant operating expenses.

61. Schlumberger, Cia De Contadores, Contadores Division, Barce-

lona, Spain. Electric, gas, and water meters. (Federico Montllonch, Barcelona, Spain.) Manufacturing lead-time reduction, 75%. Space reduction: machining, 35%; assembly, 50%. Labor savings: direct, 10%; indirect, 30%. Setup/changeover cost, 80%. Inventory investment: work in process, 75%; finished goods, 50%. Payback period, 12 months.

62. Sevel Argentina, S.A., Buenos Aires, Argentina. Fiat and Peugeot automobiles and Chevrolet pickup trucks. (David E. Stilerman, Buenos Aires, Argentina.) Storeroom space reduction: through compression, 28%; through inventory reduction, 15%. Labor reduction, 26%.

63. Stihl Moto-Serras LTDA, Sao Leopoldo Plant, Sao Leopoldo, RS, Brazil. Chain saws. (Alcides Brum, Rio de Janeiro, Brazil.) Manufacturing lead-time reduction, 75%. Space reduction: total, 30%. Labor savings: direct, 17%; indirect, 25%. Inventory investment: work in process, 61%. Capacity increase, 24%.

64. Tandem Computers, Inc., Watsonville Manufacturing Facility, Watsonville, California, U.S.A. Printed circuit board assemblies. (Edward T. Kennedy, San Francisco, California, U.S.A.) Manufacturing lead-time reduction, 85%. Space reduction: assembly, 35%; storage, 80%; total, 75%, including consolidation of other plants. Labor savings: direct, 25%; indirect, 60%; office, 80%. Setup/changeover cost, 90%. Inventory investment: work in process, 80%; total, 25%. Payback period, 6 months.

65. Teksid, Avigliana, Italy. Extruded steel automotive parts. (Federico Feyles, Turin, Italy.) Setup/changeover cost, 75%. Payback period, 6 months.

66. Walbro Corporation, Automotive Division, Caro, Michigan, U.S.A. Auto fuel pumps. (Jacque H. Passino and Warren H. Watkins, Detroit, Michigan, U.S.A.) Manufacturing lead-time reduction, 97%. Space reduction: assembly, 40%; stores/warehouse, 20%. Direct labor savings, 24%. Work in process, 99%. Quality defects, 14%. Doubled factory capacity. Payback period, 4 months.

67. White Martins, Rio de Janeiro, Brazil. Electrical welding equipment. (Aloysio Pontes, Rio de Janeiro, Brazil.) Manufacturing lead-time reduction, 40%. Space reduction: total, 51%. Inventory investment: work in process, 50%.

68. Wing Industries, Inc., Greenville, Texas, U.S.A. Doors. (Gerald Gallagher, Dallas, Texas, U.S.A.) Setup/changeover cost, 80%.

69. Xerox, Resende Plant, Resende, R.J., Brazil. Copy machines. (Aloysio Pontes, Rio de Janeiro, Brazil.) Manufacturing lead-time reduction, 61%. Space reduction: total, 68%. Direct labor savings, 51%. Inventory investment: work in process, 61%; purchases, 78%.

PROJECTS IN PROCESS

As this book neared completion, a large number of Andersen Consulting's clients had productivity improvement projects in process but had not yet implemented the changes designed. These companies and their expected benefits are as follows:

1. Brunswick, Bowling and Billiards Division, Muskegon Ball Plant, Muskegon, Michigan, U.S.A. Bowling balls. (Leroy D. Peterson, Chicago, Illinois, U.S.A.) Manufacturing lead-time reduction, 90%. Space reduction: total, 60%. Inventory investment: work in process, 90%. Quality defects, 80%.

2. Cabot Corporation, E-A-R Division, Indianapolis, Indiana, U.S.A. Ear plugs and noise dampening products. (Robert L. Christianson, Indianapolis, Indiana, U.S.A.) Manufacturing lead-time reduction, 67%. Space reduction: total, 30%. Inventory investment: 70%.

3. COFAP (Companhia Fabricadora de Pecas), Shock Absorber Division, Santo Andre, S.P., Brazil. (Aloysio Pontes, Rio de Janeiro, Brazil.) Manufacturing lead-time reduction, 71%. Space reduction: total, 16%. Direct labor savings, 18%. Setup/changeover cost, 70%. Inventory investment: work in process, 81%; finished goods, 57%. Machine downtime, 50%. Payback period, 17 months.

4. Eigen, Nevada City, California, U.S.A. Medical image processing equipment. (Thomas D. Follet, San Francisco, California, U.S.A.) Manufacturing lead-time reduction, 95%. Space reduction: total, 35%; assembly, 10%; stores/warehouse, 90%. Labor savings: direct, 25%; indirect, 40%. Inventory investment: work in process, 70%; purchases, 80%. Quality defects, 80%. (Long-term goals: see achievements to date on the list of companies with implemented projects.)

5. ENASA, Barcelona, Spain. Wheel box and axle housing, bevel pinion and crown cells. (Federico Montllonch, Barcelona, Spain.) Manufacturing lead-time reduction, 95%. Space reduction: total, 35%. Labor savings: direct, 20%; indirect, 45%. Setup/changeover cost, 70%. Inventory investment: work in process, 94%; purchases, 20%. Quality defects, 40%. Payback period, 12 months.

6. Fabricacion de Electrodomesticos, S.A. (Fabrelec), Basauri, Spain. Refrigerators and water heaters. (Raul E. Alvarado, Bilbao, Spain.) Manufacturing lead-time reduction, 70%. Space reduction: total, 34%. Direct labor savings, 33%. Inventory investment: work in process, 70%; purchases, 28%; finished goods, 48%. Merged two factories into one, freeing 270,000 square feet.

7. Fiat Geotech, Fiat-Allis Division, Belo Horizonte Plant, Belo Horizante, Minas Gerais, Brazil. (Ernesto J. Kuperman, Sao Paulo, Brazil.) Manufacturing lead-time reduction, 90%. Space reduction: total, 50%; assembly, 55%; machinery, 50%. Direct labor savings, 25%. Setup/changeover cost, 75%. Inventory investment: work in process, 90%. Payback period, 26 months. Capacity increase, 50%.

8. Fiat Geotech, Fiat-Allis Division, Lecce Plant, Lecce Italy. Earthmoving equipment. (Luca Strambio, Milan, Italy.) Manufacturing lead-time reduction, 80%. Direct labor savings, 25%. Setup/changeover cost, 75%. Inventory investment: work in process, 80%; purchases, 50%. Payback period, 18 months. Production capacity increase, 100%, with no increase in factory size.

9. General Motors Corporation, Packard Electric Division, Plant 10, Warren, Ohio, U.S.A. Wiring harness cable. (William G. Kelly, Cleveland, Ohio, U.S.A.) Manufacturing lead-time reduction, 75%. Space reduction: stores/warehouse, 10%. Direct labor savings, 15%. Setup/changeover cost, 80%. Inventory investment: work in process, 50%; purchases, 62%. Quality defects, 90%.

10. General Motors Corporation, Packard Electric Division, Plant 43 Youngstown, Ohio, U.S.A. Automobile wiring harnesses. (William G. Kelly, Cleveland, Ohio, U.S.A.) Manufacturing lead-time reduction, 60%. Inventory investment: work in process, 75%; purchases, 75%; finished goods, 50%.

11. General Motors Corporation, Packard Electric Division, Plant 44 Youngstown, Ohio, U.S.A. Wiring harness leads. (William G. Kelly, Cleveland, Ohio, U.S.A.) Manufacturing lead-time reduction, 25%. Indirect labor, 25%. Setup/changeover cost, 55%.

12. Goulds Pumps, Inc., Slurry Pump Division, Ashland Plant, Ashland, Pennsylvania, U.S.A. Industrial pump components. (Steven A. Kruger, Boston, Massachusetts, U.S.A.) Manufacturing lead-time reduction, 71%. Space reduction: machining, 26%. Labor savings: direct, 23%; indirect, 16%. Setup/changeover cost, 75%. Inventory investment: work in process, 33%; finished goods, 85%.

13. Grandes Motores Diesel S.A. (GMD), Cordoba, Argentina. Diesel engines. (David E. Stilerman, Buenos Aires, Argentina.) Manufacturing lead-time reduction, 70%. Space reduction: total, 40%. Setup/changeover cost, 64%. Inventory investment: work in process, 70%.

14. Gruppo Industriale Ercole Marelli, EMC, Milan, Italy. Electric motors and pumps. (Alessandro Falchero, Milan, Italy.) Manufacturing lead-time reduction, 80%. Labor savings: direct, 60%; indirect, 30%. In-

ventory investment: work in process, 80%; purchases, 50%. Payback period, 8 months.

15. Johnson & Johnson, Inc., Montreal, Quebec, Canada. Personal health and patient health-care products. (Stephen L. Brant, Montreal, Quebec, Canada.) Manufacturing lead-time reduction, 68%. Space reduction: total, 55%. Labor savings: direct, 15%; indirect, 30%. Setup/changeover cost, 95%. Inventory investment: work in process, 80%; purchases, 50%; finished goods, 60%. Lift trucks, 40%. Machine downtime, 95%. Quality defects, 100%. Payback period, 12 months.

16. Kendall Company, Fiber Division, Athens, Georgia, U.S.A. Nonwoven fabrics. (B. Benjamin Smith, Atlanta, Georgia, U.S.A.) Labor savings: direct, 15%; indirect, 10%; office, 5%. Setup/changeover cost, 30%. Inventory investment: purchases, 50%; finished goods, 60%. Payback period, 24 months.

17. Kendall Company, Hospital Division, Augusta, Georgia, U.S.A. Surgical dressings and related health-care products. (B. Benjamin Smith, Atlanta, Georgia, U.S.A.) Manufacturing lead-time reduction, 75%. Space reduction: total, 50%; machining, 45%; stores/warehouse, 65%. Labor savings: direct, 10%; indirect, 50%; office, 60%. Setup/changeover cost, 75%. Inventory investment: work in process, 75%; purchases, 60%; finished goods, 50%. Payback period, 24 months.

18. KICSA, Buenos Aires, Argentina. Rolled and extruded aluminum products. (David E. Stilerman, Buenos Aires, Argentina.) Manufacturing lead-time reduction, 58%. Setup/changeover cost, 77%. Inventory investment: work in process, 58%; finished goods, 60%. Payback period, 6 months.

19. Ladish Company, Inc., Ladish Pacific Division, Los Angeles, California, U.S.A. Aerospace forgings. (Douglas W. Cunningham, Orange County, California, U.S.A.) Manufacturing lead-time reduction, 55%. Space reduction: total, 40%. Direct labor savings, 20%. Inventory investment: 55%. Payback period, 24 months.

20. Larson Electronics, Inc., Portland, Oregon, U.S.A. Cellular telephone antennae. (John C. Morris, Portland, Oregon, U.S.A.) Manufacturing lead-time reduction, 43%. Space reduction: total, 50%. Labor savings: direct, 41%; indirect, 84%. Production capacity increase, 209%. Payback period, 5 months.

21. Lennox Industries, Inc., Forth Worth, Texas, U.S.A. Air conditioning and heating equipment. (Gerald Gallagher, Dallas, Texas, U.S.A.) Manufacturing lead-time reduction, 50%. Direct labor savings, 60%. Setup/changeover cost, 60%. Payback period, 14 months.

22. Holophane Company, Inc., Newark, Ohio, U.S.A. Industrial lighting fixtures. (John Rife, Columbus, Ohio, U.S.A.) Manufacturing lead-time reduction, 85%. Space reduction: assembly, 40%; stores/warehouse, 15%. Direct labor savings, 46%. Inventory investment: work in process, 60%; finished goods, 30%. Payback period, 12 months.

23. Materfer, Ferreyra, Cordoba, Argentina. Railroad cars. (David Stilerman, Buenos Aires, Argentina.) Manufacturing lead-time reduction, 57%. Space reduction: total, 37%. Labor savings, 20%. Setup/changeover cost, 60%. Inventory investment: work in process, 40%.

24. Medex, S. A., Derio, Vizcaya, Spain. Electrical appliances (differentials and disrupters). (Raul E. Alvarado, Bilbao, Spain.) Manufacturing lead-time reduction, 50%. Space reduction: total, 25%; machining, 25%; stores/warehouse, 30%. Labor savings: direct, 10%; indirect, 10%. Inventory investment: work in process, 50%; purchases, 35%.

25. Nuova Sirma, Venice, Italy. Refractory materials. (Federico Feyles, Turin, Italy). Manufacturing lead-time reduction, 70%. Direct labor savings, 66%. Setup/changeover cost, 75%. Payback period, 12 months.

26. P. T. Danmotors Vespa Indonesia, Jakarta, Indonesia. Motor scooters. (Arthur T. Stratman, Jakarta, Indonesia.) Manufacturing lead-time reduction, 85%. Space reduction: total, 58%; machining, 52%. Direct labor savings, 34%. Setup/changeover cost, 77%. Inventory investment: work in process, 84%.

27. Quality Products, Durban, South Africa. Soaps. (Herbert G. Vinnicombe, Durban, South Africa.) Setup/changeover cost, 70%. Inventory investment: finished goods, 30%. Payback period, 11 months.

28. Raychem, Wire & Cable Division, Redwood City, California, U.S.A. Wire and cable products. (Thomas D. Follet, San Francisco, California, U.S.A.) Manufacturing lead-time reduction, 80%. Space reduction: total, 60%. Labor savings, 50%. Inventory investment: work in process, 50%. Quality defects, 50%.

29. Rheem Manufacturing, Coil Fabrication, Fort Smith, Arkansas, U.S.A. Heating and air conditioning. (John G. Schoen, Tulsa, Oklahoma, U.S.A., and Neil F. Kidwell, Toronto, Canada.) Space reduction, 14%. Direct labor savings, 13%. Setup/changeover cost, 76%. Inventory investment: work in process, 72%; finished goods, 50%. Payback period, 3 months.

30. Rolland, Inc., Fine Papers Division, St. Jerome, Quebec, Canada. Business and printing papers. (Stephen L. Brant, Montreal, Quebec, Canada.) Manufacturing lead-time reduction, 66%. Space reduction: to-

tal, 30%. Setup/changeover cost, 40%. Inventory investment: work in process, 95%; finished goods, 50%. Output capacity increased, 15%.

31. Rowe International, Triangle, PWC, Bennington, Vermont, U.S.A. Wire cord sets. (William G. Stoddard, Hartford, Connecticut, U.S.A. and William A. Kapler, New York, New York, U.S.A.) Manufacturing lead-time reduction, 97%. Space reduction: total 30%; machining, 20%; stores/warehouse, 50%. Labor savings: direct, 22%; indirect, 50%. Setup/changeover cost, 72%. Inventory investment: work in process, 83%; purchases, 75%; quality defects, 70%. Payback period, 6 months.

32. SKF, San Fernando, Spain. Bearings. (Javier Tapia, Madrid, Spain.) Setup/changeover cost, 78%.

33. Union Explosivos Rio Tinto, S.A., Huelva, Spain. Lubricating oils. (F. Alfonso Capdepon and Javier Tapia, Madrid, Spain.) Space reduction: stores/warehouse, 35%. Indirect labor, 20%. Inventory investment: finished goods, 51%.

34. Unisys Corporation, Computer Systems Division, Shepard Road Plant, St. Paul, Minnesota, U.S.A. Military computers. (Peter R. Zirbel, Minneapolis, Minnesota, U.S.A.) Manufacturing lead-time reduction, 64%. Labor savings: direct, 57%; indirect, 20%. Machine downtime, 57%. Quality defects, 58%.

35. Volvo, Flygmotor AB, Trollhatten, Sweden. Aircraft engines and components. (Carl Lilljeqvist, Stockholm, Sweden.) Manufacturing lead-time reduction, 90%. Setup/changeover cost, 80%. Inventory investment: work in process, 90%. Quality cost, 50%. Space reduction: machinery, 20%.

36. Wearne Brothers Group, Wearnes Precision (Private), Ltd., Singapore. Precision machined products. (David L. Bushman, Singapore.) Manufacturing lead-time reduction, 98%. Space reduction: total, 77%. Direct labor savings, 55%.

37. Xerox, Electronic Information Products Division, Freemont, California, U.S.A. (Edward T. Kennedy, San Francisco, California, U.S.A.) Procurement lead-time reduction, 90%. Office productivity, 45%. Payback period, 1 month.

■□□

Bibliography

BOOKS

Apple, James M. *Plant Layout and Material Handling.* New York: John Wiley, 1977.

Berliner, Callie, and Brimson, James A., eds. *Cost Management for Today's Advanced Manufacturing: The CAM-1 Conceptual Design.* Boston: Harvard Business School Press, 1988.

Blache, Klaus M., ed. *Success Factors for Implementing Change: A Manufacturing Viewpoint.* Dearborn, MI: Society of Manufacturing Engineers, 1988.

Chassang, Guy. *Gerer la Production avec l'Ordinateur (Production Control in the Computer Age).* Paris: Dunod, 1983.

Dallas, Daniel B., ed. *Tool and Manufacturing Engineers Handbook.* New York: McGraw-Hill, 1976.

Duncan, William L. *Just-In-Time in American Manufacturing.* Dearborn, MI: Society of Manufacturing Engineers, 1988.

Fukuda, Ryuji. *Managerial Engineering: Techniques for Improving Quality and Productivity in the Workplace.* Cambridge, MA: Productivity Press, 1983.

Gilbreth, Frank B. *Motion Study: A Method for Increasing the Efficiency of the Workman.* Easton, PA: Hive, [1911] 1985.

Goddard, Walter E. *Just-in-Time: Surviving by Breaking Tradition.* Essex Junction, VT: Oliver Wight, 1986.

Gunn, Thomas G. *Manufacturing for Competitive Advantage.* Cambridge, MA: Ballinger, 1987.

Hall, Robert W. *Attaining Manufacturing Excellence.* Homewood, IL: Dow-Jones Irwin, 1987.

————. *Driving the Productivity Machine: Production Planning and Control in Japan.* Falls Church, VA: American Production and Inventory Control Society, 1981.

————. *Zero Inventories.* Homewood, IL: Dow-Jones Irwin, 1983.

Harmon, Roy L., and Peterson, Leroy D. *Effective Cycle Counting: A Foundation for Profitable Inventory Management.* Chicago, IL: Arthur Andersen, AD8250, item 35, 1979.

————. *Inventory Record Accuracy: Gauge of Manufacturing System Profitability.* Chicago, IL: Arthur Andersen, AD8250, item 38, 1979.

Hay, Edward J. *The Just-In-Time Breakthrough: Implementing the New Manufacturing Basics.* New York: John Wiley, 1988.

Hayes, Robert H., and Wheelwright, Steven C. *Restoring Our Competitive Edge: Competing Through Manufacturing.* New York: John Wiley, 1984.

Hayes, Robert H., Wheelwright, Steven C., and Clark, Kim B. *Dynamic Manufacturing: Creating the Learning Organization.* New York: Free Press, 1988.

Higgins, Lindley R. *Maintenance Engineering Handbook.* New York: McGraw-Hill, 1988.

Hutchins, David. *Just In Time.* Aldershot, Harte, England: Gower Technical Press, 1988.

Ishikawa, Kaoru. Translated by Lu, David J. *What Is Total Quality Control: The Japanese Way.* Englewood Cliffs, NJ: Prentice-Hall, Inc., 1985.

Juravich, Tom. *Chaos on the Shop Floor: A Worker's View of Quality, Productivity, and Management.* Philadelphia: Temple University Press, 1985.

Karatsu, Hajime. *TQC Wisdom of Japan: Managing for Total Quality Control.* Cambridge, MA: Productivity Press, 1988.

Lu, David J., trans. *Kanban: Just-In-Time at Toyota: Management Begins at the Workplace.* Stamford, CT: Productivity Press, 1985.

Lubben, Richard J. *Just-In-Time: An Aggressive Manufacturing Strategy.* New York: McGraw-Hill, 1988.

Mizuno, Shigeru. *Company-Wide Total Quality Control.* Tokyo: Asian Productivity Organization, 1988.

————, ed. *Management for Quality Improvement: The 7 New QC Tools.* Cambridge, MA: Productivity Press, 1988.

Monden, Yasuhiro. *Toyota Production System: Practical Approach to Production Management.* Atlanta, GA: Institute of Industrial Engineers, 1983.

Nakajima, Seiichi. *Introduction to TPM: Total Productive Maintenance.* Cambridge, MA: Productivity Press, 1988.

Ohno, Taiichi. (Translation not credited.) *Toyota Production System: Beyond Large-Scale Production.* Cambridge, MA: Productivity Press, 1988.

————. Translated by Dillar, Andrew P. *Workplace Management.* Cambridge, MA: Productivity Press, 1988.

——, with Mito, Setsuo, Translated by Schmelzeis, Joseph P., Jr. *Just-In-Time: For Today and Tomorrow.* Cambridge, MA: Productivity Press, 1988.

Rosaler, Robert C., and Rice, James O. *Industrial Maintenance Reference Guide.* New York: McGraw-Hill, 1987.

——. *Plant Equipment Reference Guide.* New York: McGraw-Hill, 1987.

Schonberger, Richard J. *Japanese Manufacturing Techniques: Nine Hidden Lessons in Simplicity.* New York: Free Press, 1982.

——. *World Class Manufacturing.* New York: Free Press, 1986.

Shingo, Shigeo. *Non-Stock Production: The Shingo System for Continuous Production.* Cambridge, MA: Productivity Press, 1988.

——. *A Revolution in Manufacturing: The SMED System.* Stamford, CT: Productivity Press, 1985.

——. *The Sayings of Shigeo Shingo: Key Strategies for Plant Improvement.* Cambridge, MA: Productivity Press, 1987.

——. *Study of Toyota Production System.* Tokyo: Japan Management Association, 1981.

——. *Zero Quality Control: Source Inspection and the Poka-Yoke System.* Stamford, CT: Productivity Press, 1986.

Shinohora, Isao. *NPS New Production System: JIT Crossing Industry Boundaries.* Cambridge, MA: Productivity Press, 1988.

Suzaki, Kiyoshi. *The New Manufacturing Challenge.* New York: Free Press, 1987.

Taylor, Frederick W. *The Principles of Scientific Management.* Easton, PA: Hive, [1911] 1985.

Tompkins, James A., and White, John A. *Facilities Planning.* New York: John Wiley, 1984.

Voss, C. A. *Just-In-Time Manufacture.* London: IFS Publications, 1987.

Waterman, Robert H., Jr. *The Renewal Factor: How the Best Get and Keep the Competitive Edge.* New York: Bantam Books, 1987.

Wild, Ray. *Mass Production Management: The Design and Operation of Production Flow-Line Systems.* London: John Wiley, 1972.

ARTICLES

Alvarado, Raul E. and Peterson, Leroy D. "Manufacturing Productivity: Techniques Key to Profit Improvement." American Production and Inventory Control Society, Conference Proceedings, 1982, pp. 216–220.

Alvarado, Raul. "El Renacimiento de la Industria: La Fabrica CIM." *Direccion Progreso* (Asociacion para el Progreso de al Direccion), March–April 1987, pp. 9–11.

Anderson, Steve and Lusky, Karen. "Modern Manufacturing: Is It Just-In-Time or Is It Just Too Late." *Advantage Magazine,* July 1988, pp. 24–27.

Arenberg, Thomas E. "Establishing World Class Vendor Relationships." American Production and Inventory Control Society. Congress for Progress Proceedings, 1988.

——. "Vendor Support Systems—Partners in Profit." *Readings in Zero Inventory* (American Production and Inventory Control Society), Conference Proceedings, 1984, pp. 98–99.

Azcue, Elena. "Guia Basica de la Tecnologia: Glosario de Terminos CIM." *Direccion Progreso* (Asociacion para el Progreso de la Direccion), March–April 1987, pp. 89–94.

Bergeron, Jeffrey D., and Van Hull, Peter. "Competitive Assessment Part I: Do You Know What Your Competition Is Doing?" *Chilton's Automotive Industries,* July 1988, pp. 62–64.

——. "Competitive Assessment Part II: Identifying Opportunities for Cost Reduction." *Chilton's Automotive Industries,* September 1988, pp. 73–77.

Brant, Stephen L. "Just-In-Time Requirement Planning: The Challenge of World Class Manufacturing." American Production and Inventory Control Society, Regional Conference Proceedings, March 1988.

Capdepon, Alfonso, "CIM: La Clave de la Competitividad." *Direccion Progreso* (Asociacion para el Progreso de la Direccion), March–April 1987, p. 7.

Capdepon, Alfonso, and Sirvent, Juan Ignacio. "Automatizacion Integral Flexible: Siemens-Cornella." *Direccion Progreso* (Asociacion para el Progreso de la Direccion), March–April 1987, p. 51–54.

Chassang, Guy. "A Must in Manufacturing: The Move from Financial to Management Control" (in French). *Politique Industrielle,* 1987, pp. 89–102.

Collins, Michael R., and Johnston, Roger C. "Improving Plant Productivity Through Synchronous Manufacturing." Society of Manufacturing Engineers, Autofact '88 Conference Proceedings, October–November 1988, pp. 9–19, 9–26.

Cook, James. "Kanban, American Style." *Forbes,* October 8, 1984, pp. 66–70.

Cooper, Jeffrey H. "How to Get Started With Quality Management." American Production and Inventory Control Society, 29th Annual Conference Proceedings, 1986, pp. 517–518.

Crow, David, and Storm, David. "CIM—Justifying a Strategy for Action, Not Reaction." In *Manufacturing Technology International: Europe 1988.* London: Sterling Publications, 1988.

Cuartero, Alejandro. "La Tecnologia a Punto: Sistemas Flexibles de Fabricacion." *Direccion Progreso* (Associacion para el Progreso de la Direccion), March–April 1987, pp. 21–28.

Delgado, Lucia. "Los Sistemas de Costes en la Fabrica del Futuro" *Direccion Progreso* (Asociacion para el Progreso de la Direccion), March–April 1987, pp. 85–88.

Diaz, Miguel Oscar. "Beneficios a Corto Plazo: Racionalizar el Proceso Productivo." *Direccion Progreso* (Asociacion para el Progreso de la Direccion), March–April 1987, pp. 13–17.

Dieden, Jonas, and Persson, Lars. "CIM I Verkligheten." *Saertryck ur Datornytt,* August 1987, pp. 3–4.

Evelson, Abel R. "In Argentina Just Like in Japan." *Mercado* (Editorial Coyuntura S.A., Buenos Aires, Argentina), December 18, 1985, pp. 219–220.

"Factory of the Future." *The Economist,* May 1987, pp. 3–18.

Falchero, Alessandro. "Io, Robot." *Tempo Economico,* May 1984, pp. 90–96.

Farwell, C. Robert, and Rosencrans, Bradley A. "CIM: Boon or Boondoggle." *St. Louis Commerce,* March 1988, pp. 23–26.

———. "CIM: The Road to Competitive Advantage." *Gateway Engineer,* February 1987, pp. 6–15.

———. "Implementing a Successful Supplier Program." *St. Louis Purchaser,* January 1988, pp. 20–30.

———. "Simplify, Automate, Integrate." *St. Louis Commerce,* March 1987, pp. 66–67.

———. "Trends in Material Handling." *Gateway Engineer,* April 1988, pp. 6–12.

Gallagher, Gerald R. "Materials Requirement Planning: How to Develop a Realistic Master Schedule." *Management Review* (American Management Association), April 1980, pp. 19–25.

———. "Technical Talk: Just-In-Time Manufacturing." *Integrated Manufacturing Report* (Association for Integrated Manufacturing Technology), November 1984, p. 3.

Gallagher, Gerald R., and Gullo, John J. "Developing a Closed Loop MRP System—What's In It for the Design Engineer." *Production and Inventory Management* (American Production and Inventory Control Society), Fourth Quarter 1980, pp. 21–37.

Gattermeyer, Wolfgang. "The Softside of JIT/CIM." *Proceedings of the 3rd International Conference on Just-In-Time Manufacturing,* pp. 173–179. Bedford, England: IFS Publications, 1988.

Haley, Roy W., and Piper, Bruce B. "New Inventory Management Approach Can Substantially Cut Costs," *The Practical Accountant,* February 1986, pp. 60–68.

Harmon, Roy L. "Fertigungssteuerun in Japan." *Gesellschaft fuer Fertigungssteuerung und Materialwirtshaft* (Jahrestagung), January 1981, pp. 61–79.

———. "Update 1982: U.S. Adaptation of Japanese Techniques." American Production and Inventory Control Society, Conference Proceedings, October 1982, pp. 179–182.

Hronec, Steven M. "Cost Management." *Automation,* August 1988, pp. 30–32.

Salcedo, Jesuś. "Automatización de Oficira: Un Enfoque Hacia la Productividad Total." *Avianca, el Mundo al Vuelo,* January 1, 1989, pp. 38–44.

Jaikumar, Ramchandran. "Postindustrial Manufacturing." *Harvard Business Review,* November–December 1986, pp. 69–76.

Kruger, Steven A. "In Pursuit of World-Class Productivity." *Rochester Business Magazine,* May 1986, p. 28.

Leffin, John W. "Group Technology Analysis and the Microcomputer: Tools for Manufacturing Cell Design." American Production and Inventory Control Society, Fall Seminar Proceedings, September 8–10, 1986, pp. 473–477.

——. "Improving Machining Process Flow: The Application of Group Technology to Manufacturing Cell Design." Computer Integrated Manufacturing and Flexible Manufacturing Systems, Seminar Proceedings, April 24–26, 1985, pp. 97–100.

Lizarralde, Pedro, and Diaz-Caneja, Emilio. "Estrategia de Almacenamiento en un Entorno Just-In-Time." *Manutencion y Almacenaje* (Compania Espanola de Editoriales Tecnologicas Internacionales S.A., Barcelona), July/August 1988, pp. 43–48.

Montllonch, Federico, and Cardona, Javier. "Estrategia CIM en Cables Pirelli." *Direccion Progreso* (Asociacion para el Progreso de la Direccion), March–April 1987, pp. 57–62.

Nellemann, David O. "Gaining Competitive Advantage," pp. 1–25, Chicago: Arthur Andersen, June 1986.

——. "Gaining Competitive Advantage Through Technology." *Commline: The Journal of Computerized Manufacturing,* Winter 1987.

Nellemann, David O., and Smith, Leighton, Jr. "Just-In-Time vs. Just-In-Case Production: Concepts Borrowed Back From Japan." *Production and Inventory Management* (American Production and Inventory Control Society), Second Quarter, 1982, pp. 12–21.

Peterson, Leroy D. "Reinventing the Factory." Hitchcock Publishing, April 1986.

Peterson, Leroy D. and Harmon, Roy L. "Masters of Production Scheduling." *ICP Interface Manufacturing & Engineering,* Spring 1983, pp. 22–26.

Piedra, Carlos. "Quien Dirige a Quien? Los Recursos Humanos y la Tecnologia," *Direccion Progreso* (Asociacion para el Progreso de la Direccion), March–April 1987, pp. 81–84.

Piper, Bruce B., III. "Robots Yield Significant Benefits in Assembly Cells." Society of Manufacturing Engineering, Autofact Proceedings, 1988.

Romanosky, Jack. "Creating the Computer Integrated Manufacturing Factory: Key Management Decisions." *P&IM Review* (American Production and Inventory Control Society), November 1986, pp. 33–34.

Rosencrans, Bradley A. "Can There Be CIM Without AI?" *Gateway Engineer,* December 1988, pp. 11–12.

——. "A Plan Is Needed." *Gateway Engineer,* August 1988, p. 14.

——. "Simplification Sets the Stage." *Gateway Engineer,* January 1989, pp. 12–13.

——. "Using Technology to Improve Engineering Productivity." *Gateway Engineer,* September 1988, pp. 25–26.

——. "Why Cellular Manufacturing?" *Gateway Engineer,* February 1989, p. 11.

Rubio, Andres, and Hernandez, Pedro J. "Una Isla en la Fabrica: La Funcion de Ingenieria." *Direccion Progreso* (Asociacion para el Progreso de la Direccion), March–April 1987, pp. 72–75.

Ibañez, Juan J. "Cómo Lograr en Colombia la Productividad Total." *La Repúbica,* February 27, 1989, p. 7.

Skinner, Wickham. "The Focused Factory." *Harvard Business Review,* May–June 1974, pp. 113–121.

Smith, Leighton, Jr., and Harmon, Roy L. "Closed Loop Systems in Japan: Techniques of Worldwide Applicability." American Production and Inventory Control Society, Conference Proceedings, October 1981, pp. 105–108.

Smith, Scott A. "Managing Change: The Softside Aspects of Implementing JIT Principles." American Production and Inventory Control Society, Logistics Conference, April 1988, pp. 1–2.

Starke, Bengt. "Modellfabrik Visar Moejligheterna." *Verkstaederna,* April 1988, pp. 20–24.

Stevens, Mark E. "Cost Accounting in the Factory of the Future." American Production and Inventory Control Society, Fall Seminar Proceedings, October 10–14, 1988.

Stilerman, David S. "The Japanese Approach." *Clarin,* (Buenos Aires, Argentina), November 17, 1985, p. 12.

——. "Storage and Movement of Materials." *Tecnica y Industria* Indutec (Buenos Aires, Argentina), December 1986, pp. 31–33.

Stoddard, William G. "Productivity in Manufacturing: Survival Strategy for U.S. Industry." *Material Handling Engineering,* January 1985, pp. 54–64.

Stoddard, William G., and Rhea, Nolan W. "Just-In-Time Manufacturing: The Relentless Pursuit of Productivity." *Material Handling Engineering,* March 1985, pp. 70–76.

——. "New Guidelines for Factory Automation." *Material Handling Engineering,* May 1985, pp. 104–108.

——. "People Make Manufacturing Productivity Work." *Materials Handling Engineering,* September 1985, pp. 84–92.

——. "We Need to Change the Role of MRP in Manufacturing." *Materials Handling Engineering,* July 1985, pp. 104–108.

Strambio, Luca, and Falchero, Alessandro. "La fabbrica del futuro e' Ancora Lontana?" *Tempo Economico,* January–February 1987, pp. 64–69.

———. "E'il Momento del Group Technology." *Tempo Economico,* May 1986, pp. 80–85.

———. "Una Strategia Per Competere Meglio." *Tempo Economico,* April 1986, pp. 71–75.

Strambio, Luca, and Tarizzo, Guido. "Il J.I.T. Manufacturing Come Preparazione per l'Automazione di Fabbrica." *Logistica d' Impresa,* May 1986, pp. 447–453.

———. "Produzione Senza Scorte." *Logistica d' Impresa,* March, 1985, pp. 181–188.

Sundstrand, Orjan. "Just-In-Time Tillverkning inom Svensk Verkstadsindustri." *Mekanresultat* (Sveriges Mekanforbund), February 1987.

———. "MPS Och Japansk Producktionsfilosofi." *Verkstaederna* (Sveriges Verkstadsforening), April 1985, pp. 21–24.

———. "Overgripande Resursplanering." *Verkstaederna* (Sveriges Verkstadsforening), October 1986, pp. 38–40.

Tapia, Javier. "El Camino Hacia El Futuro: Migracion CIM." *Direccion Progreso* (Asociacion para el Progreso de la Direccion), March–April 1987, pp. 65–70.

Tarizzo, Guido. "La Ricerca Dell' Eccellenza: Casi di Successo di Gestione d' Impresa." *L' Impresa,* May 1986, pp. 87–89.

Teschner, Rainer, and Gattormeyer, Wolfgang. "The Softside of CIM—An Automobile Perspective." In *Manufacturing Technology International: Europe 1988,* pp. 266–272. London: Sterling Publications, 1988.

Thurwachter, William A. "Simplified Integrated Manufacturing: A Byword for Operational Strategy." *Industrial Engineering Magazine,* November 1986, pp. 74–82.

Vassal'lo, Luis. "La Fuerza Motriz de la Fabrica: Sistemas de Planificacion." *Direccion Progreso* (Asociacion para el Progreso de la Direccion), March–April 1987, pp. 31–38.

———. "El Mantenimiento: Usted Tambien Piensa Que Es Poco Importante?" *Direccion Progreso* (Asociacion para el Progreso de la Direccion), March–April 1987, pp. 77–80.

Vizoso, Fausto. "En la Frontera de los 90: Tecnologias de la Informacion." *Direccion Progreso* (Asociacion para el Progreso de la Direccion), March–April 1987, pp. 41–49.

Whitney, Daniel E. "Real Robots Do Need Jigs." *Harvard Business Review,* May–June 1986, pp. 110–116.

Willis, Roger G., and Klich, Michael J. "The Simplify-Automate-Integrate Approach to CIM and Competitive Advantages." Society of Manufacturing Engineers, CIM Tech Conference Proceedings, March 24–26, 1987, pp. 215.1–215.5.

Index